# THE END
## OF
# CONVENTIONAL CHRISTIANITY

# The End
## of
# Conventional Christianity

*by*
W. H. van de Pol

*Translated by*
Theodore Zuydwijk, S.J.

NEWMAN PRESS
New York, N. Y.    Glen Rock, N. J.
Amsterdam    Toronto    London

A Newman Press edition, originally published under the title *Het Einde van het Conventionele Christendom* by J. J. Romen & Zonen, Roermond, The Netherlands, © 1967.

Published by Newman Press
*Editorial Office:* 304 W. 58th St., N.Y., N.Y. 10019
*Business Office:* Glen Rock, N. J. 07452

# Contents

# Introduction

The first lines of this book were written on that memorable day when Pope Paul VI traveled to the United States to address the United Nations with a message of peace. He asked all the nations of the world to restore and preserve peace. He did not distinguish between friend or foe. He asked for peace, purely on the basis of a mutual sharing in being human. While the Pope was, of course, fully aware of his apostolic mission to the world, he wanted to fulfill this mission as a human person among his fellow men.

Even though in the past there had been occasions when popes set forth on trips, the papacy had come to be regarded as an office whose holder should remain within the confines of the Vatican walls. Pope John XXIII and Pope Paul VI put an end to this conventional idea of the papacy.

Infinitely more important however is that both these popes also brought about a definitive change in the attitude which popes had traditionally adopted toward those who preached "dangerous" religions, philosophical and scientific teachings, toward those who spread "pernicious" social and political theories, toward schismatic and heretical Christians, nazis, communists, and atheists—in short, toward all those who in one way or another placed themselves in opposition to the "rights and the teaching authority of the Church which Christ founded."

Earlier papal allocutions and encyclicals contained expressions of a sincere desire for the return of those who had gone astray. There had been assurances that they would be received back with open arms. But these words had never quite rung true in the ears of those to whom they were addressed. Instead of the moving voice of charity and love, it was the voice of justice and authority that was heard. There was always a greater awareness of the threats of excommunication and of the loss of eternal salvation.

Within the Church, this had become the commonly accepted

1

situation. One saw it in a conventional aspect of the papacy. And yet, by their very manner of going out to meet the people Pope John and Pope Paul put a stop to this age-old conventional attitude toward those of other convictions. We now find ourselves at the beginning of a totally new functioning of the authority of the pope. We are at the beginning of an entirely new relationship between the papacy and Christianity, between the papacy and the world, between the papacy and the individual. The one all-important motive of the pope is once again the love of Christ, a love without qualification and without limitation.

We are here faced with profound changes which were not anticipated and which in the future will prove to be of immense value, just as they have been a source of surprise up till now. This is not a book about the papacy. But what has thus far been said about the end of certain aspects of the papacy, which had practically come to be considered conventional, is symptomatic of everything that has to do with the Church, Christianity, and religion. In fact, it is symptomatic of everything that concerns our present and future human existence in all its common and individual forms and expressions. In an ever-quickening tempo, that which was old is about to disappear, and that which is new finds forms that are totally different from those we anticipated. In ever-widening circles there is a growing awareness that in all aspects of our human existence we have arrived at a turning point in the history of our civilization. This is certainly true also for the religious aspect. Conceptions and convictions, teachings and manners of behavior which only a brief time ago were considered obvious suddenly appear to be outdated.

No matter whether it concerns the speculation, formulation, explanation, and proclamation of the content of faith, or whether it concerns the expression of faith in religious services, in spirituality, in everyday life, in the relationship between Christians, and in the manner of being a Christian in the world, the transitions now taking place are so far-reaching that the final outcome cannot yet be foreseen.

At any rate, we are involved in a phenomenon not thought up and propagated by one person or another. It is rather something that happens to us, whether we like it or not. We did not see it coming; we are just barely trying to get used to it; yet we are sure that we are unable to stop it; in fact, it is becoming more and more evident that we are willy-nilly very personally involved in the spiritual and material transitions now taking place.

What is happening in our days is something that affects all mankind in all its dimensions. We cannot avoid it. We are constantly finding out that all things are interrelated. The transitions in the religious realm are not isolated. On the contrary, they find their source in all that is going on in the scientific, philosophical, social, and technical fields—in short, in any and all of the areas of the individual and communal life of man on this earth. It is only in this entire context that the contemporary religious situation can be understood and assimilated. In this cultural revolution, the role played by radio, television, and all modern means of communication and transportation can be compared to the role played by the invention of the art of printing in the transition from the Middle Ages to modern times.

We are witnessing the birth of a world in which mankind is knit together more closely than ever in a worldwide culture that embraces everything and everyone. Neither the religious nor any other dimension of human activity can escape its influence. Many of the age-old, conventional forms of Christianity have become obsolete and untenable. An antiquated, conventional Christianity has rapidly come to a definitive end. This presents all Christians of all the Churches all over the world with the common task of casting Christian life and belief in new forms. This will have to be done in such a way that in the emerging world of the future the Gospel will continue to be a divine force really contributing to the edification of a new world and the coming of God's Kingdom among all. In other words, ecumenics comprises the entire world.

As sharers in a common Christianity, we find ourselves today in a transitional phase with all the obscurities and uncertainties necessarily connected with such a transition. We are still living in the anxiety and tensions that necessarily accompany the end of conventional Christianity. We cannot yet quite perceive what precisely is happening, what we are to do, and where it is all going. This book is an attempt to treat of the end of conventional Christianity, of its causes, its characteristics, its consequences.

Fortunately there are many indications of a new beginning and a new future. But at the same time it cannot be denied that the unexpected and rapid changes in the ecclesiastical and religious areas have caused concern, uncertainty, and anxiety among many Christians. It could even be said that the most striking feature of the present religious situation is found in mutability, mobility, uncertainty, and unrest. This is an established fact, and evidently not much can be done about it. Solutions are attempted and moratoriums are proclaimed, but these are no more than provisional, and a little later all is adrift again. This simply happens to be our situation, and it does not seem that we have once again arrived at definitive solutions and returned to the tranquility and stability fervently desired by so many.

In the past five or ten years numerous books have appeared in which the authors attempted to trace the causes that have led to the present religious situation. These writers endeavor to arrive at accurate analysis and diagnosis. Not surprisingly, they mostly fall short in suggested therapies. It is highly doubtful whether one single person is capable of tracing out a new future which can actually be realized. This new future will gradually be given to us if we are prepared to labor toward it as Christians of all the Churches, in a common effort and in obedience to the guidance of the Spirit of God. This surpasses the capacities of one single theologian or of one single Church leader. Rather, all Christians depend on each other in a close sense of unity and collaboration.

Obviously the first question must be how it is that we as Christians of the most diverse Churches have together arrived in the present religious situation. This is the question this book is concerned with. It is not so difficult to indicate a number of complex causes which have exercised their influence. Some of these influences have existed for several centuries, others for longer or shorter periods. The fact is that causes have accumulated, so that finally all of them together have created the present religious situation. It could be said that there is one common denominator inasmuch as the cause for the religious unrest must be looked for in the gradual process by which conventional Christianity is being undermined.

We find ourselves in this situation because we have experienced both the collapse of realities that had been fixed for centuries and the consequent rapid and definitive end of what we have called conventional Christianity. In all this it matters little that in the past four or five centuries Christianity has had a Roman and Protestant form. For Roman as well as for Protestant Christians, conventional Christianity has come to an end, with all the consequences that this entails. Certainly, in this respect we share the same common problem.

All Christians alike, therefore, share in the same situation and transition to a new expression and practice of the Christian faith. In the light of what will be said in this book it is possible to predict that this situation and transition also will indirectly put an end to the antithesis between Rome and the Reformation. The antithesis is becoming antiquated. It will gradually fade away and finally dissolve in the future Christianity now being born.

The time is past when attempts were made to conquer the antithesis between Rome and Reformation in theory by means of theological constructions on paper. Nor should one expect to see the antithesis ended by a "return" or capitulation of the Protestants. It is rather by profound changes which both sides will undergo that gradually the separation will lose its significance. All those involved will have to adjust themselves more and more to the course of affairs. It no longer has any sense to continue trying to restore unity by polemical or apologetical activities, by proselytizing or by conversions from one side to the other. Nothing but a joint effort toward a renewed Christianity of the future will bring about a *rapprochement* between Christians of different Churches, until finally, as the fruit of this labor, we shall be able to rejoice in a new and complete unity and communion.

Theological and ecclesiastico-juridical differences hardly touching on the essence of Christianity have too long made us, Roman and Protestant Christians, try to match each other's apostolic zeal for conversions. Too long has Christianity suffered under the contrast between Rome and Reformation with its attendant polemic and separation, even though both sides sincerely strive for a continued catholicity in an authentic way.

This antithesis, not willed by Christ, has inflicted immeasurable harm to the realization of Christ's command to proclaim the Gospel and extend the reign of God among all the nations to the very limits of the earth. I do not by any means intend to underestimate the questions involved in the antithesis between Rome and Reformation. Nevertheless, these questions should never have separated us Christians, and in the future we shall have to try together to provide a new answer, neither Roman nor Protestant. It will be new in accordance with our present understanding of the bible, and with our present insight into the nature of belief, Church, and religion.

## Genesis of the Book

At this point I should make a few observations with regard to the genesis, method, purpose, and composition of this book. For a proper understanding of the book, it is most important that the reader should form a clear picture of its aims.

As far as the genesis of the book is concerned, it has, like my other works, its origin in lectures and courses I have given. Its great advantage is therefore that it arose from a living contact with an audience which one can see, to which one must constantly adjust, and which is capable of showing its reaction. Further, discussions at home and abroad, with persons known and unknown, of varying ages and religious orientations, have also contributed to the origin of this book.

In the fifties I was frequently asked to speak about the causes of what used to be called the "silent" defections from the faith. With each new lecture, subsequent discussions seemed to add to the number of causes, and new aspects of the problem of belief were uncovered. Ultimately it appeared to me that the faith could in our times be attacked in so many hitherto unknown ways and on so many serious and varied grounds, that I lost the courage to continue lecturing on this topic.

A provisional effort to give at least a global picture of the background to the problem of belief, and to give at the same time some positive suggestions how one could arrive at faith, led to the publication of my book *Ways unto Faith*.[1] After tracing out three ways, one based on thought, another on biblical witness, and another on conscience, I attempted a synthesis under the heading of "The existential nature of belief."

Much of what the book contains is still valid today and can be a real help in the struggle toward a genuine living faith. Yet, at the same time it evidently does not provide sufficient security to modern man's many and varied questions concerning the content and concept of faith.

[1] W. H. van de Pol, *Wegen tot Geloof* (Romen & Zonen, Roermond, 1952).

In the past ten years I have constantly been preoccupied with the question of how it is that the faith has become the cause of much concern and temptation in the lives of so many persons. I have looked for a method which might lead to the formation of a true and real picture of the present problems of faith in which all the actual causes and aspects might be justly represented.

It was in 1962 that I began to deal with this matter in my annual courses to the students of the various faculties at the Catholic University of Nijmegen. That there was a constant increase of material published in this connection is known to all, and can be seen from the reading list at the end of this book. For reasons already indicated, I entitled this course *The End of Conventional Christianity*, a title which was the result of my investigations into all that was taking place in the field of contemporary religious life and thought.

Shortly after I had started lecturing on this topic, Bishop Robinson's book *Honest to God* appeared in March 1963.[2] The fact that this book was very soon translated into many different languages is a typical indication of the religious situation in which we now find ourselves. Many Christians were at a loss with what to do with the conventional faith they inherited from their parents. At the same time they regretted that it no longer had any meaning for them. These Christians quite evidently found that Robinson had understood their confusing situation, and thus the book was a challenge for many to rethink their faith. This latter fact is indeed more important than the book's content itself. Anyone who would seriously and scientifically want to go into the problems which Robinson touches upon would have to begin reading, among others, the works of Tillich, Bonhoeffer, and Bultmann.

Dr. Robinson himself would be the 'first to admit that his book is not a standard scientific work. In fact as a New Testament scholar he left the field of his special competence. Therefore he did not write the book as a professional, but as a bishop who had an acute daily awareness of the defections from the faith, of the problem and tragedy of belief in his own diocese. It is to his great merit that he wanted to understand, that he wanted to show he understood, and that he, as bishop, was willing to admit that all of us these days are struggling with challenges to our faith.

[2] J. A. T. Robinson, *Honest to God* (S.C.M. Press, London, 1963).

Of course it was far from Robinson's mind to think that his book would provide the definitive answer. Nor did he intend to do away with God. It seems to me that those who have spoken disparagingly of his book are still in too conventional a phase to understand its importance. Obviously they are totally unaware of what goes on in the minds and hearts of millions who simply have no idea what to do with the religion they inherited, and who are therefore completely estranged from conventional Christianity.

While my inspiration to lecture on this subject and to write this present book did not come from Dr. Robinson's book, I must say that I welcomed it as a clear symptom of the situation in which we find ourselves. It certainly also pointed to certain problems in connection with our own theme which we cannot afford to lose sight of, and which we may not purposely ignore. Moreover, there are other important indications that the end of conventional Christianity, and the religious problems, uncertainties, and unrest connected with it, must be taken very seriously.

The Roman Catholic Church has always been considered as the unassailable, impregnable, and invulnerable fortress of unchangeable stability. Therefore, when suddenly everything in this Church seems to have been dislocated and unsettled, and when so many items previously considered sacrosanct are being subjected to critical discussion, one cannot escape the conclusion that even in this Church something is going on with regard to conventional thought and the life of faith. The Second Vatican Council has come to an end, but many are convinced that the renewal of thought and the confrontation with the demands and problems of our time are only beginning. Rather than considering the Second Vatican Council as finished business, we must see it as an initial impulse which only prepared the way toward a lasting stimulation.

The Council made it clear that in our day there are spiritual forces at work compelling us to make a final settlement of accounts with all that has become antiquated and to concentrate on present and future tenets, functions, and structures. Consequently, even the Second Vatican Council can be seen as a symptom of the end of conventional Christianity.

If I may be permitted another personal observation in this connection, I must say that it has always been my conviction that if a person dedicates his life to study and research, in religious as well as in other areas, his findings may every now and then force him to change his opinions and viewpoints. If, after a long life of research, a person still has the same ideas about everything as when he began, one is inclined to ask what good all the research has served.

Rather than being surprised when a theologian decides he must change his allegiance from one Church to another or from one modality or theological direction to another, I have always been amazed that there were so few such instances. It almost seems as if for most theologians their study is no more than a means of proving that predetermined unchangeable positions and convictions are correct. This attitude has resulted in newly-found facts and arguments being considered dangerous as soon as it appears they might shake the foundations of perennially fixed religious convictions. These convictions are seen as fixtures to which one is bound for life, and which must be protected and defended at all costs.

The reason for this attitude is the supposition that a particular position is based on revelation from God, and "surely God knows better than man." But what is lost sight of is that all religions have recourse to authoritative revelation, and that all Christian Churches are convinced that their own confession is in all points in agreement with biblical revelation. Even among biblical scholars and exegetes who avail themselves of the best sources it is a rare phenomenon that they are unable to make their exegesis agree with the position of the Church they belong to. A preordained and preconceived interpretation is simply identified with the actual content and meaning of God's word, and thus it is given a seemingly impregnable authority which in fact belongs to God alone, and not to the *interpretation* of God's word.

A truly impartial consideration of what is taking place these days in the Churches (Roman Catholic, Anglican, and Protestant) and in the spiritual and religious world outside these Churches must, in my opinion, lead to the conclusion that much of what was fixed and stable is not so firmly founded as we thought it to be. That which is truly from God is firm and stable, but this does not apply to the human margin in our convictions and practices. And this human margin is very large indeed.

In our days conventional Christianity is being attacked and undermined by an accumulation of factors of the most diverse nature and origin. Many Christians are quite susceptible to the

many facts, discoveries, events, and arguments that come upon us
from all sides, so that they cannot help but be changed by them
in many respects. For myself, I am ready to acknowledge that
over the past five or ten years my views on Church and religion
have undergone more profound changes than ever before. And it
is really this fact which is the reason for this book, written for all
those who in our contemporary situation are confronted with
similar facts. How has all this come about? Precisely what is the
situation like? What are we going to do about it? These are the
problems to which this book addresses itself.


*Approach to the Problem*

   Secondly, a word must be said about the approach to the problem. The method I have followed is strictly the phenomenological method proper to my profession. Unless this is constantly kept
in mind, one is liable to misunderstand the scope and content of
this book.
   I realize that there are theologians who believe this method is
unacceptable or of very little value. They hold that a theologian,
in bonds of strict fidelity, must strive for the deepest and purest
possible understanding of the truth which God has revealed, and
which is no other Truth than Jesus Christ, the Incarnate Word to
which the Holy Spirit witnesses by means of the sacred scriptures. For them, the theologian's method is exclusively the
exegetico-dogmatic method. He is personally committed to the
truth he discovers. The phenomenologist, on the other hand, con-
ducts himself as a non-committed spectator. Some theologians
hold that as far as truth is concerned, this attitude is not to be
permitted, since the phenomenologist thus remains outside the
Truth without participating in it.
   If theology is seen in this light, it follows that phenomenology
is a science which does not strictly pertain to theology. But this
does not mean that the phenomenologist cannot have personal
convictions of faith. What it does mean is that the nature and
method of his profession require that in his research he bracket
his personal convictions. As a Christian he is just as seriously
and completely concerned with the truth as the theologian in the
precise sense of the word. As a phenomenologist, however, he is

concerned, in an uninhibited but scientifically responsible fashion, with the religious truths for man on this earth, regardless of the Church or religion to which the man belongs. He is also concerned with the manner in which these truths function in the person's life, independent of the question of whether one is here dealing with truth or not. Such a judgment does not fall within the competence of the phenomenologist precisely as phenomenologist.

Because of the proper aim and method of his profession, the phenomenologist occupies himself with the study of religious expressions as such. His task is to observe these expressions as given phenomena, to describe them exactly, to analyze them, and thus to arrive at an explanation from within, as it were. It is not his task to estimate the content and value of religious teachings and practices. This he must leave to the biblical exegete, the dogmatic and the apologetic theologian.

Consequently, the present book does not intend to determine or defend a Christian truth. Its purpose is to investigate phenomenologically the facts and events and any other factors which have caused the present religious unrest.

It might be asked what the sense of all this is if the real truth is left out of consideration and thus fails to come to light. Of course for the Christian precisely as believer, and in fact for anyone, truth (and as a result, theology) is of much greater value than phenomenology. This, however, does not mean that the phenomenologist cannot render an important service to the Church, to the mission of the Church, to ecumenical discussion, and to the individual Christian. In fact, the mission of the Church and ecumenical discussion could become much more fruitful if one would profit fully from the results of phenomenological investigation. Fruitful spiritual labor is possible only when one has a clear insight into the nature of the spiritual milieu and of the spiritual situation in which the work is done.

## Purpose of the Book

After this brief exposé of the phenomenological method it should not be difficult to understand the intention of this book. Its intention is by no means polemic or apologetic. Neither does it intend to carry on propaganda. The writer does not even intend to oppose certain opinions, practices, and conditions, or to defend or praise others. He does not even intend to argue that an end should be put to conventional Christianity or to suggest what should take its place. If such prominent ecclesiastical meetings as the Second Vatican Council, the Lambeth Conference, or an assembly of the World Council of Churches, require years of preparation, lengthy discussions, and the assistance of learned experts in order to solve the pending religious questions and to determine a new course of action for the future, it would be all too audacious to try to do this on one's private initiative. Therefore, the intention of the author is much more modest than that.

On the basis of an extensive investigation, the book tries to find an answer to the question of why it is that conventional Christianity has become so undermined that we are experiencing its collapse. With the aid of the phenomenological method the book tries to point out how it is that in our days we find ourselves in the present religious situation which is so confused, problematical, changeable, restless, and uncertain, not only in Christianity but also in all world religions.

How has this come about? That is the question. It is, therefore, a matter of explaining, clarifying, throwing light on a religious situation which is a fact, and which therefore must be treated as such. Even the final chapter about the present and the future does not intend to plead for a personal ideal or program. It only draws conclusions from what is actually taking place, and it suggests on the basis of the data in what direction the new course of Christian faith, thought, and action (being a Christian in the world) is moving. The only exception to this are the two final paragraphs of the last chapter.

## Composition of the Book

The first chapter will consist of a detailed analysis of the idea of conventionality. From this it will become evident that the end of the age-old conventional Christianity cannot possibly mean that from now on any form of conventionality will be excluded. Christianity of the future too will gradually adopt conventional forms.

Apart from conversions and transfers which take place at a more mature age because of personal development, religion for most men is something one receives with one's formation at home. Every man is born into a definite religious or possibly areligious milieu. From the very first moments of our existence we undergo impressions of a religious nature. From a very tender age we grow up in a definite religious milieu, so that it becomes, in a way, part of ourselves. Normally a person cannot imagine himself, from a religious point of view, other than he is from birth. A Protestant *is* a Protestant. He experiences himself *as* a Protestant He cannot imagine that he would ever be anything else. It is part of his being. He would no longer continue to be himself if he were something else. This is true also, *mutatis mutandis*, for the Roman Catholic; not only is it true for the Christian, but also for the Jew, the Mohammedan, the Buddhist, the Hindu. It is because of this that transfers and conversions come about so painfully, and only after a long and difficult process of conversion. In other words, religion normally has a conventional character.

When, therefore, because of an accumulation of very different factors, an age-old conventionality in the religious area is attacked and undermined at a definite point in history, this is necessarily seen as a serious and apparently mortal crisis. This is what we are witnessing today in the entire world, even among non-Christian religions. Much of what will be said in this book will also be true for religion in general. It will become obvious that at all points we arrive at the fundamental and central question about God. Who is he, if he does exist? Where is he? Where can we find him? Is a relationship, a communion with God possible? If so, how?

I am limiting myself to Christianity, and in particular to the Protestant part of Christianity. However, what happens here is symptomatic also for the religious existence of all of mankind.

In the first chapter an attempt will be made to analyze the nature of conventionality in the area of religion. The second chapter will consist of an effort to determine the content of Christianity before it was attacked and undermined by the combination of causes discussed in the third and fourth chapters.

Because of an accumulation of very different factors, conventional Christianity has been gradually undermined, so that in our day we are experiencing its end. This fact is at the basis of the religious unrest which has become so serious that it sometimes seems as if Christian existence itself is at stake.

In this connection one could divide Christians into three groups. The divisions between these groups run throughout the various Churches. Former contrasts have been replaced by new ones. There are Christians who try to conquer the present unrest by clinging to the old, traditional teachings and practices. They consider it their vocation and duty to protect and keep the treasures of the past. There is also a wide middle-group who with great seriousness and devotion dedicate themselves to an *aggiornamento* of the old Christianity. Essentially they consider the Christian faith to be unassailable, and therefore they do not find that even in the present situation it is under attack. They say it must find better expression, and in particular it must be lived out in a form which is adapted to our changed and changing world. There is yet a third group. This is a group of Christians who emphatically desire to be and remain Christians, but who see sharp contrasts between conventional Christianity which in their view is radically obsolete, and the manner in which man can and must be a Christian in the future. They speak of Christianity without religion, and in some places even of Christian atheism.[3]

Meanwhile it is becoming more and more evident that the problem born from the end of conventional Christianity is ever more concerned with the problem of God. What is faith in God? What is atheism? Does not atheism at least have this positive meaning that it has unmasked the idols? Chapters five, six, seven, and eight deal with this emphasis of the religious problem of God. These chapters are the core of the book. They are intended to point out what precisely is at stake in the present religious unrest. Following this, the ninth chapter deals with the question about the absoluteness of Christianity and with the question about the positive significance of other religions. The synthesis contained in the tenth chapter is followed by an effort, based on the facts and events which have been considered, to look into the future of Christianity.

[3] T. J. J. Altizer, *The Gospel of Christian Atheism* (Westminster Press, Philadelphia, 1966).

# 1. Religious Conventionality

The word "conventional" is derived from the Latin verb *convenire*. This means to come together, to speak together, to agree, to be convenial to. A convention is a meeting, an agreement, a pact. And finally, convention also receives the meaning of "custom." When people agree on something or other and conduct themselves accordingly, such conduct slowly develops into custom. What in certain communities has been agreed upon will almost unconsciously determine and dominate the conduct of all those who belong to that community. In the long run, this will result in a conventional conduct and in conventional viewpoints, attitudes, motives, norms, and judgments.

Precisely insofar as such a complex has become typically conventional, those concerned are not aware of how the convention came about, possibly in the distant past. There is a tacit supposition that it has always been so, and that it will also have to remain so forever. Imperceptibly, the convention becomes something to which in everyone's opinion everyone will have to adhere, even if the reasons for it are usually hidden.

Conventions are found in every community. It could even be said that it is precisely these conventions which keep the members of a community united and which distinguish the community from other communities with other conventions. Without any express motivation, the conventions of one's own community are held to be the only correct ones. No consideration is given to the fact that members of other communities think likewise about *their* conventions. As long as conventions are observed by everyone, and as long as no one calls their validity into doubt, the unity of the community is safeguarded. But at the very moment that one convention after another is attacked, there will be a manifestation of unrest, tensions, and conflicts within the community. Oppositions will develop, and this in turn will threaten the unity and continued existence of the community.

Conventionality does not occur only in the area of religion. There is a conventionality in fashion, in forms of conduct, and in other expressions of culture. We are, however, limiting ourselves here to conventionality in religion.

Not only Christianity, but all religions everywhere, and at all times, have been strongly characterized by conventionality. This is partly due to the fact that religion generally belongs to the masses. In this respect there is a remarkable difference between religion on the one hand, and philosophy and science on the other. There have been instances in which philosophers, explorers, and researchers had difficulty overcoming conventional insights which had become untenable in their respective areas. The facts and arguments, however, soon proved to be stronger than the conventional concept. Hence we find progress in science. Hence too, the danger which science presented to religious conventions.

Religion has always been the concern, not of individuals, but of communities, even to the extent that diverging opinions of individuals were generally regarded as suspect. Although the origin of most religions must be traced back to an individual founder who gathered disciples and followers around him, any one of these religions in the long run proved to be a mass-phenomenon.

Philosophy and science have always been the concern of individuals or of small groups. But religions have been confessed by an entire people, or even by many peoples who all belonged to one area of culture. Religion is a social phenomenon *par excellence*. Religion is also a cultural phenomenon in the sense that it has always arisen within a certain culture and has had a decisive influence on the further development of that culture or on the rise of a new culture. Therefore it is possible to speak of a Christian, an Islamic, or a Buddhist culture. The character and forms of these cultures can be understood only from within the religious context at the basis of that culture.

Among primitive peoples, religion is so much an ethnic phenomenon that it is obvious for all the members to belong to the tribe's religion. The ties between religion and tribe, people, or nation have been so firm that during and even long after the religious revolutions of the sixteenth century, princes and magistrates tried to preserve the unity of religion in their country or city. The idea of a state or national Church is of primitive origin and continues to exist in conventional Christianity.

What does the conventional aspect of religion consist in? In general it can be said that religion is conventional insofar as the religious convictions and practices are held to be true and valid primarily because they were taught to be true and valid, either at home, at school, at church, or in the religious milieu in which a person grew up and to which he always belonged, and not because their truth and validity were grasped as a result of personal thought, personal experience, and personal conscience.

This of course does not exclude the fact that various religions and Churches have always had some believers who personally appropriated and practiced the religion of their milieu. In fact the conventionality of religion was often threatened by such conscious believers. These conscious believers, aware of their personal responsibility for their religious convictions and action, are the ones most seriously afflicted now that conventional Christianity is being undermined and attacked from so many sides.

## Further Analysis of Religious Conventionality

The first and most noticeable characteristic of religious conventionality is the matter-of-factness with which one accepts and practices everything that is taught and prescribed. As soon as the slightest doubt arises about this matter-of-factness, conventionality is finished in principle. Whenever an individual in a religious society begins to reflect on the religious teaching and practice in that society, conventionality is affected for himself personally, and to that same degree he becomes a danger to the conventionality of the society. This does not necessarily mean that the teaching and practice concerned are also rejected. But they have lost their conventional character because they are no longer accepted as a matter of fact, and for the sole reason that it has always been so taught and done.

The immediate consequence of the matter-of-factness with which in a given milieu certain conventional teachings and prescriptions are accepted is that they are considered immune to any attack. Should contrary facts and arguments be presented from without, they are *a priori* rejected as being unworthy of consideration. One does not wish to hear them. If one has any dealings with members of other religious groups, he limits himself to an attempt at convincing the other that he is simply wrong and that he should be converted.

The principal function of religious conventionality is that it gives a feeling of rest, safety, and security to human existence. Now, human existence is in every man, precisely as man, characterized by an existential tension, concern, and uncertainity; but these are entirely or for the greater part silenced by religious convictions and practice. For in all religion it is a matter of man being in the clear with God (with the gods, with the universe, with reality). As long as a person's religiousness is in a conventional stage, nothing is so dangerous for his peace of mind as an attack and undermining of the conventionality of religion.

As long as possible, man resists disturbance of his peace of mind. He simply cannot bear being endangered. This explains why an attack on religious conventionality is usually countered, not with calm and relevant arguments, but with passionate vehemence and indignation. Psychologically it is an unmistakable sign of religious conventionality when parents, teachers, and priests react with infuriation and threats—instead of with control and well-considered arguments—to the insights, ideas, and conduct, or even open criticism of their children, pupils, and parishioners. This kind of impassioned sensitivity usually betrays a secret fear that one's own security, based as it is on conventionality, is endangered.

The nature and function of religious conventionality is also characterized by an invincible stubbornness. Conventions in other areas of life, such as fashions, manners, ways of living, and so on, may be given up with reluctance, but this is done only because they are not related to the security a person needs in order to live in peace with his human existence as such. On the other hand conventionality in the religious area does have that relation, and thus there are reasons for the stubbornness which characterizes religious conventionality. It takes bulldozers to raze a stronghold of religious conventionality. In the long run, only an accumulation of irrefutable facts and arguments can fulfill this job.

Yet, on further reflection it appears that in spite of its stubbornness religious conventionality also has casual and arbitrary characteristics. This becomes obvious only when individual believers for some reason or other are taken out of their familiar conventional milieu. It often happens that people in such circumstances are spiritually and religiously uprooted unless they are capable of making the transition to the religious conventionality of their new environment.

In such circumstances people experience that teaching and conduct can, in many respects, differ from what they have always heard and seen. What had, as a result of a commonly acknowledged and accepted conventionality, up till now been considered as self-evident and irrefutable, suddenly is seen to be less certain and secure than one had thought.

It is clear that the modern means of publication and communication, the frequent emigrations and widespread travel to all parts of the world, all contribute to the notion that convictions and conduct are not the only true and correct ones merely because they are valid in one's own personal environment. Communication with the world at large is not very conducive to the continued existence of conventional religiousness. It is therefore easy to understand why religious and ecclesiastical leaders have tried as much as possible to prevent communication between the believers entrusted to their care and "those of other convictions." It is precisely for this reason that in some circles objections are raised against ecumenical *rapprochement*. As long as the faith and the life of faith are not based on personally acquired convictions there is indeed a danger in communication with the outside world.

Therefore a positive significance of religious conventionality lies in its function of preserving and protecting. As has been noted before, every religion has the characteristics of being a cultural mass-phenomenon. The percentage of those prepared and able to form their own judgment in religious matters depends on the level of culture that has been reached. A short time ago ecclesiastical authorities apparently did not think this percentage was very high. Individual efforts to reflect personally on questions which arose were suspect. Many "believers" still prefer to follow conventional ideas and practices. They evidently do not realize that conventionality is not quite a guarantee of the possession of the truth. For people with this attitude the shock is therefore all the more severe when firmly fixed truths based on "generally accepted" conventional grounds, are suddenly discovered not to be so firmly fixed at all.

While it can be admitted that under certain circumstances and at a certain stage of culture, religious conventionality has a preserving and protecting function, this very function can also lead to very unfortunate isolation. What is taught and done within a given religious society is absolutized, and thus there is a total lack of interest, love, and understanding of the religious life and needs of those who do not belong to one's own circles. Narrow-mindedness and intolerance are inevitable disadvantages of any religious isolation. Here again, it is a matter of seeing the speck in the eye of another, but not the log in one's own.

Quite obviously, religious conventionality is a serious obstacle to fruitful religious contact between members of different religious societies. It seems to be just as self-evident that the other's position is unacceptable as it is that one's own position is beyond reproach. Not infrequently this becomes clear at ecumenical gatherings. Once such a meeting has been mutually arranged, those who take part in it for the first time are hesitant and ill at ease. Such people often act in the supposition that they are defending personally acquired convictions, whereas in reality they are still caught in the shackles of an age-old conventional vision proper to the group they belong to. We do not always believe as personally and think as independently as we sometimes imagine. We are more conventionally determined and limited than we realize. We are the products of our environment, children of our time, servants to one or another religious and theological trend. Without being clearly conscious of it, we all live, believe, and think from some religious or spiritual isolation.

Precisely because it is so extremely difficult to effectively break out of this isolation, it is a rare occurrence to establish a true dialogue between representatives of different religions or Churches; it is rare that people really listen to each other, that they really allow themselves to be informed, corrected, and enriched by what the other has to offer. Usually it is a matter of a monologue, during which each of the parties waits for the moment that the other capitulates and acknowledges that he is wrong or not altogether right. Mutual suspicions prevail that the other is not sufficiently open-minded or sincere. Each party loses sight of the fact that they, themselves, are rather incapable of delivering precisely what the other is so easily expected to produce. When it comes right down to it, we are all part of "blind humanity." [1]

It would be a mistake to maintain that intellectuals in general and religious leaders in particular are less conventionally bound than those who may be counted as belonging to the popular masses or the masses of the faithful. It is generally known that intellectuals outstanding in their particular science or research frequently are no less conventional than anyone else in the religious area.

As far as religious leaders are concerned, they usually consider it their duty to defend and maintain at any cost those conventional convictions and norms which are held in the community entrusted to their care. Usually they do this by strongly emphasizing the immaturity of the masses of the people. They distinguish between the "knowledgeable" and the lay people. The knowledgeable, whether they be priests, ministers, theologians, or engaged in pastoral care, are the ones in authority; the lay people are those who must be guided, instructed, and exhorted, and who are to accept all this in due submissiveness.

A growing self-awareness of the lay people not only constitutes a danger to the conventional exercise of authority, but is also a threat to the conventional concept of religion. In our days we are witnessing a conflict between maturity and authority, and an immediately related conflict between maturity and conventionality.

No one will be foolish enough to think that we have reached the point where all adult people are also mature and capable of forming independent judgments in all areas of life. Such a point will, in fact, never be reached.

At the same time, it is an established fact that everywhere and in every increasing tempo a growing percentage of the population is in the process of reaching true maturity. Illiteracy is practically non-existent in all fully developed nations. All persons have enjoyed primary and secondary education and have had sufficient training to understand that judgment and action require prior reflection. Advanced education is received by more and more members of the younger generation. Through press and pocketbooks, through radio and television, everyone can constantly be informed about significant events everywhere. People

[1] E. de Greeff, *Notre destinée et nos instincts.*

with sufficient intelligence, interest, and energy want to be conversant with current affairs, to reflect on questions which arise, and think out possible solutions. Even where people depend on the judgment of experts they still like to appropriate the knowledge made available and the counsel given.

On the level of politics this growth in maturity has long since resulted in an acceptance of democracy, at least in the free countries. Today it is no longer possible to demand that a person sacrifice his intellect and conscience, his experience and expert knowledge, in order to submit unconditionally to any authority in any field whatsoever. This is true also from the religious point of view. If ecclesiastical and religious authority is to continue to function properly, it will have to be adapted to the growing maturity of the faithful.

However, with this growing maturity and self-determination of the faithful, it is no longer possible artificially to maintain conventional notions, practices, and conduct by pressure from above if their meaning and necessity are not seen by seriously thinking people. A growth of maturity goes hand in hand with an increase in the undermining of conventionality.

In this respect a development is taking place which cannot be stopped. This development will have a determining influence on the structures of authority in any Christian Church or community. The number of the faithful who would unconditionally believe and accept things without reflecting on motives and arguments is dwindling. They cannot continue to believe simply because the bible, the Church, the pope, the council or the synod, the pastor or the minister says so. The legitimacy of these authorities is not called into doubt, but people rightly expect answers to questions, and insights into the meaning, the value, the acceptability, the plausibility of what is taught and prescribed. In other words, there will be more confidence in the legitimacy of claims to authority if that which is taught and proclaimed really addresses the entire person more strongly and more personally.

Finally in this analysis we must speak of the inevitable but detrimental connection between conventionality and prejudice. It is clear that the different characteristics of conventionality are closely interrelated. Aloofness and seclusion promote narrowmindedness. When these qualities are joined to immaturity one finds a predisposition to prejudice. However, the deepest source of prejudice lies in the fear of a possible attack against conventional convictions and practices, which might in turn result in a loss of religious security.

It is clear, therefore, that prejudice is not the same as misunderstanding. With a certain amount of goodwill on the part of those involved, a misunderstanding can be cleared up by supplying further information or a better explanation. A misunderstanding is of an intellectual nature. But intelligence has little to do with prejudice. Most intelligent people are capable of a sudden display of incradicable prejudice when it concerns a group unsympathetic to them.

A prejudice always has an affective and emotional nature. It is not a casual and accidental opinion, but rather a conviction which, though contrary to reality, is so deeply anchored in the entire structure of a given personality or pattern of life that the person concerned is unable to relinquish his prejudice without endangering his personal integrity. "To change it, the whole pattern of life would have to be altered." [2] This is particularly true when religious prejudices are involved. Prejudice shares in the emotionality as well as in the stubbornness of religious conventionality: "It is easier to smash an atom than a prejudice." [3]

Prejudice plays havoc with the process of knowing. If we are prejudiced toward a group which differs from our own, our prejudice hinders us from acquiring a proper knowledge and a true judgment of that group.

In the first place, we are either not at all or only very vaguely conscious of our prejudice. Without motivation, we proceed from the supposition that our prejudice is not prejudice but a self-evident and correct judgment. This unmotivated supposition is in fact an illusion. At no price will we be robbed of this illusion. Newman called these "our preconceived ideas." We refuse *a priori* to test these preconceived ideas against facts and arguments. It is therefore quite according to the very nature of a prejudice that it prevents us from arriving at a better insight or a more correct judgment.

[2] G. W. Allport, *The Nature of Prejudice* (Doubleday Anchor Book [abridged], New York, 1958), p. 384.
[3] *Op. cit.*, p. 9.

In the second place, our prejudices are closely connected with our talents, our mentality, our actual knowledge, our norms—in short with who we are and what we have become by our education and our environment. No two persons are exactly alike in all possible respects. But for that very reason no two persons have the same vision, identical in all details, of the reality they are confronted with. But to the extent that prejudice is involved we are unable to see and admit that our vision and our judgment are incorrect and that those of another might be correct.

In fact, our knowledge and our judgment depend entirely on what we have and are. What comes to light in our knowledge and in our judgment is not the known and judged reality, but our being such as we are and not other. In this connection, Allport cites Plato: "The light within meets the light without." [4] It is precisely when we are prejudiced that our vision and judgment of the other person or of the other group says more about ourselves than about those whom we think we know and judge. Without our being aware of it, prejudice excludes true knowledge and correct judgment.

An exact investigation into the origin and nature of the prejudice, which every person suffers from in one or more respects, would have to be based on numerous tests and inquiries. About the results of such investigations many clarifying and worthwhile observations can be found in the work of Allport, and also in Carlyle Marney's *Structures of Prejudice*.[5] Of particular interest is the part played by heredity, character, environment, and education, in the origin of a prejudice. "A prejudice is often organic, inseparable from the life process." [6]

Prejudices are rarely of a purely individual nature. On closer inspection, even personal prejudices usually appear to be fostered by group-prejudice. Therefore, if by "conventional religion" we understood religion insofar as it is not based on personal reflection, experience, and practice, but on the current conviction and practice of a certain religious society, religious conventionality

[4] *Op. cit.*, p. 161.
[5] C. Marney, *Structures of Prejudice* (Abingdon Press, New York, 1961). Allport's study is mainly concerned with prejudices of a social nature (race, class, party). Marney's is mainly concerned with an analysis of religious prejudices, with reference to the present religious situation, in particular in the Protestant world.
[6] Allport, *op. cit.*, p. 371.

can be considered a group-prejudice. Of course this does not mean that religion as such, or a communally confessed and lived faith is, because of its being communal, nothing but a prejudice of a religious nature. What is meant is that the custom-aspect by which the religion is characterized acts, in relation to other groups, as a group-prejudice.

Religious conventionality as a group-prejudice must be considered the principal obstacle on the road to ecumenical *rapprochement* and collaboration between the Christian Churches and the world religions. It is the prejudice in the religious areas, more than the actual teaching and the actual religious practices, which keeps people separated from each other. God excludes no one from his love and care, from his forgiveness, his reconciliation, and his salvation. God excludes no one from the catholicity which is meant by *oekumene*. It is we ourselves who exclude each other from it. And the principal reason why we do so lies in our religious conventionality and in the group-prejudice inevitably connected with it.

Conventionality cannot be separated from prejudice. Neither of them is based on facts and arguments, but on a presupposed vision and opinion. Neither conventionality nor prejudice wishes to be convinced of being incorrect; both of them demand or expect only that others will allow themselves to be convinced of their being wrong. Therefore neither of them is prepared for dialogue or collaboration, since these might endanger the conventionality and the prejudice.

In the course of Church history, conventionality and prejudice have repeatedly given rise to threats and the application of cruel and unjust punishments and actions that had more to do with hate than with love. In our own time the different Churches are more prepared to forgive, to encounter, to listen, to dialogue, to pray together, to collaborate, and to strive together toward a new unity and communion. Because of religious conventionality and prejudice, many are still resisting this ecumenical development. However, the very fact that this development continues to grow is one of the many signs which indicate that the end of conventional Christianity has come.

After this attempt to analyze the nature of religious conventionality, we must now look for the concrete form and content of conventional Christianity.

# 2. Conventional Christianity

It will be clear to the reader that in the preceding analysis of the nature, function, and consequences of religious conventionality we have touched only the surface of the theme and the problem presented in this book.

We must now proceed to examine the meaning of conventional Christianity, or at least what I mean by it when I speak of it. What is it in the concrete? How are we to imagine conventional Christianity according to its form and content, this conventional Christianity undermined to such a degree that it is no longer tenable and acceptable, this conventional Christianity of which we are experiencing the definitive end, an end which is, in turn, the principal cause of today's religious unrest? What is understood by conventional Christianity, and what is not understood by it?

In the first place, conventional Christianity does not mean the Christianity of the Christians, i.e., the Christians of the first three or four centuries. Christianity at that time was not yet conventional; it was still in a process of becoming, a process accompanied by much friction and tension. One only has to think of the letter to the Romans, in which Paul is at pains to unite the Jewish Christians and the gentile Christians into one community. One can think of the letter to the Corinthians where there is mention of different factions which considered each other as inferior and incomplete, and of a number of opinions and practices which remind one more of unbelief and paganism than of the message of Christ and a Christian manner of living. One could further think of the letter to the Galatians which shows how difficult it was for the Judeo-Christians to remain faithful to the Gospel message, or of the letter to the Thessalonians which shows the community's unrest with regard to the *parousia* of Christ. One could finally recall the statements contained in practically all the letters of Paul, in which he exhorts the Christians to a unity of mind and spirit and to a way of life proper to Christians.

In post-apostolic times, teachers arose occasionally who presented their own interpretation of the meaning of the person, the message, and the work of Christ. It took the Christian Church four centuries before she succeeded in describing the "Catholic" faith exactly and distinguishing it sharply from the many and varied heresies which gave evidence of different visions of the meaning and content of the Gospel. It was also in the course of the first three of four centuries that the canon of sacred scripture, the organization of the Church, and the manner of the weekly celebration of the Lord's supper received more fixed and definite forms. It is extremely difficult for us now to form a clear picture of precisely what the Christians believed and how they lived in those centuries when Christianity, as a new world religion, was still in the process of developing a stable form.

Christianity of the first few centuries was originally a strange element in the Hellenistic-Roman culture and world. It gradually developed into a new religion with its own identity and character. Increasingly it felt the influence of the surrounding pagan culture, not only externally but also from a religious and ethical point of view.[1]

Christianity sprang forth from a Judeo-Semitic milieu and had its roots in the religious faith of the Old Testament. Yet in the formulation of the faith, in the growth of the ecclesiastical structure, in the functioning of authority, in the definitive form of the cult, and in the creation of a new morality, Christianity as a new world religion was also strongly influenced by Greek thought, and especially by the Roman spirit of legalism and strict discipline.

When, as a result of the conversion of Emperor Constantine, Christianity was established as a state religion, and paganism, even among the greater masses of the people, was within one generation replaced by Christianity, it was only to be expected that the content of the faith as well as liturgical and sacramental practices would in many respects be interpreted from a pagan viewpoint.

This occurred even to a greater extent when, mostly in a short time and at the order of their prince or ruler, the peoples of Western Europe were forced to transfer to Christianity. Sometimes this was the result of the conversion of the king; at other

[1] M. Gough, *The Early Christians* (Thomas and Hudson, London, 1961).

times it was the consequence of incorporation into a realm which had already been Christianized. But in every case it was a case of sudden mass-conversions, and not of deliberate individual transitions. It was not through reading the bible and studying the faith that the population came in contact with Christianity, but through the reception of the sacraments and the attendance at church services. It is true that great missionaries went about preaching, and that nations were transformed into Christian nations through new Christian legislation, but inevitably many elements of Christianity were conceived in the former pagan manner. This was particularly true with regard to priesthood and sacrifice, and in general with regard to liturgical, sacramental, and devotional actions. From a religio-phenomenological point of view this course of events is to be considered more or less inevitable; therefore it should not amaze us.

Yet as a result of this development there was an increasing tension and discrepancy between the biblical religious faith and the official teaching of the Church on the one hand, and the images of belief and the religious practices of the people on the other. During the second half of the Middle Ages in particular, legendary stories of the saints occupied an increasingly important place in the imagination of the people. Furthermore, the original sacramental practice was more and more replaced by sacramental devotions and devotions to the saints. The distance increased between the princely bishops on the one hand and the lower clergy and the people on the other, and in particular there was a widening of the gap between the clergy who had pursued studies and the people who were ignorant and underdeveloped. It is ultimately these tensions and contrasts that are to be considered as the principal cause of the sixteenth century Reformation.

This very brief historical summary is required because an understanding of what conventional Christianity is must be seen against this background. Conventional Christianity is the Christianity of the entire Christian people. This does not necessarily mean that it is the Christianity of the bible, in the sense that it corresponds in all respects to the content and meaning of sacred scripture. It is even possible that a crisis comes about in conventional Christianity when there is a growing suspicion, or even conviction, that the current Christianity should be tested anew against the bible. Nor is conventional Christianity the same as the official Church teaching, liturgy, and sacramental practice, or the same as the theology of the Fathers of the Church and later theologians. What is understood by conventional Christianity in this book is Christianity as it has been conceived and practiced by the Christian people since the beginning of the christianization of Western Europe globally. The sixteenth century Reformation was a severe jolt for the Christianity of the Middle Ages, but since that time it is still possible to speak of a conventional Christianity in Roman and Protestant variations.

## Characterization

In the phenomenological characterization of conventional Christianity which follows, we are thinking of Christianity as it existed within the Christian countries of Europe during the ten centuries which history usually refers to as the Middle Ages. This serves to define it clearly in time and place. Such defining is not arbitrary. It is used because we must discuss conventional Christianity in its original and pure form. One could also say that this was conventional Christianity in its genuine state. It was this way until about the end of the Middle Ages when the first traces of an undermining began to appear. Since that time Christianity has continued to exist in its original form, but not without having to adapt itself on some points to the rise and development of a new culture.

The principal general characteristic of conventional Christianity was that in the consciousness of the people it was felt to be something irrefutably established because of divine origin. What the Church taught and prescribed was based on a direct revelation, i.e., on a communication or command of God himself. Because of that it was not subject to doubt and could not be meddled with. Whoever had the audacity to assert something against the judgment of the Church was a heretic. The arguments and motives of a heretic would not be heard. A heretic was nothing; he was burnt at the stake.

A second general characteristic was that the image which the people formed of the teaching and practice of Christianity was based not on a reading and study of the bible, but on belonging to the Church. What was heard and seen in the Church determined the picture which people formed of the Christian religion. It determined religious images and convictions as well as religious actions and the moral conduct. This could hardly be otherwise, because prior to the invention of the art of printing people could not afford the price of a book; moreover, people were generally still illiterate.

The religious images and convictions of conventional Christianity were closely connected with the primitive and prescientific idea of the world and of man. Though scientists knew the earth was a globe, people in general imagined the world as a flat surface. Above the earth was the vault of the firmament with the stars of heaven. There God was seated on his throne, with the Lamb, surrounded by an innumerable multitude of angels and blessed who watched the conduct of man and assisted the faithful by their prayers and by actually rendering help and protection. It was therefore a matter of course to invoke the intercession of the saints and to count on their help and assistance in time of need.

Below the earth was the netherworld with the fire of hell, the dwelling place of the devil and his cohorts and of the souls who were damned. From this netherworld the devil and evil spirits went forth to plague and tempt the people on earth. While man lived on earth, the good and the evil spirits were in constant battle over the possession or the salvation of his soul. By means of frequent invocations of Mary and the saints, the guardian angels and the other angels, the faithful, by means of aspersion with holy water and making the sign of the cross, tried to keep themselves within the sphere of influence of the sacred, to keep the devils at a distance, and to exorcise the fearful evil powers.

The soul was conceived as a spiritual, invisible being which could exist by itself, but which, as long as man is on this earth inhabits the body, gives life to it, makes it function; in short, the soul "animates" the body. A living person was an animated body. At death, the soul left the body and was led by the angels to the place prepared for it: heaven, paradise, purgatory, or hell. At the resurrection of the dead the soul returned to the body and continued its existence in the body as though nothing had ever happened.

*Tenets of Faith*

Within the framework of this conventional image of the world and man one must place the tenets of faith by which conventional Christianity was originally characterized. They are the same tenets of faith expressed in a concise form in the apostolic creed and in the more elaborated creed of Nicea (the creed of the Mass).

Everything that exists, heaven and earth, the world which we can see and touch, the world above and below us—and around us insofar as it remains hidden to our perception—is the work of God's hand. In conventional Christianity this was accepted as a fact by everyone without much reflection and as something rather obvious. Everything that exists gives, by its very existence, a clear witness to the greatness, the goodness, and the omnipotence of God. It is as if God's existence could be perceived with the senses. If God did not exist, then obviously nothing would exist, and we ourselves would not be in existence either. This dependence and relation was so evident that conventional Christianity had no place for any doubt about the existence of God. Nor was there any doubt about the fact that it was the really existing, one and only, truly and eternally living God who made everything which existed. To doubt this would have been the same as to doubt everything, including oneself.

This belief is not limited to Christianity. Outside Christianity too there is belief in a God who created everything. But insofar as it is specific to conventional Christianity, and insofar as it was accepted by every Christian as obvious, religious belief has a content which must be further determined.

The world and man, as God created them, were good. The present state of man and the world is contrary to God's initial act of creation. Something has intervened—a power which spoiled everything. This is the power of satan.

The first human couple, Adam and Eve, lived in perfect innocence and in undisturbed happiness of paradise. But God wanted to test the obedience, fidelity, and love of man. Man was allowed to eat the fruit of all the trees except the fruit of the tree of the knowledge of good and evil. Satan, the prince of disobedient and fallen angels, made use of this prohibition to tempt man, to make him fall into sin, to separate him forever from God, and thus to plunge him into eternal damnation. As a consequence of the sin of Adam and Eve, sin entered into the world. As an inalienable evil, original sin was transferred to all humanity and brought with it, as a necessary result, deprivation, sickness, death, and all possible kinds of anxiety, affliction and suffering for humanity, with eternal death as the final prospect. However, even before man was expelled from paradise, God added to his word of punishment the promise of ultimate salvation and redemption for man, the promise of the coming of the Messiah, the Christ, the Savior or Redeemer of the fallen and condemned human race.

These events, literally and historically understood, form the background to the Gospel of Jesus Christ, i.e., the good news with which the Christian teaching of salvation is concerned. At least this is the way conventional Christianity always understood it, very concrete and very real. It concerns something that God has done, something that actually happened. The Christian faith is not a matter of abstract considerations about God. It is a historical event, a salvation history in which and through which the same God who made heaven and earth and who dwells in an inaccessible light that renders him invisible to anyone has made himself known to man, has revealed himself. Quite in accordance with the New Testament teaching, conventional Christianity always imagined this event of salvation as follows.

As a result of original sin man was no longer the child of God, he lost "supernatural grace." But God did not relinquish him to total ruin. From the very beginning God had a special predilection for some particular men, such as Abel and Noah. Noah's family was saved by God when the flood wiped depraved humanity from the face of the earth. Later, God chose Abraham as a friend, and in Abraham, Isaac, and Jacob he chose their entire progeny as a people specially dedicated to him. This was the people of the Old Testament, the chosen people of Israel.

To this people, chosen from all the peoples of the world, God gave, through Moses, his sacred law after he had delivered them from slavery in Egypt. God spoke to his people through the prophets. From this people, finally, the Savior was born, Jesus Christ, the Son of God, conceived of the Holy Spirit, and born of the Virgin Mary, as it is confessed in the creed of the Church.

It was entirely in accordance with the testimony of the New Testament and the proclamation of the faith of the Church in all times and in all parts of the world that conventional Christianity understood the coming, the conception, and the birth of Jesus Christ as a totally unique event in the history of mankind, and at the same time as a totally incomprehensible and ineffable mystery.

The angel Gabriel came down from heaven and announced in human language the joyful tidings to Mary that she who did not know man would give birth to a son who was to be called Son of the Most High.[2] This was the only Son of God, who was from all eternity in the bosom of the Father, who is one with the Father, and through whom God created everything that is. In the womb of the Virgin Mary this Son of God took to himself a human nature and was born as man. As man: but by virtue of his divinity he would reconcile mankind to God, bring to mankind salvation, redemption, justification, sanctification, make man participate again in eternal life as a child of God. And all this was to be understood in the literal and complete meaning of the word as an actual and historical event.

For thirty years Jesus lived a hidden life. He played with the children in the streets of Nazareth; in the company of his parents he visited the temple in Jerusalem; with his foster father Joseph he worked in the carpenter's shop. No one became aware of Jesus' divinity. Then Jesus left the parental home, was baptized by John the Baptist, and was tempted by the devil. He then gathered a group of disciples around himself and went with them from city to city, preaching the need of conversion and the coming of the Kingdom of God. He corroborated his preaching by means of amazing healings and other miracles.

Deaf mutes who had never been able to hear a human word were suddenly capable of speaking the Aramaic language; the dead, whose bodies had begun to decay, rose from the dead and lived as though nothing had happened; devils by whom the possessed were tortured were driven out and went into pigs who rushed into the lake and were drowned; a huge amount of fish was caught where the disciples had labored all night in vain; and the storm which threatened the lives of the disciples was calmed by the command of Jesus.

What Jesus preached and did is described in the four gospels of the New Testament. However, the gospels seemed to place the main stress on the last few days of Jesus' life, on the institution of

2 Lk. 1, 32.

the last supper as a lasting meal "in commemoration of me," on the agony and capture of Jesus in the garden of Gethsemane, on the interrogation and judgment by Caiphas, the Jewish high priest, by Pontius Pilate, the Roman governor, on Jesus' suffering and death on the cross, and finally on the resurrection on the third day together with the subsequent apparitions of the risen Christ to Mary Magdalen, to the disciples, and ultimately to more than five hundred on one day, most of whom, as Paul states in one of his letters, "are still alive, but some have fallen asleep." [3]

Not only the gospels but also the ten sermons reported in the Acts of the Apostles as well as the letters of Paul place the main stress on the death and resurrection of Christ. It might even be cause for surprise that in his letters Paul never cites from the preaching of Jesus. The message of salvation is the message of the atoning, suffering and death of Christ, followed by the resurrection of Christ as a confirmation that all powers of sin, death, and hell, have been definitively conquered in Christ as the pledge of our own future resurrection on the last day when Christ shall come again to judge the living and the dead, and when he shall establish his reign in a new heaven and a new earth, a reign which shall not end. In conventional Christianity, in accordance with the testimony of sacred scripture and the proclamation of the Church, all this too was taken as actual events in the literal and full sense of the word; as actual events which at the same time infinitely surpass human understanding.

This is the salvation which the Church, throughout the ages, from the very beginning until the present, has announced and has celebrated in her liturgy. In particular it was always celebrated in the holy Eucharist, the supper of thanksgiving and commemoration which forever is the repetition of the last supper of Christ with his disciples on the evening before he suffered and died, a repetition and commemorative celebration until the day of his return. It is for this reason too that in the liturgical year the main stress is laid on the three sacred days of the institution of the last supper, on the passion and death on the cross, and on the resurrection and the empty tomb.

In the testimony of sacred scripture, as well as in the proclamation of the faith of the Church and the liturgical celebration of the redemption, it is a concentration on the death on the cross

[3] 1 Cor., 15, 6.

and the resurrection. These two are inevitably linked together. They are related to each other as an indivisible unity; one cannot be without the other. On this one central event of the death on the cross and the resurrection of Christ, central to all of human history, the salvation of all mankind is based. The proclamation of the cross and resurrection is the core of the Christian and ecclesial *kerygma*, the Christian and ecclesial message of salvation. Conventional Christianity, in all the dimensions of the Christian people, has always understood it thus.

However, the work of salvation has not reached its completion in Christ's death and resurrection, understood as a unity. This completion lies in man. Salvation must come to reality in the human person. No matter how fundamental and central Easter is, it must be followed by the Ascension and Pentecost. Forty days after Easter, Christ, before the eyes of his disciples, ascended into heaven where he is seated at the right hand of the Father. Only then could the Holy Spirit come down from heaven and be poured forth over the disciples in the form of flames and a driving wind. This was the moment of the birth of the Church, the Body of Christ, animated by the Holy Spirit.

Only at that point could the proclamation of salvation be begun. Only then could those who believed be baptized in the name of Jesus, be incorporated into the Body of Christ, and participate on the first day of each week in the eucharistic supper in union with Christ and fellow Christians. In this manner did the work of salvation reach its final end in the life of the individual believer and in the life of the Church in its entirety—the Church which in God's plan of salvation was destined ultimately to embrace all mankind in its universality, when "the whole earth will have become full of the knowledge of the Lord." [4] Conventional Christianity never doubted the manner in which salvation was to be realized. On this point, too, faith was based on the testimony of the bible and on the proclamation of the Church.

Thus far our characterization of conventional Christianity has concerned itself with what Christians always believed because it could be read in sacred scripture and was thus proclaimed in the Church. It was this faith which in the second half of the Middle Ages found intellectual expression in the imposing systems of the theologians, and an artistic expression in sculpture, in painting,

[4] Is. 11, 9.

and in the magnificent cathedrals of France, England, and Germany.

There is yet another aspect of conventional Christianity which we must necessarily include in our characterization. This is the aspect of the Christian concept and conduct of life, the aspect of being-a-Christian as it found expression in devotional and moral life. It is quite true that the Reformation did bring about a change on this point, but in the life of devotion—especially of the pietists and the methodists—and in the attitude toward fellow men, Protestant Christianity in its conventional form does not differ significantly from pre-Reformation Christianity.

If in our day conventional Christianity is under attack, it is directed in large part against the manner in which most Christians have conceived of their being-a-Christian and have put it into practice in the world.


*Piety*


The piety of conventional Christianity has usually been marked by a dualism between heaven and earth, between God's kingdom and the world. Evidently it is a matter of "despising the terrestrial and loving the heavenly," as expressed in some liturgical prayers.

The piety of conventional Christianity means denying the world, self-abnegation, ascetics, prayer, meditation, and mystical experiences. In spite of the opposition levelled against this piety, mysticism, and religious experience, particularly by the Swiss theology of the twenties,[5] it can hardly be maintained that there are no foundations in sacred scripture for these characteristics of Christianity. For is it not written: "Do not love the world or the things that are in the world. If anyone loves the world, the love of the Father is not in him," [6] or "No one can serve two masters; for either he will hate the one and love the other, or else he will stand by the one and despise the other. You cannot serve God and the mammon"? [7] Or do we not read: "So also none of you can be a disciple of mine without taking leave of all his posses-

[5] Emil Brunner, *Die Mystik und das Wort* (Zurich, 1924).
[6] 1 Jn. 2, 15.
[7] Mt. 6, 24.

sions," [8] or "If anyone wishes to be a disciple of mine, he must leave self behind; day after day he must take up his cross and come with me. Whoever cares for his own safety is lost; but if a man will let himself be lost for my sake, that man is safe"? [9] What did Jesus say about the dangers of riches, about selling all that one has, about not being concerned over food and clothing, about food and drink that never perish but last unto eternity, about gathering a treasure in heaven?

Furthermore, does not scripture speak of a "being hated by the world," and of a "being in the world but not of it," [10] of a seeking what is above, where Christ is seated at the right hand of God? "Mind the things that are above, not the things that are on earth. For you have died and your life is hidden with Christ in God." [11] Does not Paul also speak of chastising the body, of running a spiritual race in the arena in order to attain the prize, of self-denial in everything, of praying without ceasing, and of such mystical experiences as "being caught up into paradise and hearing secret words that man may not repeat"? [12] Does not the entire bible point from earth to heaven? This could be extended considerably, and therefore it is extremely difficult to assume that conventional piety as we meet it in the Churches of the Catholic type and in the pietist movements, in Methodism, and in other Protestant orientations, has no basis in sacred scripture. Can it therefore not be said that the varied and widespread system of religious orders and communities is a rebellion against the secularization of Christianity, [13] and that the call to the silence and emptiness of the desert is an authentically biblical vocation? [14]

After these examinations, affirmations and questions, however, we come face-to-face with a surprising and possibly critical phenomenon in the general attitude toward life by which conventional Christianity has until now been characterized: this is the current notion that a person can be a Christian in two different manners. Being-a-Christian can evidently be divided into two

8 Lk. 14, 33.
9 Lk. 9, 23-24.
10 Jn. 17, 15-16.
11 Col. 3, 1-2.
12 2 Cor. 12, 4.
13 A. M. Allchin, *The Silent Rebellion, Anglican Religious Communities* (S.C.M. Press, London, 1958), p. 11.
14 P. F. Anson, *The Call of the Desert* (S.P.C.K., London, 1964), pp. 2-7.

areas, the sacred and the profane. One can lead a life in the world and a life in the Church, a life on Sunday and a life during the week, a life dedicated to a profession and a life dedicated to piety and devotion. It is even possible to choose between two different states of life, both of which are valid for the Christian. One can choose between a religious and a secular way of life as if in principle it does not matter whether a Christian leads a religious or a worldly life provided the latter does not conflict with the demands of morality.

## Morality

This matter leads us to the area of morality, a rather perilous matter. Conventional Christianity bears the stamp of an apparently generally accepted, conventional concept of the nature of Christian morality. There is scarcely a facet of Christianity on which public opinion is at once so sensitive and so unanimous—and therefore so easily touched, if not severely shocked, when the convention is attacked—as that of Christian morality. And yet at the same time there is scarcely a facet of the Christian attitude which cannot be shown to be in accordance with what Jesus said in his preaching.

What is conventional morality? It is the morality of men who would not for anything in the world transgress even the least of the divine or ecclesiastical precepts, but who evidently are not aware of the fact that they are in constant danger of trampling and deadening the law of God, which is the law of love, through their very strict and literal observance of the outward law. In the New Testament this is the morality of the scribes and pharisees, perfectly correct and decent men whose conduct was literally blameless in the sight of the law, and who prided themselves on being renowned as such before God and men. "God, I thank you that I am not like the rest of men, greedy, dishonest, adulterous. . . . I fast twice a week and I pay tithes on all I get." [15] Jesus calls these men hypocrites, fools, and blind men, "whitened sepulchres which outwardly appear beautiful, but within are full of dead men's bones and all uncleanness," [16] i.e., full of hatred, sensuality,

[15] Lk. 18, 11-12.
[16] Mt. 23, 27.

avarice, lust for power, and self-complacency. Why this disastrous judgment over men who have fame and a good reputation, and who are admired and praised for their faultless manner of living, their piety, and their strict obedience to the law?

Must, then, the law of God not be honored? Is it good, then, to transgress the law? By no means, Paul would answer. But what, then, is wrong with these honorable and highly praised men of the conventional and bourgeois morality?

We touch here on a very sensitive point of conventional Christianity. It is questionable whether on this precise point conventional Christianity differs at all from the conventional Jewry of the days of Christ. And yet, it was precisely because he constantly attacked conventional morality that Jesus was violently hated, that the pharisees and sadducees, the scribes and high priests—in short, the leaders of the people—delivered him into the hands of the Roman governor, who put him to death.

Had not Jesus, quite unnecessarily, undermined the prestige of the priest and the levite by his parable of the good Samaritan? [17] Had not Jesus, by his preaching, undermined the authority which the scribes and pharisees enjoyed with the people? Had not Jesus in all sorts of ways transgressed the law of Moses—by curing the sick on the sabbath, by not fasting, by not observing the law of purification? Was it not a veritable desecration of the holy law that Jesus ate and drank with public sinners and despised tax collectors who were extorting money from the people on behalf of the Romans? Did he not protect a woman taken in adultery and then proceed to allow her to kiss his feet in the very company of his host and fellow guests? Did not Jesus endanger the entire social order by his criticism of the rich, by his exhorting the rich to shun members of their own social class and invite the poor and the destitute, the dregs of humanity, to dinner? Was it not against all convention for Jesus to converse in a friendly manner with women and Samaritans? Were not the grievances of the leaders of the people well founded and just?

On the other hand, what did Jesus mean when he said "Do not judge that you may not be judged; because with the judgment with which you judge, you too will be judged, and the measure which you use will also be used against you"? [18] Is it possibly

17 Lk. 10, 30-37.
18 Mt. 7, 1.

because we neither really know our own heart nor that of another? Or perhaps it is because we are all sinners and stand in the
same need of God's forgiveness, and that only God has the right
to judge. Did Jesus ever exhort his disciples to make sure they
judged everyone who might be guilty of wrongdoing? Or did
Jesus ask his disciples to be always ready to forgive, even seventy
times seven times, even if the wrong done had been perpetrated
against themselves?

Was not Jesus concerned to educate his disciples and followers
to a radically new norm of judgment, to a radically new attitude
toward their fellow men, to a life not according to the letter but
according to the spirit of the law—in short to a life based not on
justice but on love? In the parable of the prodigal son, did Jesus
take up the cause of the elder son who served his father faithfully
for so many years? Did not Jesus, in spite of what would seem to
be a justified admonition of the elder son to the father, take up
the cause of the younger son who, having learned his lesson the
hard way, had returned home? [19] In short, did not Jesus state
explicitly "I tell you, if your justice does not surpass that of the
scribes and pharisees, you shall not enter into the Kingdom of
Heaven"? [20] With all this, did not Jesus indicate that the Christian's attitude toward his fellow man should be of a totally different, new, and higher order than that of the current morality of
conventional Jewry?

The question is whether in all sincerity we can maintain that
the radical transition of all norms regarding human relationships,
which is the core of Jesus' preaching, has in fact found expression
and application in the traditional bourgeois morality of conventional Christianity. Or should we rather say that the great seriousness with which conventional Christianity has tried to bring
*faith* into agreement with the testimony of the bible has been in
inverse proportion to the slight efforts to inculcate the *manner
and conduct of life* intended by Jesus?

If one were to ask about the nature and content of the morality
of conventional Christianity, one would have to conclude that it
has not distinguished itself in any respect from that of the Jews
and the Gentiles. It is nothing but the morality of the Ten Commandments, the morality of natural law, of the law which, as Paul

[19] Lk. 15, 25-32.
[20] Mt. 5, 20.

says, is written in the heart, not only of the Jews who have the external Law, but also of the Gentiles who "although they do not have the Law, do by nature what the Law prescribes." [21]

This general human morality is the official morality of conventional Christianity. It was only the exceptional saints whose actions surpassed it. For the "ordinary man" who was ready in all humility to admit "that he was not a saint," there was only this bourgeois morality. More could not be demanded or expected of him.

Now what is involved when a person arranges his life according to the demands and norms of the official morality of conventional Christianity?

In the first place, a man must keep the sixth commandment and contest against any notion, idea or deed which opposes the general traditional interpretation of this commandment. This commandment in conventional Christianity has received such prominence that many are inclined to think of a "moral life" as exclusively the sexual life of man. Sin is any fantasy, any desire, any action, any relationship which is against sexual morality, particularly when it concerns something that also must be branded as being against nature. It is really amazing how violently and uncontrolled some people can react when cases in this area come to their knowledge or are discussed. In comparison, murder, theft, and deception seem to be of very little significance.

Yet, at the same time, there is practically no aspect of human existence which can be so carefully protected against publicity as sexuality. When at one time or another something does come to light, it is only a slight reflection of what is possible or what is actually taking place. As a result we are easily inclined to camouflage our sexual desires and conduct, to sublimate sexual guilt feelings, to acquire a good name by a public show of indignation and disgust, and to judge harshly anything we think to be a sexual transgression. This is no doubt the reason why Jesus said to the scribes and pharisees who brought him a woman caught in adultery, "Let him among you who is without sin, cast the first stone." [22]

A second virtue which conventional Christianity has always given strong emphasis to is the virtue of justice. A Christian must render everyone his due. The norm for this was always justice,

[21] Rom. 2, 14.
[22] Jn. 8, 7.

not love which goes to the farthest extremes. It is not a matter of going to any extremes but of staying within limits. It is a matter of the strict demands of justice and duty, but in such a manner that no one can be asked or expected to render more than what he is obliged to in justice.

Since numerous everyday conflicts make it important to determine what the demands of justice are and what a person's strict duty to another is, the need arose for a complicated legislation which would cover all the aspects of man's life. And this was accompanied by an equally complicated jurisprudence. Strictly speaking, there is no reprimand for the Christian as long as he has observed all the rights and duties in his human contacts. Anything over and beyond rights and duties is at most a praiseworthy addition, but in the eyes of many it is naive and foolish. Under no condition can a person be called a "bad Christian" just because he never did more than he was obliged to do in strict justice.

Likewise, man's relation to God in the bourgeois morality of conventional Christianity has been considered a matter of justice. It is fitting and just that the Christian render God the honor which is due to him. This means that one must not give honor to idols, but only to the true, living God. This is done in the first place by participating in the weekly divine service, secondly by using the name of God with respect, and finally by not transgressing God's commands: honoring father and mother, not killing, not committing adultery, not stealing, not giving false testimony against one's neighbor.[23] The prescript against lying, however, is put into practice with certain reservations: i.e., as long as it is not to our own disadvantage. This is true also for promises. Promises are fulfilled as long as the circumstances remain unchanged. Usually one does not consider oneself bound to fulfill one's promises if it would involve some unforeseen and heavy sacrifices at the cost of one's own happiness in life. In such circumstances one would consider oneself excused and would transfer the consequences to the other, hoping that he will be able to find the necessary help and assistance with someone else.

For centuries, one of the most striking features in the morality of conventional Christianity was the complete absence of social consciousness. The happy awakening of this consciousness in our own day is a rather late phenomenon among Christians, and even

[23] Ex. 20, 12-16.

then it was for a large part due to pressure from the outside, from the suppressed, exploited, excluded, and persecuted peoples, races, classes, and religious or social minorities.

Who would dare affirm that the numerous wars waged among Christian peoples, culminating in the last two world wars, that the manner in which Christian nations have colonized and have been trying to expand their power over the entire world, and that the fate of the working classes since the industrial revolution of the eighteenth century, correspond in any way to what Jesus taught and intended?

The bourgeois morality of conventional Christianity is based on the natural law and the Ten Commandments. Under all circumstances it relies exclusively on justice and adheres as much as possible to principles. Neither charity nor sound reason is capable of doing anything against the juridical mentality of morality.

If we compare this legalistic morality to the parables, to the sermon on the mount, and particularly to the eight beatitudes of Jesus, the radical difference becomes at once obvious. The same holds true in a comparison to the admonitions which Paul gives in his letters.

If the beatitudes are the norm, Christians should in all circumstances of life strive to belong to the poor in spirit, to those who weep, to the meek of heart, to those who hunger and thirst after (social) justice, to the merciful, to the pure of heart, to the peacemakers and to the persecuted. According to conventional morality, however, Christians are above all attached to principle; they insist on their right, they live according to the letter of the law and the corresponding duty. It never occurs to the principled and proper man of the bourgeois and official morality to consider that sometimes charity may demand that one does more than what is right and of duty, in fact that charity may even demand that the law be transgressed. Conventional Christians evidently are unaware that Jesus preached a radical revolution precisely with regard to conventional morality.

It is of course quite true that at all times there have been individual Christians whose lives transcended by far the justice of bourgeois morality as held in conventional Christianity. Nor can it be denied that the campaign against the slavery of the Negroes in America, and later the opposition against racial discrimination, were launched by Christians. In this connection we must also keep in mind the social gospel preached in England and America. Of great importance, finally, is the social witness as heard with unmistakable clarity in the world conferences on Life and Work, in the meetings of the World Council of Churches, and in the sessions of the Second Vatican Council. However, all these glad tidings are more like protests against current moral standards than reflections of an age-old, self-evident, traditional morality as practiced by official and conventional Christianity.

## General Observations

In the preceding pages I have tried to present an analysis and description of the faith, the piety, and the morality as conceived for centuries by the faithful who lived in the sphere of influence of conventional Christianity. While doing this I have tried to abstract completely from the theological reflection which took place from the very earliest times.

If in this effort I have been a little more elaborate on the point of morality than on the points of faith and piety, this is due primarily to the fact that conventional belief and piety appear to have recourse to the Gospel message proclaimed in the New Testament, whereas this can hardly be said of the morality of conventional Christianity.

But a second reason for this stress is that it has become increasingly clear to me that the criticism and attack which Christianity now experiences from many younger people, from representatives of colored races and non-Christian nations, as well as from humanists, communists, and other modern groups, are directed more against traditional Christian morality than against the tenets of faith which might be unacceptable to modern man. In this criticism and attack, the latter are considered secondary. Finally, if objections are presented against certain forms of Christian piety, this is due primarily to the otherworldliness represented in these forms.

We shall have to say more about this in our final chapter, but it can now be stated that the theme of this book and the problem connected with it concentrate mainly on the question about God. In the final instance the undermining of conventional Christianity has resulted in a question about the possibility and the eventual nature and reasonableness of belief in God. Moreover, the purpose and content of the lectures from which this book resulted demanded that the main emphasis should be given to the problem of God as it occurs in our time, due to the undermining of conventional Christianity. It would, of course, be quite possible, and in fact very important, to give more attention to the practical questions of piety and morality. But it is not feasible to deal fully and professionally with all the facets of the present religious crisis. A conscious onesidedness is inevitable. Moreover, the problems are so numerous and the available literature so extensive that here, too, a certain amount of selectivity is necessary. It is therefore more a matter of using examples to typify and clarify our present religious situation than of presenting a comprehensive treatment of it.

Finally, a remark about the significance of the sixteenth century Reformation. There is no doubt that the Reformation was a severe shock to conventional Christianity in the form it had had for a thousand years in Western Europe. Particularly with regard to piety and sacramental practice, considerable changes had occurred in the second half of the Middle Ages. Popular piety had become magical, mechanical, and anthropocentric. A separate volume would be required to go into this in greater detail. But it is important to realize that the Reformation was primarily directed against these defects for practical reasons, not because of theological speculation.

The Reformation was made possible by the spread of translations of the bible, which in turn was a result of the invention of the art of printing, and meant a return and recourse to sacred scripture. The authority of ecclesiastical tradition was replaced by the exclusive authority of the bible. In many respects this meant a change in faith, piety, and morality whenever and insofar as the Reformation insights into the bible seemed to demand it. No matter how important and necessary, a theological justification based on the bible came about only gradually. For the Reformation it was primarily a matter of purifying the divine service and devotion of unbiblical images and practices, which were seen as pagan, and establishing a relation to God and a Christian manner of life based on the pure and genuine Gospel.

However, the Reformation version of conventional Christianity corresponded rather well to the post-Tridentine Roman Catholic Church's version of it, especially in regard to the idea of literal inspiration, the historicity and genesis of the bible, salvific events and their interpretation, the otherworldliness of piety, and individual and social morality.

## Farewell to Religion and Christianity

Practically in all parts of the world there is now taking place what in our day is being referred to as a "silent defection from the faith." However, of at least an equally serious nature is the religious unrest, a feeling of attack and uncertainty among a large segment of the faithful who would not for anything in the world want to lose their faith, but who at the same time are thoroughly confused about it. They are disturbed by the numerous and often far-reaching changes which Churches make in church life. They are disturbed by the new theological insights they hear and read about, and by the objections to the current beliefs in God brought to everybody's attention through novels, scientific books, radio, television, the press, and forums.

It would be a kind of self-deception if pastors and believing Christians were to pretend that only a small number of intellectuals are occupying themselves with these questions, that the masses of the faithful are "happily" uninterested. Such indifference to what is taking place in spiritual and religious matters would, if it were true, be an ominous sign indeed. The large-scale indifference which is actually found among students and many others could be a sign that not only conventional Christianity but religion and Christianity as such have come to an end. All too often, and on all sorts of occasions, people say that "we are totally uninterested."

People of whom it was not expected are asking questions such as: "Have we left the era of belief behind us forever? Could it be that religion belongs only to the past? Does Christianity still have any sense?" Of course to hear these questions one has to go outside the circle of likeminded faithful and speak with others openly and without reserve about Christianity and Christian morality. Anyone who does this discovers very quickly that the circle of those who are still at peace with the general conventional Christianity of the past has become very small.

Only a highly self-assured and self-satisfied theologian would be unwilling to admit that it is no longer possible to formulate a facile answer on the spur of the moment to questions that come from the ignorance of the uninitiated. We theologians have the perfection of all knowledge! But that is precisely why we no longer understand the questions of the "common man." Perhaps it would be far better to say: "I do not know either. I know that I believe, but my faith is under attack; let us search together."

Some time ago a book appeared in Germany with the title *Farewell to Christianity?* [24] This rather alarming title would not at first sight suggest that the book is a collection of articles presented by a number of friends to a bishop on the occasion of his sixty-fifth birthday. It seems a strange idea, not particularly suited for festivity, to present a bishop with the question of whether the time has come to say farewell to Christianity—in other words, whether we are at present experiencing the end of Christianity.

The bishop who received the book is Lutheran Bishop Hans Lilje, well known in ecumenical Christianity. In the introductory chapter he is called "the bishop of those who are doubting, asking, and searching; the bishop of those who actually no longer belong." [25] He is called "a bishop who counts skepticism among his Christian virtues, a healthy skepticism which, being directed at one's own heart, acknowledges that God is greater than our heart, thus leading from one truth to the other." [26] The question of the end of Christianity can be asked of a bishop who has not pledged himself once and for all to a system, a bishop who knows that he, too, is a believer subject to attack and temptation, one who forever asks questions and continues to find new answers.

In any case, it concerns a question. The reason why the question is asked, so the writers tell us, is because our present historical situation is from the religious point of view characterized precisely by this question. Whether one is ready to hear and acknowledge it or not is the serious question facing Christianity in the present circumstances. Many causes have contributed to the fact that we are no longer in a position to let the question go by unnoticed.

[24] Seeberg-Zahrnt, *Abschied vom Christentum?* (Furche Verlag, Hamburg, 1964). This book is to be regarded as an answer to Gustav Wyneken's book *Abschied vom Christentum*, which appeared in 1963.

[25] Seeberg-Zahrnt, *op. cit.*, p. 14.

[26] *Op. cit.*, p. 9.

Fortunately, we are concerned with a question. "As long as man continues to ask questions, there is hope. Only when he stops asking questions is Christianity over and done with; but then man too is done and over with, for he denies his origin and his very being." [27] If this has ever been true, then it is particularly true in our own time. We find ourselves at a decisive stage in the history of mankind. Nothing is so alarming as the fact that evidently there still are unruffled, self-assured, purely conventional Christians immune and indifferent to the entire problem. Precisely because conventional Christianity has come to a definitive end, no Christian can continue to be a Christian without knowing that he is involved in the present problem with the future of Christianity at stake. We are faced with a new dilemma: either no Christianity or a radically renewed Christianity. If this were not true, then there would have been no Second Vatican Council and we would not be experiencing all the things now taking place in Christianity.

"The all-important religious line of demarcation no longer separates Christians from non-Christians, but the self-assured from the perturbed, the indifferent from those who live in expectation, the content from those who doubt, those who ask questions from those who have given up asking." [28] Consequently, the best books now appearing are those that deal with the questions that count in the actual problematical situation without anticipating the solution by premature answers. The solution to the present situation can never be given by one single person. It will have to be found by Christianity in its entirety. Even then it can be found only gradually, not in a self-assured confinement but in a continuous, open-minded, and sustained dialogue with all mankind, with those who believe in God and with those who do not.

The contemporary Christian is a man of belief and unbelief, a man of question and answer. The dialogue he is involved in is not his own dialogue. It is the dialogue which God carries on with all mankind in the decisive situation which is taking place in the world now. For this reason it is a matter of an ecumenical dialogue *par excellence*, a dialogue in which the entire *oekumene*— all mankind in its widest range—is involved, a dialogue between Christians, between all religions, between believers and unbelievers.

[27] *Op. cit.*, p. 12.
[28] *Op. cit.*, p. 10.

Previous answers are frequently no longer tenable; new answers have hardly been found. One question, however, is the same everywhere. That question is man himself, simply because he is that strange being: "man." This is the central truth of humanism, that man is man, and that he must ask himself what this fact means to his existence. However, does the question of man transcend man, and does it lead to the Other whom we call God? Among all men in the whole world, and of whatever religion, any answer to this question merits full consideration.

We shall have to begin by listening to each other. The unbeliever will have to listen to the believer, and the believer must listen to the unbeliever. We shall have to give serious consideration to each other's questions and answers. If the unbeliever recognizes God's call and God's coming in this dialogue, he will have to listen to God together with the other; together with the other he will have to go forward to meet God. But no man in the world, whoever and wherever he may be, profits from preconceived, self-assured answers. God still walks with mankind. We ask about him; we hope to encounter him.

If this book is dealing with the end of conventional Christianity, the emphasis is placed on the word "conventional." The title is not intended to suggest that the end has come to Christianity as such, to genuine Christian belief and living. The term "conventional Christianity" does not mean the Doctors of the Church, mystics, religious founders, reformers, missionaries, and theologians. It means Christianity in general as it has been understood and practiced for centuries by ordinary Christians. This sort of Christianity has come to a definitive end. It has been undermined and is collapsing. Because conventional Christianity has been the Christianity of "the masses," its collapse results in mass defections, or at least in a general religious unrest.

Since many people identify conventional Christianity with Christian faith and practice as such, there is a general opinion that the end of conventional Christianity is also the end of any form of Christianity, and possibly the end of any form of religion. It is not my intention to demonstrate apologetically that this is not so. As a phenomenologist I ascertain that many people have this opinion. But it must also be pointed out that those authors who write about the end of religion and Christianity are usually attacking *conventional* Christianity. In only a few instances are their attacks directed against Christian faith, life, and thought in their optimal form.

This, however, should not lead the reader to conclude that books which attack and reject the current narrow forms of Christianity do not constitute a real challenge for the serious Christian, and that therefore these books can simply be disregarded. The real question at issue is whether religion and Christianity are coming to an end. If we are convinced that this is not true, then we must ask ourselves how religion and Christianity will be renewed in order to have meaning and significance for future mankind.

There is a number of people who hold that Christianity, and possibly religion in general, are now coming to a definitive end. For instance there is the English scientist Bertrand Russell, generally known through his book *Why I Am Not a Christian*.[29] His position is similar to that of Gerhard Szczesny who wrote *The Future of Unbelief; Contemporary Reflections of a Non-Christian*.[30] Correspondence concerning this book between the author and Friedrich Heer was published under the title *Belief and Unbelief; Christian or Non-Christian*.[31] In Germany appeared Otto Flake's book *The Last God*,[32] and Gustav Wynekens' *Farewell to Christianity*.[33] In France, Henry Fesquet published a book called *Catholicism, Religion of Tomorrow?*[34] He dedicated this book "to all those who, not believing in Christ, have helped me understand him better." In 1963 a collection of lectures was published under the title of *Objections to Christian Belief*,[35] written by Christians aware of the present religious unrest. Of far greater importance is the non-theological prophetic

[29] Bertrand Russell, *Why I Am Not a Christian* (Allen and Unwin, London, 1957).

[30] G. Szczesny, *Die Zukunft des Unglaubens* (List Verlag, Munich, 1959).

[31] Heer-Szczesny, *Glaube und Unglauben* (List Bücher, Munich, 1959).

[32] O. Flake, *Der letzte Gott. Das Ende des theologischen Denkens* (Rütten und Loening, Munich, 1961).

[33] G. Wyneken, *Abschied vom Christentum* (Szczesny Verlag, Munich, 1963).

[34] H. Fesquet, *Le catholicisme religion de demain?* (Grasset, Paris, 1962). English tr.: *Catholicism, Religion of Tomorrow?* (Holt, Rinehart & Winston, New York, 1964).

[35] Vidler, and others, *Objections to Christian Belief* (Constable, London, 1963).

and poetic witness of Werner and Lotte Pelz, called *God Is No More*.[36] The book has a preface by Canon Carpenter of Westminster. Perhaps this religion-less witness concerning Christ could be considered as an elaboration of Bonhoeffer's vision.

The books by Russell, Szczesny, Flake, and Wynekens are indications of a total break with any form of Christianity and religion. The last two books mentioned show a deep insight into the motives which at present frequently lead to defections from the faith, as well as a clear understanding of the necessity of a radical renewal of the Christian's religious life and practice. Periodicals in many countries show that these insights are shared by a good number of Christians.

Particularly encouraging is the increasing distaste for proselytism and for the biased apologetical attitude in which people had nothing else in mind than to defend their own position without having any serious intention to understand and appreciate the arguments and motives of others. It is also good to see particularly among the younger generations that there is much less inhibition and much more openness and sincerity when it comes to manifesting difficulties and doubts. Fortunately there exists a growing dislike of forms of ecclesiastical discipline and censorship which give the impression that all is well with the faith and the life of faith, and which, by all sorts of measures, silence precisely the most sincere people.

In some instances this new honesty is more important in itself than what is being said. Many frank expressions merit attention precisely because they bring to light the hidden worries and doubts which until recently were usually kept secret. For too long have we kept up appearances, misleading not only ourselves but others as well. Regardless of the question of their positive values, books such as Robinson's *Honest To God*,[37] Pike's *A Time for Christian Candor*,[38] Baxter's *Speak What We feel*,[39] and Novak's *The Open Church*,[40] have great merit because of

---

[36] Werner and Lotte Pelz, *God Is No More* (Lippencott, Philadelphia-New York, 1964).

[37] J. A. T. Robinson, *Honest to God* (S.C.M. Press, London, 1963).

[38] J. Pike, *A Time for Christian Candor* (Harper and Row, New York, 1964).

[39] Baxter, *Speak What We Feel* (S.C.M. Press, London, 1964).

[40] M. Novak, *The Open Church* (Darton Longmans and Todd, London, 1964).

their honesty. For those who are willing to understand, this type of publication creates an entirely new climate in which pastoral care and dialogue begin to show a much more open, honest and meaningful character.

It now seems that the focus of the discussion concerning the question of whether there shall be an end or a rejuvenation of Christianity and religion has shifted in two different respects.

The first is only indicated in passing here. Since the Second Vatican Council, the focus has unexpectedly been shifted from Protestant to Roman Catholic Christianity. This does not mean that Protestant Churches do not occupy themselves with the question about the future and renewal of Christianity. But in the Roman Catholic Church the question has suddenly become acute, actual and central in a manner which only a short time ago seemed quite impossible. It seemed impossible because for centuries the Roman curia, by means of the Holy Office, exercised a spiritual discipline in the Church which was unequaled in obstinacy and inviolability.

This formidable, almost tyrannical spiritual power was born from a deep sense of responsibility to safeguard the substantial content of the faith against any form of attack. While it was worthy of praise for this reason, it seriously restricted the spiritual freedom necessary for progress, and for as long as possible it blocked any renewal of Christian thought. Today this is no longer possible. There is no place for such a form of authority in the Church of the future. Collegiality and frequently consultation in which freedom of expression is guaranteed will put an entirely new stamp on the manner in which the Church of the future will carry out its task of proclaiming the faith.

The second shift in focus in the question about the end or rejuvenation of Christianity merits more thorough consideration. This is where the question culminates in the problem of God, particularly as it has occurred in the United States. There are several reasons why this discussion has shifted from Europe to the United States. It is due first of all to the profound changes regarding the position of Europe in the world. The era of colonialism and imperialism has ended. The apparently meek submission of Asiatic and African nations to the supremacy of their overlords has been replaced by criticism, rebellion, and antipathy, if not by outspoken hatred. The guidance and advice of the

whites is no longer wanted. The repercussions of this transition in
the relations between whites and colored are also felt in missionary work. Added to this is also a new confrontation between
Christianity and the non-Christian religions. This will be further
dealt with in the ninth chapter.

The fire which was kindled all over the world by Western
man during the era of imperialism has become a real world con-
flagration which now threatens the continued existence of the
white race. As far as Europe is concerned, it has become hedged
in by two strong world powers, the American and the Asiatic
blocs. In all respects Europe has to rely on American support.
Within the Western sphere of civilization the cultural leadership
has shifted more and more from Europe to the United States.
This shift is now making itself felt also in the area of religion and
Christianity.

It cannot be denied that as a result a certain fatigue and fatalis-
tic acquiescence predominates in Europe. In some parts there are
manifestations of a psychosis of decline. There is a widespread
notion that the role of Europe has ended forever. In some places
believing Christians speak out against this acquiescent defeatism.
They are deeply aware of the European Christian's responsibility
for all that Europe has done to the world: "It is we who have
made this world the way it is now." [41]

Europe seems to be seized with spiritual fatigue with regard to
religious and theological discussion. Certainly, the stimulus given
by the Second Vatican Council is encouraging, but Protestant
discussion has practically come to a standstill. For almost a half
century this discussion was dominated by the theological revival
and transition of the Twenties. The names of Karl Barth, Emil
Brunner, Rudolf Bultmann, and Paul Tillich are known to everyone. All these men lived to be about eighty, and even now their
names are dominating the discussion. In this connection mention
must also be made of the names of Heidegger and Jaspers.

But in more recent years the younger generation of preachers
and theologians has become disappointed. The influence of Barth
is on the wane. From all sides there are manifestations of growing
resistance to the exclusivism of Barth's basic theological principle.
There are still many who admit that during the Twenties it was
Barth who saved the Reformation in Europe. But at what price?

[41] Thus: Heinz Beckmann in *Abschied vom Christentum?* p. 47.

It is said that it was done at the cost of many valuable religious aspects which cannot be disregarded without irreparable damage to the foundations which religious belief and life are based on. John Cobb voices a widespread opinion when he says that "few men in our age or in any age have come so near succeeding in confronting us with a final choice for or against faith. If Barth has failed, as I believe he has, his failure has been one of the most brilliant failures of all times." [42] Here Cobb touches on the deepest cause of the fact that particularly in the United States the problem of God and the question of the tenability of the Christian faith has been raised in an entirely new manner.

In Europe the accent in the theological discussion has shifted from Barth to Bultmann, and at the moment there is a growing tendency to find a satisfactory solution in the theology of Tillich. In the United States the accent has shifted in the opposite direction. Paul Tillich, emigrated from Germany to the United States in 1933 and dominated the theological discussion there for a long time. The younger generation has gradually come to show more interest in Bultmann and finally also in Bonhoeffer. The latter's well known prediction concerning the approach of a religionless era,[43] in which a totally secularized Christianity will find a hearing and following, has met with wide approval. This prediction became the most important stimulus for the God-is-dead movement.

Apart from this stimulus however, the modern analytical philosophy of Wittgenstein [44] and the new method of linguistic analysis have given an impetus to the discussion of the problem of God. Particularly because the discussion takes place within the Christian Churches it has disturbed many people. The discussion centers around the question of whether and how a synthesis is possible between the original core and meaning of the Christian proclamation and the atheistic mentality of modern society. The theologians who favor this synthesis are professors of different divinity schools where future pastors are trained. They are firmly

[42] J. B. Cobb, *Living Options in Protestant Theology* (Westminster Press, Philadelphia, 1962), p. 197. Cobb belongs to the group of American, German, and Swiss theologians who together edit the series *New Frontiers in Theology* (Harper & Row, New York).

[43] Dietrich Bonhoeffer, *Widerstand und Ergebung* (Kaiser V. Munich, 1962), p. 182.

[44] C. A. van Peursen, *Ludwig Wittgenstein* (Wereldvenster, Baarn, 1965).

convinced that the God of conventional Christianity no longer exists in the consciousness of modern man. Altizer even published an entire gospel of Christian atheism.[45]

A final cause of the shifting of the focus of theological discussion from Europe to the United States is the youthful openness and vitality by which the United States is distinguished from Europe. In one of his autobiographic narratives Paul Tillich tells of the differences in mentality and attitudes between Germany and the United States which he saw upon his arrival as an immigrant in 1933: "I saw the American courage to go ahead, to try, to risk failures, to begin again after defeat, to lead an experimental life both in knowledge and in action, to be open toward the future, to participate in the creative process of nature and history." [46]

The American has a natural repugnance of any form of heteronomy, of any restriction to the freedom of expression, of being tied down to tradition, convention, and authority. This predisposes him to explore really new ways in all areas, including those of culture and religion. It is quite true that the United States is also known for extreme forms of obstinate orthodoxy, but it seems that in this respect there exists a remarkable contrast between the older and the younger generation. In any case, as far as our theme is concerned we shall not be able to limit ourselves to Europe; we shall have to pay due attention to the possibly strange if not alarming direction in which the discussion about our problem is moving at the moment in the United States.

The phenomenologist of religion Wilfred Smith has written an extensive and well documented study about the concept of religion, entitled *The Meaning and End of Religion*.[47] After dealing with the history of this concept Smith attempts to show that a clear distinction must be made between the action of Jesus, Mohammed, and Buddha on the one hand, and the world religions that claim to be allied to them on the other. His criticism of the current concept expressed by the word "religion" finally leads him to suggest that this misleading and confusing word be abol-

[45] T. J. J. Altizer, *The Gospel of Christian Atheism* (Westminster Press, Philadelphia, 1966).

[46] Kegley-Bretall, *The Theology of Paul Tillich* (Macmillan, New York, 1952, p. 20).

[47] W. C. Smith, *The Meaning and End of Religion* (Macmillan, New York, 1963).

ished. He also pleads for the abolition of the names Christianity, Mohammedanism, and Buddhism. These religions, as cultural products, are not the proper means of understanding the message, witness, or teaching of these founders of religion; in fact they are really an obstacle to understanding.

As the point of departure for his reflections, Smith selected a paragraph from the dogmatics of Karl Barth, entitled *Religion as Unbelief*. The paragraph he selected is found in the chapter about *God's Revelation as Abolition of Religion*.[48] He also adopted Bonhoeffer's vision of a future religion-less Christianity. We shall not go further into this question here. For the moment our intention is only to make clear that the question about the fture of religion and Christianity is being seriously considered in the United States.

The importance and effects of the discussion about this question are frequently apparent in many periodicals, such as *The Christian Century*, *Religion in Life*, *Theology Today*, *Christianity and Crisis*, and *Religious Studies*, as well as in the growing number of publications in book form, many of them in pocket format.

The American weekly *Time* in 1966 spectacularly popularized the God-is-dead movement. Reactions varied from "The existence of God is not in question" to "The God myth is dying, with our energetic help." The actual religious situation of our time was perhaps best expressed in the following reaction: "The most provocative article you've ever printed. We shall never find God in this life; that is what makes life tragic. But to stop searching for God, that makes life meaningless."

The first impulse for this new, sensational, and sometimes disturbing discussion concerning the question about God came from Gabriel Vahanian's book *The Death of God*.[49] Published in 1961, it carried the subtitle *The Culture of Our Post-Christian Era*. The book is intended as a study of the history of culture based on the presentation of undeniable facts. That "God is dead" might be a purely cultural phenomenon. It might result from modern man's notion that official Christianity seems to contradict the original "Christianity" of the New Testament. Furthermore, a modern immanentist culture is quite unable to acknowledge any

---

[48] *Op. cit.*, p. 125; Cf. Barth's *Kirchliche Dogmatik* (Zurich, Vol. 12, 1945), pp. 324ff, and note 44.

[49] Gabriel Vahanian, *The Death of God* (Braziller, New York, 1961).

meaning in a supposedly transcendental reality. Vahanian concludes that "the death of God may be only a cultural phenomenon as though only our religio-cultural notion of God were dead. But this makes even more serious the question whether the transcendental views of man and his culture, as set forth in the Bible, have any chance of surviving the modern presupposition that God is dead." [50]

It is all too superficial to try and shake off this increasingly important question by saying that it is nothing but a fad, called to life by an insignificant small group, by a handful of young, radical theologians. The problem is based on real facts and causes that are at the very root of the undermining of conventional Christianity.

The God-is-dead movement has a six or seven year history. In 1961 William Hamilton published his book *The New Essence of Christianity*.[51] It was meant to be a reflection of and "a laying claim to those few things that are certain." Hamilton's problem, too, is how, in an era of the death of God, it is possible to believe.

Here we touch on an important point of the new and paradoxical "God-is-dead theology." For the theologians of this group deliberately wish to continue being *theologians*. They also want to continue referring to themselves as Christians. In fact, it could be said that the more convinced they are of the death of God, the more they hold fast to Jesus of Nazareth as the only one in whom they have found support for their human existence. Hamilton has explained this in an article in *The Christian Century*, in the series "How I am making up my mind." [52]

The same applies to Thomas Altizer who in his book about *Mircea Eliade and the Dialectic of the Sacred* approaches the problem from the religio-phenomenological aspect, and in *The Gospel of Christian Atheism* from the philosophical aspect.[53] According to Altizer, "the proclamation of the death of God is a Christian confession of faith," and "the radical Christian affirms

---

[50] *Op. cit.*, p. 231.

[51] William Hamilton, *The New Essence of Christianity* (Association Press, New York, 1961).

[52] William Hamilton, in *The Christian Century* (Oct. 1965).

[53] T. J. J. Altizer, *Mircea Eliade and the Dialectic of the Sacred* (Westminster Press, Philadelphia, 1963). *The Gospel of Christian Atheism*, cf note 45 above.

that God has died in Christ and that the death of God is the final and irrevocable event." [54]

The conviction that the collapse of conventional Christianity is as inevitable as the death of God is closely tied up with the conviction that conventional Christianity with its official, bourgeois morality is a radical denial of the message of Jesus of Nazareth. This conviction led Pierre Berton, author of *The Comfortable Pew*, to sever his connections with every Christian Church.[55] Yet he did not break his relations with Jesus of Nazareth! Conventional Christianity is being more and more sharply contrasted to the preaching of Jesus. This applies also to the highly captivating book of Werner and Lotte Pelz to which we have referred.[56]

God is dead. But Jesus of Nazareth is his representative. This is the leading idea in Dorothee Sölle's book *Stellvertretung*.[57] In our present, earthly, human existence we have to do with Jesus of Nazareth. Jesus takes the place of God. But he also keeps the place of God open. And it is here that the possibility of Christian hope lies.

At the basis of the spiritual and religious unrest of our day lies the fact that the undermining of conventional Christianity, which has been going on for a long time, has now come to its final stage. One cannot argue against facts. We have to begin by accepting them, and then we must ask what we are to do. Once again, we want to emphasize that this book has a strictly phenomenological character. It is not intended to attack or defend anything. This is not a weakness, but rather a necessary self-control. The situation in which we find ourselves is so complicated and so hard to fathom that we cannot be sufficiently discreet and prudent.

[54] T. J. J. Altizer, *The Gospel of Christian Atheism*, pp. 102, 107. Note: Altizer and Hamilton published together a collection of essays under the title of *Radical Theology and the Death of God: The Ferment of Protestant Thinking* (Bobbs-Merrill, Indianapolis, New York, 1966).

[55] Pierre Berton, *The Comfortable Pew: A Critical Look at Christianity and the Religious Establishment in the New Age* (Lippincott, New York, 1965). Note: This book was written at the invitation of the Anglican Synod of Canada. The same firm published a collection of reactions, edited by Wm. Kilburn, entitled *The Restless Church* with a foreword by Martin E. Marty.

[56] Cf. note 36 of this chapter.

[57] Dorothee Sölle, *Stellvertretung; Ein Kapitel Theologie nach dem 'Tode Gottes'* (Kreuz Verlag, Stuttgart, 1965).

# 3. The Changed Image of World and Man

The end of conventional Christianity has not come upon us suddenly and by surprise. Nor is it an event which took place at a certain point of time which can be accurately determined. What can certainly be said is that it concerns a religious near-disaster which we are now experiencing. There are some who have seen this coming for a long time; there are others who have been overwhelmed by it suddenly; there are yet others who are quite unaware of what is going on.

It is an ever accelerating process which will be completed in the life span of two generations at most. The process has not artificially been called into life; it is happening to us whether we like it or not. We are right in the midst of it without being able to foresee where it is all leading. No apologetical reflections and no ecclesiastical measures are able sto stop the definitive collapse of conventional Christianity. No one can withdraw himself from it.

What we are at present experiencing in the religious area is the inevitable final outcome of an undermining process which began several centuries ago. By an ever increasing accumulation of different causes, this process gradually gained in force and influence, and now finally in our own time it is stepping up its pace toward the end.

The first group of causes consists of the numerous facts and connections which have come to light as a consequence of the rise and development of the natural sciences, of psychology and other modern anthropological sciences. The profound changes in the image of the world and man which resulted from this knowledge could not possibly fail to affect the primitive religious images and practices that date from a prescientific stage of development. The third chapter will deal with this group of causes.

A second group of causes is formed by the amazing results

61

which modern biblical sciences have yielded, and by which an entirely new vision of both the content and the meaning of the bible has developed. Connected with this are the results of research into the earliest stages of Christianity and into the various influences—including non-Christian ones—which played their part in the gradual rise of Christianity as a world religion. This group of causes will be dealt with in the fourth chapter. At the end of that chapter we will add a summary treatment of a group of different causes. This third group comprises the various, often revolutionary, changes which Western civilization experienced since the end of the Middle Ages. At first these changes were hardly noticeable, but they increased as a result of the shock of the Enlightenment and the French Revolution, followed by a rapid succession of events in our own age. These revolutionary changes are now resulting in a growing process of secularization which has gripped all mankind.

A fourth and extremely influential group of causes which affects the reflection on the content and meaning of religion in general, and of Christianity in particular, comprises the changes which Western thought has undergone in the last few centuries. These changes took place particularly as a result of the so-called "Copernican revolution" of thought brought about by Immanuel Kant's critique of knowing, subsequently by Kierkegaard's criticism of the speculative idealism of Hegel, and in our century by the existentialist manner of thinking linked to Kierkegaard. The fifth chapter will deal with the connection between philosophy and the problem of God. The sixth chapter, under the title of "Existence and Existents," will be devoted entirely to the thought of Martin Heidegger.

The seventh and eighth chapters, too, will deal with contemporary questions about the problem of God in the religious situation of the twentieth century. The seventh chapter, entitled "Revelation and Faith," will be devoted entirely to the manner in which Karl Barth has posited, approached, and answered the problem of God. Under the title of "Existence and Revelation," the eighth chapter will deal with the correlative philosophico-theological approach of Paul Tillich.

A final group of causes of the present undermining of conventional Christianity has not yet been mentioned. This group will be dealt with in the ninth chapter, entitled "Confrontation with the Non-Christian Religions." The modern means of communication and the nascent world culture based on it are the causes of closer and more frequent encounters between Christians and non-Christians.

## Introductory Remarks

Primitive man could do nothing else than rely, in complete impartiality, on the impressions he received from the reality that surrounded him. He could not have recourse to methodical investigation and systematic reflection. Phenomena and events which he could not understand were attributed to the action of invisible forces, spirits, and gods.

This is why, from the very beginning of man's consciousness, an immediate and inseparable connection existed between religion and the manner in which man experienced and "explained" nature. It was not science but religion which supplied the answer to questions about the origin of things, how it is that everything is the way it is, what forces and powers are to be blamed for what happens. Likewise it was religion that had to supply the answer to the practical question of how disasters could be avoided and how the invisible powers could be made to serve the interests of man.

The phenomenologist of religion who occupies himself with this matter has no great difficulty seeing how a good number of images, religious opinions and practices in the great world religions—and therefore in Christianity too—are related to the original connection between religion and nature as it existed in the consciousness of primitive man.

Of course it could very well have been that the rise of modern sciences, with their methodical experiments and the resulting explanations of phenomena, might have led to a confirmation of the entire prescientific vision of nature, and therefore to a confirmation of the effectiveness and acceptability of the religious images and practices based on this vision of nature. However such a confirmation and corroboration did not happen.

In fact, the contrary is true. Primitive man's vision of the nature and causes of natural events was continually proved to have been very simple and provisory. This awareness grew with the development of more methodical and exact observation of nature, with the growing understanding of the relation between various phenomena, and with the penetration into the secrets of nature which made it possible to explain the new wonders of nature whenever they appeared. Quite obviously the radical transition in the understanding of nature—including man himself —necessarily involved certain consequences regarding the acceptability and the effectiveness of all religious images and practices related to the primitive manner of experiencing nature. In the long run it is not possible to lead two lives, rejecting in the religious area those achievements of science which in other areas are accepted as self-evident.

As we have stated, the religious customs of the primitive peoples originated in a prescientific manner of thought and attitude which no longer corresponds to the evident achievements of modern science. The same is true for many images and practices which continue to exist in the great religions of the world. There can be no conflict between science and religion in the true and deepest sense of the word, but this does not exclude the possibility of conflict between science and certain forms by which religion manifests itself.

In apologetics two different methods have been used to try and remove this conflict. We can be fairly brief about the first method, since it no longer has much meaning in our own time. Not too long ago it was a favorite pastime to ridicule science, with Darwin as a particular target for his theory of the origin of man. There were frequent references to the inconsistencies of science. Statements which one day might, with the greatest conviction, be made by some scientist, might evaporate the next day by the reasonings of another scientist. In the meantime science has made steady progress in all fields and has proved the reliability of this progress by numerous amazing discoveries. The apologetical distrust of science has therefore lost all meaning.

The second means used by apologetics to remove fears of a possible conflict between science and religion is of a more general, abstract, and speculative nature. It begins with a frank admission that both science and religion are concerned with genuine truth. But, it is pointed out, truth is of a twofold nature; truth is attained in two different ways. Scientific truth is based on exact observation, whereas religious truth rests partly on speculative thought and partly on divine revelation. However, since it is impossible that truth contradicts truth, there can never be a conflict between real science and real religion. If it should appear that there is a conflict, then science is based on human judgment and religion is based on divine affirmation. And surely, God is more worthy of belief than man!

In such reasonings many facts and questions are disregarded. For example, scientifically determined facts are compared to what are called facts of revelation. But in science we are dealing with verifiable "knowing," whereas in religion we are dealing with "believing" that cannot be strictly verified. Revelation is received by faith. It cannot be ascertained and checked; it can only be believed. The believer has convictions which he accepts as based on revelation from God and therefore as true.

Modern man, with his scientific way of thinking, asks questions. Now it is clear that what religion teaches and proclaims is based on divine revelation. Since all religions claim to be based on revelation, could it be that what religion teaches and proclaims is either entirely or partially of human origin? Supposing that not everything is based on revelation. How can it be known what in a religion is based on revelation and what is not? What must a person do when the "facts of revelation"—which are accepted as absolutely true because revealed—conflict with what is scientifically accepted as true or possible? Could the passing of time make it become clear that the entire notion of "revelation" is a remnant of a prescientific stage of culture? Has the time come when something is irrefutably true only when it can be scientifically documented and proved? Is the cardinal difference precisely that in the prescientific stage man in his desire for explanation looked to revelation and had recourse to fantasy, whereas scientific man looks to discoveries and has recourse to exact scientific investigation and research? What is revelation? Might Duncan Howlett be right when he says that "the doctrine of revelation is perhaps the most pernicious idea ever invented by the human mind"? [1]

According to the nature of his conventionality, the typical conventional Christian usually reacts to such questions and remarks with indignation and ridicule. He simply does not want to hear them and has no intention of seriously considering them. But this

[1] Duncan Howlett, *The Fourth American Faith* (Harper & Row, New York, 1964), p. 197.

does not get us anywhere. In the meantime thousands have definitively turned against religion and Christianity because such questions have never been answered to their satisfaction.

In this chapter we shall not consider these problems in further detail. We shall try to do this later. What we are concerned with here is to see how conventional Christianity has become more and more undermined. In any case, the objections and questions suggested before are by no means the last word. It would be unreasonable to think that there is an insurmountable contradiction or hostility between Christianity and science. It would seem so only if we confront the narrowest conceptions of Christianity with the narrowest conceptions of science. Moreover, the objections against religion, particularly against miracles in the bible, are as old as the bible itself. When the question is raised about the possibility of conflict between laws of nature and divine miracles, we have really not advanced beyond the point of the rise of modern science; the question is the same as it was in the days of Job.[2]

If we want to say something meaningful about the relation between Christianity and science we shall have to confront the two as they present themselves at their best. As far as Christianity is concerned, we shall have to eliminate the widespread opinion of conventional Christianity which holds that Christianity is a matter of revelation in the sense of a miraculous and infallible communication of a number of truths which must be unconditionally accepted because they come from God himself. In that case "to believe" is to affirm truths which God has made known and which are "presented by the Church as truths to be believed." However it seems to me that no outstanding theologian Roman Catholic or Protestant—is content with such a presentation. Therefore we must ask what Christianity understands when it speaks of revelation and faith.[3]

As far as science is concerned we must be on our guard lest we become the victims of antiquated or popularized science at its worst. Science, too, knows its conventions, prejudices, and dogmas. Here also a methodological principle can degenerate into a law of nature, and something that is no more than a provisional

---

[2] R. Hooykaas, *The Principle of Uniformity in Geology, Biology, and Theology* (Brill, Leiden, 1963), p. 228.

[3] Cf. Chapters seven and eight.

working hypothesis can become petrified into a static dogma. In science, too, the necessary openness for the unexpected can disappear.[4]

It cannot be denied that, just as many of the old firmly established statements of conventional Christianity have been undermined, many of the old affirmations of conventional natural science made in our youth have undergone the same lot. Although developments in various branches of natural science of the past fifty years are for the greater part beyond my understanding, I think I have understood enough to be able to see that there is great reluctance to absolutize former achievements.

As a result of Einstein's theory of relativity, Planck's quantum theory, and the progress of nuclear physics, biochemistry, and radio astronomy, natural science has reached borderline areas of the total material reality where things are not as objective and absolutely fixed as was previously supposed. It is becoming more and more evident how little we humans really know and understand and how far we are from a complete and definitive unfolding of the inscrutable mystery of material reality in its deepest sense.

Consequently no one who has any idea of the level which science has now reached can possibly affirm that science has proved once and for all that God does not exist. Science can neither prove nor refute God's existence. "Religious questions will never be decided by science or philosophy." [5]

Nor does it seem to be in line with the present state of science to think that natural science has shown once and for all that only a materialistic view of life and the world corresponds to scientifically ascertained reality. The question about the nature of material existence has, precisely because of the newest developments in the science of elementary particles, become an unexplained and unanswered question. Therefore, with Carlyle Marney, we could consider materialism rather as a "prejudgment of reality," [6] i.e. as a form of prejudice.

The greater the successes which science has been able to achieve in the past twenty-five years, the more reserved the real

[4] A. van Melsen, *Evolutie en Wijsbegeerte* (Utrecht, 1964), p. 40. English tr. *Evolution and Philosophy* (Duquesne University Press, Pittsburgh, 1965).

[5] *Op. cit.*, p. 226.

[6] Marney, *Structures of Prejudice* (Abingdon Press, New York, 1961), pp. 23ff.

scientists have become. "The more we penetrate matter by experiment and analysis, the less we can say what it really is." [7] Whether or not we can speak of a covenant between Christianity and natural science, the present state of affairs certainly does not allow us to speak of an everlasting bond between natural science and materialism.

On the other hand, it is no less premature to suppose that the results of science may have little or no influence on conventional Christianity as commonly understood. It is also premature for apologetes to abuse the recent development of natural science by giving the impression that there is no longer "any danger" to religion, as if now we could peacefully return to points of view that were unjustly considered to be overcome, and as if science itself had now proved "that the bible was correct after all." [8] It is not nearly as simple as that.

Both on the side of science and on the side of Christianity many persons are guilty of an all too simplistic view of the present state of affairs. The problems which arise at the borderline of these two areas are much more difficult and of a much more serious nature than many seem to realize. [9]

In any case, I have not made the preceding observations to take sides, but to prevent the reader from drawing conclusions which would be as premature as they would be unfounded.

After these precautions we shall now go on to examine which results of the modern natural and anthropological sciences have, since the Middle Ages, increasingly contributed to the gradual undermining of the conventional concept of Christianity. Even though a sharp distinction is frequently made between the unchangeable core of the Christian faith and the time-conditioned, changeable periphery, it is still difficult to maintain that the undermining of conventional Christianity affects only the periphery.

Christianity is a religion of revelation. The source for a knowledge of God's revelation is sacred scripture, the bible, the book of books. That the bible is the absolutely trustworthy source of

[7] Hans Reinhard Rapp, a member of a group of young physicists and theologians at the atomic reactor institute of Karlsruhe, in *Abschied vom Christentum?* p. 65.

[8] Werner Keller, *Und die Bibel hat doch Recht* (Econ Verlag, Vienna, 1961).

[9] This became once more quite clear to me while reading van Melsen's excellent work. Cf. Note 4 above.

God's revelation has in conventional Christianity always been attributed to the fact that this book, a collection of Old and New Testament writings, came into being in an entirely special manner. The writers of the bible were inspired by the Holy Spirit in such a way that the bible was, as it were, written by God's own hand. Therefore the bible is in all respects a completely infallible and trustworthy book.

Nowadays most theologians tend to make a distinction between the word of God, i.e., what God in his work of revelation has to say to people, and the human, time-conditioned form in which the word of God comes to us in the bible. According to them the primitive world picture found particularly in the first eleven chapters of Genesis belongs to this human, time-conditioned form. The acknowledgment of the non-binding, purely human character of the biblical world picture is a necessary capitulation before the evident achievements of natural science. Almost all Christians have accepted this capitulation. Only fundamentalists are resisting it. However until the rise of modern science every Christian was perfectly convinced that even as far as the facts concerning nature and history were concerned the bible was a strictly trustworthy and authoritative book.

## The World Picture of Natural Science

From what has been said thus far it can easily be seen that the first real shock which conventional Christianity had to endure from the side of natural science was the discovery that the biblical world picture was in no respect in keeping with evident reality.

According to the creation narrative the earth is older than the sun, the moon, and the stars (which came into being only on the fourth day of creation). And this is in spite of the fact that light was created on the first day, independently of the celestial bodies. The blue vault of heaven was seen as a physical dome, the firmament. Above this firmament, as well as under the earth, there were water supplies. When in the narrative of the deluge even the tops of the highest mountains were flooded, this was caused by the water gates of heaven and the earth being opened. The earth was considered to be a flat disk, above which stood the dome of heaven. Across this dome moved the sun, the moon, and the stars in their daily rising and setting. Even if it is granted that the narrative of the creation is more a song of praise than a scientific explanation, the fact remains that this extremely primitive world picture is the world picture of the bible. Probably as a result of external influences, one also meets New Testament descriptions of a netherworld below the earth where a fire is burning. This idea is the basis of the threefold partition of heaven, earth, and hell mentioned in the creed.

### Earth and Heaven

It was probably the Greek philosophers who on the basis of some simple perceptions—such as the widening of the horizon when a person climbs to a higher altitude—became aware of the fact that the earth was shaped as a globe. Through the writings of Aristotle this notion became the commonly accepted fact among the theologians of the Middle Ages. In fact the Ptolemaic system, which dates from the second century and which had its origin in Egypt, must have been known in the Roman Empire and therefore to Western European scholars. This system was a completion of Aristotle's world picture insofar as it was able to give an ingenious explanation of the remarkable, sometimes loop-like movements made by the five planets, each at different times, along a course between the fixed stars, and counter to the course of the daily rotation of the celestial globe.

Clearly, this world picture was a considerable progress over the primitive world picture of the bible. Yet this progress was evidently not felt as a conflict. The earth remained the focal point of the universe, and compared to its enormous size all celestial bodies were merely small lights. Primitive ideas about the nature of these lights continued to exist. The fire of hell was thought to be somewhere within the earth. Until the end of the Middle Ages, illiterate people kept to the primitive world picture as presented in the bible.

Toward the end of the Middle Ages the humanists displayed some doubt about the correctness of the Ptolemaic world picture. The first scientific refutation of the system came from Nicolas Copernicus, a canon attached to the cathedral of Frauenburg. He was born in Poland, traveled much, and was known as a mathematician, astronomer, medical scientist, and theologian. Between the years 1497 and 1529, this versatile man produced a number of publications in which he maintained that the explanation of the remarkable courses of the planets could be made more simple and more obvious if the earth were conceived as a rotating globe which in a year's time travels in a circular course around the sun. In that case the moon would be the only heavenly body which would travel around the earth in a circular course. The planets would then, like the earth, travel in a circular course around the sun, in periods of different duration. The daily rising and setting of the sun, the moon, the planets, and stars would then, as a result of the rotation of the celestial globe, be no more than the reflection of the daily rotation of the earth on its axis. This is the Copernican world picture. Through the action of his pupils and friends the insights of Copernicus were gathered together in a work entitled *De Revolutionibus Orbium Coelestium* (About the Revolutions of the Celestial Globes) which was published in 1543, the year Copernicus died. The geocentric world picture had definitively been replaced by the heliocentric world picture of Copernicus.

This was corrected and amplified by Johannes Kepler during his terms as professor at the Universities of Prague and Linz. Kepler gradually discovered the three laws to which his name has been given, and which were ultimately published together in 1619 in a work called *De Harmonice Mundi* (About the Harmony of the Universe). The first law of Kepler states that the planets (including the earth) do not travel in circular, but in elliptic courses around the sun. The sun is not at the central point, but in one of the two focal points of the elliptic course. The second and third law of Kepler refer to the duration of the planets' revolutions.

It is an irony of history that the progressive Copernicus received an indignant letter from the reformer Luther who referred him to the text from scripture "O sun, stop at Gibeon; and thou moon, at the valley of Aijalon" (Jos. 10, 13). In Linz Kepler came into conflict with the Lutheran Church council and was denied admission to the Lord's supper because of his heretical views.

This leads to the question dealing with the connection between the radical revolution in the world picture outlined above and the

Christian faith. Why was the transition to the heliocentric world picture the first real shock that began the undermining of conventional Christianity? That this transition to a new world picture was finally considered to be an undermining of conventional convictions of faith is clear from the Inquisition's treatment of Galileo (1564-1642) toward the end of his life. Since the appearance of Copernicus' publications, many persons had defended the heliocentric world picture for almost a century with impunity. Consequently these people hold that in the conflict between the Holy Office and Galileo it was purely a matter of prestige.[10] But it was also apparently a matter that concerned faith. The great difference between Copernicus and Galileo was that the former worked only theoretically, whereas the latter worked on a practical basis. For Copernicus it was a matter of speculation; for Galileo the world picture was based on experiment and perception. Copernicus and Kepler reached only their fellow scientists. The danger presented by Galileo was that he tried to convince the non-initiated of the correctness of the heliocentric world picture, being the first to use a telescope in his experiments.

With the aid of his telescope Galileo could show the phases of the planet Venus to anyone who was willing to look. This meant that he was able to show that Venus is a globe which receives its light from the sun, and which moves around the sun. In 1611 he even got so far as to have the pope look through his telescope. Some cardinals and monsignori refused to follow the pope's example because they feared for their faith. Some preachers even went from town to town, preaching on the text from the Acts of the Apostles: "Men of Galileo (instead of Galilee) why stand there looking up into the sky"! This course of events was too much for the Holy Office. One of its consultors expressed the opinion that all the heresies of Luther together were not as dangerous as the teaching of Galileo. Apparently this consultor saw that Galileo's action was the beginning of an entirely new threat to conventional Christianity, and that Galileo's discovery, based on experiment, was only the first of many troubles. The consultor was the great cardinal and theologian Robert Bellarmine.

In 1611 Copernicus' book was placed on the Index. Galileo did not make his reaction known to only the initiated and in Latin,

[10] For example, C. F. Weiszäcker, *Die Tragweite der Wissenschaft*, (Stuttgart, 1964). Vol. I, p. 114.

but to the entire population and in Italian. His reaction was contained in a writing with the title *Dialogo sopra i due massimi sistemi del mondo: Tolemaico e Copernicano*. At first an *imprimatur* was granted to this writing, but a conflict with the Inquisition could not be avoided. Galileo was detained and in 1633 he was forced to declare under oath that he abjured, damned, and destested his erroneous opinion about the rotation of the earth. In spite of his capitulation Galileo was kept under control for about eight years, until shortly before his death in 1642. Apparently Galileo was considered to be an acute danger to the faith. It was not merely a question of prestige but a question of faith.

The reason why I have dwelt somewhat in detail with the case of Galileo, which is generally known but often presented incompletely, is that we are dealing with the prototype of a number of later cases up to our own time. These cases are indications that conventional Christianity has been undermined during the past three centuries by the advance of modern science. I do not make any judgments but limit myself to ascertaining facts.

If by analogy with words such as thermometer, barometer, pressure gauge, and so on, the word "conflict gauge" could be introduced, it would have to be said that the most sensitive conflict gauge for the determination of the relationship between conventional Christianity and developing modern sciences was until very recent times the Holy Office.

One has to have the greatest admiration for the skill and sense of duty with which the Holy Office for centuries exercised its task of protecting faith and morals. Only when the Holy Office was seriously convinced that the integrity of faith and morals was at stake was attention given to a question, and possibly disciplinary measures were taken. It was always the concern of the Holy Office to protect conventional Christianity in its Roman Catholic manifestations. The Holy Office was always extremely distrustful of a distinction between the divine and the human aspect of the Church, between the form and the content of a declaration, between what was essential and what was accidental. What counted was the preservation of the whole without distinction.

With regard to the threat which conventional Christianity has had to endure during the past few centuries from various sides, three different points of view are possible.

The one extreme point of view is that of the Holy Office: as far as doctrine and theology, piety and morality are concerned, conventional Christianity must be preserved and protected at any cost against undermining of whatever nature and from whatever side.

The other extreme position is that of an ever growing number of believers: it is apparent that conventional Christianity has in so many respects and so many ways become undermined that it is no longer possible to accept it. Therefore it is better to leave it behind altogether, either with regret or with definite aversion.

Between these two extremes is the middle of the road which the Second Vatican Council and the synods and world conferences of the non-Roman Catholic Churches try to take. This position makes a sharp distinction between the essence and the formulation of the Christian faith, between what is essential and what is accidental in the practice of the Church and the personal living of the faith, between authority and the personal conscience, between charity and justice, between the human and the divine aspect—in short between the immutable core and the changeable, partially antiquated exterior of conventional Christianity. It seems to me that this position has been adopted by the great majority of believing Christians in practically all Churches.

Those who have adopted this position are quite willing to admit that conventional Christianity has gradually become undermined and is therefore in need of a drastic restoration and facelifting. They consider such restoration necessary not only for their own religious life and practice, but also with a view to contacts with other Christian groups, with non-Christian religions, and with non-believers. It is particularly necessary to win back those who have left Christianity and to protect others against defection.

In this connection, however, there is a serious problem which, as far as I can ascertain, many are not sufficiently aware of. This is the problem of what norm must be used to establish—without falling into error—where the borderline lies between the unchangeable core and the changeable exterior. It seems to me that our contemporaries find it self-evident that the achievements of any science and of culture in general should, insofar as they are firmly and surely established, be taken seriously; they should be accepted, and the inherited and conventional forms of Christi-

anity should be confronted with them. Facts which have been
certainly ascertained and insights which are founded on proper
bases cannot be ignored and left aside simply because they seem
to present some threat to conventional Christianity, just as the
phases of Venus could not be ignored once they had been verified. This is an extremely serious matter. In my studies of the
religious and spiritual situation, the impression has grown that the
core is becoming ever smaller, and that the outer layers are ever
increasing.

We should now return to the case of Galileo and continue our
bird's-eye view of the past three centuries. It is not difficult to
ridicule the Galileo case by asking what it matters to religion
whether the earth revolves or whether it stands still. To those
who speak in this way the words of Christ could be applied:
"You understand nothing." If the transition from the geocentric
to the heliocentric world picture had not constituted a threat to
the more than ten centuries old conventional Christianity, the
Holy Office would not have become so upset and would not have
made it so difficult for Galileo.

If we ask where the threat precisely is, the first answer is that
the adoption of the heliocentric world picture affected the authority of the bible as it had always been understood. Three
possibilities were therefore open: either preserve the authority of
the bible by rejecting the heliocentric world picture, or accept
this world picture and discontinue believing in the infallible authority of the scriptures, or both accept the new world picture
and yet continue to adhere to the authority of the scriptures. The
latter combination, however, would be possible only if the concept of biblical authority could be subjected to a drastic revision.
It was not immediately obvious that such a revision of the nature
and extent of the authority would affect only the outer layers of
the faith and the practices founded on it. Similar and even more
serious situations have *mutatis mutandis* arisen in the past few
centuries. All one has to do is recall the farreaching consequences
of acknowledging the fact of evolution for an understanding of
the bible, the Christian faith, and human existence.

In the second place, the adoption of the heliocentric theory
placed new and great demands on man's powers of imagination.
Previously it was not so difficult to imagine that God, the angels
and the saints attentively followed everything that happened on

earth. It was not so difficult to imagine that Jesus came down from heaven to become human, that after having been buried he descended into the realm of the dead to proclaim the Gospel there, that after having risen from the dead and after having appeared on several occasions to the disciples he ascended into heaven. But what has become of heaven and hell? The greater the advance of astronomy, the more difficult it became to form some idea of heaven and hell.

Here too, as always, arise the three possibilities we have mentioned: either retain the old images, or reject the entire faith together with the old images, or combine the rejection of the old images with the retention of the faith. But we must try to realize what this last possibility means. It means that the literal and dimensionally conceived heaven and hell lose their realistic character and take on the aspect of symbols. Does this not necessarily include the idea that the coming on earth and the ascension into heaven become symbolic images instead of historical events? And does this not finally flow over into all the salvific events? It is not possible to stop somewhere arbitrarily for the reason that otherwise the conventional belief would be too strongly affected. But supposing the courage to acknowledge the ever new and evident achievements of modern science, and thus the necessity of being consistent in the pursuit of the way of symbolization, does this not ultimately result in conceiving God as a symbol?

If by the force of circumstances we follow the way of symbolization because we accept the achievements of science, philosophy, and cultural development just as we accept the content of the Christian faith, we must realize that while we do know where we begin, we do not know where we shall finish. The point where we shall end cannot be artificially constructed. Only with continued exertion can we reach this point by being completely faithful to any truth of any nature we meet along the road.

In the third and final place the adoption of the heliocentric world picture meant that anyone who wanted to preserve the Christian faith would also have to accept a profound change in his religious attitude and mentality. This change implied that in the future the person must respect the results of experimental research. Thus resulted the problem of the relation between religious, ecclesiastical, and scientific authority. The problem cannot be avoided by affirming that religion and science are incomparable units that have nothing to do with one another. For it is not a matter of religion in general, but of this concrete conventional Christianity, characterized by a definite ecclesiastical structure, doctrine, theology, liturgy, piety, and morality. It is for that reason quite possible that new achievements of science and culture might endanger conventional forms of Christianity.

It is likewise quite possible that in such instances, just as in the case of Galileo, a conflict might arise between a certain concept of biblical or ecclesiastical authority and the authority of irrefutable facts, discoveries, and insights from the scientific area. In such instances should a believer be expected to follow Galileo's example and do violence to his scientific conscience, or should he be expected to form for himself a new idea of the nature and extent of biblical or ecclesiastical authority which makes it possible for him to be true to his scientific conscience? Such a change of attitude and mentality may have consequences that cannot now be foreseen; the beginning is known, but the end is not. Once a person takes this road, he can only allow himself to be guided by a dynamic openness to the future.

## The Mechanization of the World Picture

We have now come to the unexpected facts which have been laid at the doorstep of conventional Christianity by natural and anthropological sciences. The preceding reflections can be applied to any of these unexpected facts; the application is left to the reader.

A second shock conventional Christianity had to endure was the result of the mechanization of the world picture. The first tendencies in that direction go back as far as the mathematical and scientific speculations of Greek antiquity. But Galileo can be considered to be the person who "has probably contributed the most to the rise of classical natural science." [11] Therefore he can be seen as the person who gave the first impulse to the modern belief that all natural phenomena follow certain laws, leading therefore to the mechanization of the world picture and the technologizing of Western culture.

[11] E. J. Dyksterhuis, *De Mechanisering van het Wereldbeeld* (Amsterdam, 1950), p. 368.

Primitive man experienced nature around him as a living and at the same time capricious, unpredictable, and often awe-inspiring reality. He saw everywhere the manifestation and action of invisible forces—of gods, angels, spirits, and souls. The most unexpected and amazing events were considered possible if forces dwelt in or made use of objects, trees, or animals. Animals that could speak (such as the serpent in paradise or Balaam's ass) presented no difficulty for the apprehension of primitive and prescientific man. It was in the stage of primitive religion, so closely allied to the primitive experiencing of nature, that the first religious images and practices of the great world religions arose. A good number of religious opinions, feelings, attitudes, and customs which for centuries were accepted as obviously belonging to conventional Christianity go back to the primeval age of the first religious awakening. The bible is full of them, as are the ecclesiastical, liturgical and devotional practices.

The entire complex of religious notions, myths, legends, and practices has its origin in the prescientific experience of nature; therefore, they have meaning and are worthy of belief only in their original context. For modern thought they are enigmatic relics of a far distant world of belief and feeling which people today do not know what to do with.

This difficulty cannot be pushed aside by general and abstract considerations about the radical difference between religion and science. In themselves such considerations have some value, but we are not dealing with religion and science in the abstract. We are dealing with two diametrically opposed concrete worlds of thought and action which clash whenever they meet. This does not mean that there have been no religious scientific researchers. What it does mean is that certain concrete religious images and practices cannot be brought into harmony with the modern mechanistic notion of nature. It is true that Kepler still thought that angels kept the earth and planets in their revolving movement, but from this fact it is impossible to conclude that "belief in angels" could be harmonized with the world picture of natural science.

The mechanistic world picture is based on an entirely new way of considering nature. This consideration is characterized by "the experiment (instead of speculative thought, poetic fantasy, or divine revelation) as the source of knowledge, mathematical formulation as the means of description, mathematical deduction as the sign pointing to new phenomena that must be verified by experiment." [12]

This method has not been limited to natural science only. It has been widely applied in psychology and other modern sciences of man. It is based on such notions as uniformity and laws by which everything we perceive and experience in this world is interconnected. The unpredictable gods, angels, spirits, and forces have made way for constant characteristics and reliable laws. The necessary consequence was a new vision and experience of everything that takes place in nature and human life, a new vision of what is possible and what is impossible, and new ways in which man tries to influence and dominate what happens and tries to put the given reality at the service of his interests through technology.

It is true that a problem exists concerning a religious understanding and technological use of the "God-created reality," but this does not mean that a religious person is permitted to establish criteria which do not fit into the scientific world picture: "It is not possible to utilize light and radio, to apply modern medical and clinical means in cases of sickness, and at the same time believe in the world of spirits and wonders of the New Testament." [13] Anyone infected by rabies who has recourse to eating St. Hubert's bread as a precaution and who also goes to see the doctor lives in two entirely different stages of culture at the same time without realizing that the stages are mutually exclusive. The primitive, prescientific world picture has definitively had to make way for the mathematical-mechanistic world picture of modern natural science.

This remains true in the latest developments of natural science which introduce the researcher to border line areas where the notion of the law of nature has apparently been dethroned. For these newly discovered borderline areas are entirely different from the world of unpredictable forces, spirits, and gods which primitive man believed in. Insofar as certain notions, practices, and customs of conventional Christianity have been undermined by the mechanistic world picture, there is no possibility of a return to the customs and practices of the primitive world. The

---

[12] *Op. cit.*, p. 1.
[13] H. W. Bartsch, ed. *Kerygma und Mythos* (Hamburg, 1951), Vol. I, p. 18. English translation by Reginald H. Fuller (S.P.C.K., London).

question of which elements in the biblical manner of presentation have been definitively eliminated is not a leftover of an antiquated liberalism; it is a lasting question of very real import.

## Evolution

A third and very serious shock which harassed conventional Christianity had its origin in the birth of the notion of evolution around the middle of the last century. Here it is not a matter only of a new vision of the structure of the universe and a law-regulated nature, but of a profound change in the manner of approaching, ordering, and explaining all reality, natural as well as cultural, that surrounds us and of which we are a part.

The rise of the teaching of evolution is rightly ascribed to Charles Darwin (1809-1882) and to his book *The Origin of Species*.[14] The book appeared in 1859. It was based on a number of investigations and discoveries during a journey around the world aboard the *Beagle* from 1831 to 1836. For a quarter of a century Darwin, in collaboration with Alfred R. Wallace and others, occupied himself with the study of the material before he dared publish his book. Darwin's theory of evolution was not the fruit of an arbitrary fancy or fantasy but the result of a laborious effort to explain methodically on the basis of concrete data the origin and the enormous variety of forms of living beings that populate the earth.

A clear distinction must be made between the fact of evolution and the theory or hypothesis which tries to give an explanation of this fact. Darwin's teaching about the origin of species was no more than a hypothesis, even if it was based on exact observations and clearly ascertained facts. Darwin was well aware of this, and in the sixth and seventh chapters of his book he offers a number of difficulties that were still to be solved.

It has gone on like this to our own day; one theory of evolution has followed another. Until now two of the greatest difficulties lie in the fact that it has become evident that characteristics acquired because of a change of environment are not hereditary, and in the fact that no examples have been found of an actual

[14] Editions: Everyman's Library, Nr. 811, Dent and Sons (London, 1956) and Mentor Books MT 294 (The New American Library, 1958).

breakthrough of the boundaries by which one species is distinguished from another. Added to this is the fact that the newest genetics has found impoverishment instead of enrichment of the species when circumstances such as radioactive radiation cause a mutation in the genes. Consequently, even after an entire century, the scientific effort to give a satisfactory factual explanation of evolution is still experiencing great difficulties.

However if anyone were to conclude from the hypothetical character of the existing theories of evolution that evolution itself is not a definite fact he would obviously have very little insight into the idea of evolution. Thousands of facts and discoveries have long since changed the increasing probability of evolution into complete certainty. Biologically this fact means that the great variety of living beings of lower and higher development—including man—which now populate the earth have in the course of millions of years developed from minuscule unicellular existence to their present richness of forms by way of numerous stages of development. Through the partnership biology has made with geology and paleontology it is no longer possible to doubt the fact of evolution.

The profound and farreaching transition caused by the notion of evolution means that the previous static character of reality has had to make way for a totally new vision of the dynamic, constantly evolving (possibly in certain cases and circumstances degenerating) character of all that exists. Nothing originates suddenly in its fully grown state. All living beings, earth-forms and celestial bodies have gone through a lengthy history of becoming. This is true for individual beings and for total complexes such as the universe, the layers of the earth with their minerals and stones, the world of plants, the world of animals, the world of humans with all its differentiation in races, peoples, languages, and cultures. Everything has gradually developed from a tiny beginning to the present day.

Within a few years the idea of evolution began to dominate all areas of science. From biology, paleontology, and geology it went into anthropology and ethnology, subsequently to the sciences of law and history, the philological sciences and literature, and finally found its application in the research into the origin of the bible and the wide area of the modern science of religion. Many theologians vehemently resist such a profane approach to the sacred science of theology. But for the scientific person it is not clear why questions should not be asked about the factors which influenced and determined the origin of the bible and the rise and development of Christianity and the other religions.

Physically and psychologically, as well as culturally and from the religious point of view, man has been put into the full light of evolution. Man was not created a few thousand years ago, full and ready-made such as he is now. Man was not an initially perfect being who through an act of disobedience passed on his imperfection to posterity. Man comes from an extinct branch of primates. During "a million years of man" [15] he gradually developed into a natural and cultural being. His ability to speak, his thinking, his aesthetic sense, his ethical consciousness, and his religious expressions have developed from primitive beginnings through numerous stages to the height they have reached in man today.

The rise and wide application of the notion of evolution caused a transition in the vision of nature and man, a comparison to which the transition to the heliocentric world picture and the discovery of the regulation of events by laws of nature was a mere trifle. Hence the reason why conventional Christianity has as long as possible resisted the acknowledgment of the fact of evolution. This resistance has not yet been conquered in all Churches and sects. It is clear that on many points of doctrine the only possible choice is between a conventional and an evolutionist point of view. The Christian will have to make up his mind: either he must keep conventional teaching and reject evolution, or he must accept the fact of evolution and adapt Christian teaching to it.

Theologians are correct when they point out that creation, sin, redemption, *eschaton*, and final destiny are terms and notions of a specifically religious nature, and that science cannot say anything about these, pro or con. The possibility of conflict between faith and science would be excluded if religious notions were not so closely connected in the bible with facts and events which conventional Christianity always understood in a literal and historical sense. The salvation proclaimed in the bible is presented in the form of a salvation history. This made salvation into a historical

[15] Richard Carrington, *A Million Years of Man* (Weidenfeld and Nicholson, London, 1963).

and even a cultural phenomenon. Creation corresponds to a creation narrative; sin corresponds to a narrative of the fall and the deluge; redemption corresponds to a story of the coming, the passion and death, the resurrection and ascension of Christ; the *eschaton* and final fulfillment corresponds to a story of the expectation of the return of Christ, the resurrection of the body, the last judgment, the new heaven and earth, and life eternal.

If all these are taken as events in the literal and historical sense, then the literal and historical conception is tenable only if it fits into the picture which scientific man has formed in the light of evolution.

If the biblical picture of creation, the fall, the deluge, of ancient languages and people, and of the origin of culture could not be brought into harmony with the evolutionist picture of man and the world and with the numerous facts on which the theory of evolution is based, then it is not surprising that those who wish to be true to both faith and science should change the narratives —previously taken in an historical sense—into myths and legends that have value as signs and symbols of the religious truths they indicate. But once this road is taken it is not easy to see why pure conventionality should prompt men arbitrarily to call a halt somewhere. Shouldn't they be consistent and consider as signs and symbols even the stories of the redemption, *eschaton*, and the final destiny which previously were considered to be historical? Such a question is not the fruit of skepticism or unbelief. It simply urges itself inevitably on anyone who wants to adapt belief in the message of salvation to the modern vision of the history of the development of man and mankind based on the fact of evolution.

Copernicus, Galileo, Bacon, Newton, and Darwin were the principal thinkers who heralded the birth of the natural and anthropological sciences. They are surrounded by a crowd of witnesses and collaborators who together paved the way for a definitive rise and development of all those sciences which in the past hundred years have advanced with such enormous strides. Man's method of observation, his thought, experiencing, and application have taken on an essentially new character. Modern man has become thoroughly unfamiliar with the aprioristic, generalizing, abstract, and speculative approach to reality found in prescientific man. Whether we like it or not, it is an established fact that the scientific way of thinking has changed man. He finds it increasingly impossible to live partly in the past and partly in a future world of thought.

In the few pages reserved for the purpose here it would be impossible to give a sufficient idea of the achievements of the modern natural sciences and the amazing technical successes which have followed as a result. As a natural consequence of these achievements our environment and our way of life have undergone such drastic changes that they necessarily had to influence the general attitude of modern man toward religion and the forms of religious practices. In order to get a clear insight into the character of our time with its many new possibilities and dangers one would have to study one or more works written about the history of natural science.

Even at the beginning of the seventeenth century William Harvey had, in his book about the circulation of the blood, laid the foundation for the rise of the modern medical sciences. There has always been a close contact between the medical sciences and the natural sciences. Whenever the latter took an important step forward the possibilities of the former were increased. Finally the parallel development of these two groups of science culminated in numerous technical methods of healing and admirable surgical achievements by which in our own day a great number of people have their lives lengthened, or at least their suffering mitigated. As a result man has been able for a great part to control his own life.

The development of the natural sciences during the past century suffices to recall how discoveries have grown in extent and significance in the field of chemistry, and how these discoveries have been applied in the industrial, pharmacological, and medical fields. We have but to think of the rise and development of the science of electricity with its many applications in the field of illumination, traffic, and industry; of microscopics and bacteriology based on it, with its significance for the care of health and medical therapy; of the invention of aircraft and the development of modern air transportation; of the discovery of radio waves and the resulting radio and television transmissions; of the development of radiology and x-ray techniques with their medical applications; of the development of atomic science with the resulting discovery of atomic fission and the generation and application of atomic energy; of the rapid flight of biochemistry with its inventions of numerous medical preparations; of modern genetics; of the most recent discoveries in the field of radioactivity; of radio astronomy; and of theoretical natural science.

Man continues to penetrate ever further into the secrets of nature. It would seem, however, that the secrets of nature itself, of what life is, what consciousness is, what thought is, what spirit is, continue to elude man's capacity for research and knowledge. The mystery of all being, and in particular the mystery of man himself, has become more awe-inspiring and inscrutable. It does not seem that we shall ever experience the solution of this mystery on earth.

Meanwhile the development of the modern natural sciences has taken place so gradually and—at least for the uninitiated—so unnoticed, that it is impossible to speak of new shocks to conventional Christianity (such as the three we have spoke of earlier), at least not in the area of natural science. We still have to mention shocks of a different kind which have their origin in the areas of psychology, biblical science, philosophy, and the science of religion.

However, in conclusion of this section about what natural science contributed to the undermining of conventional Christianity, a word must be said about the changes in man's concepts of time and space brought about by geology and astronomy.

## Time and Space

Whether they are conceived as Kant's aprioristic forms of sensibility or not, time and space belong to the secrets of human consciousness. The greatest secret of human existence, which never exhausts our thinking, lies in the fact that man not only exists but that he is aware of knowing that he knows that he exists. This is the inscrutable mystery of human self-consciousness. Self-consciousness is the basis for the fact that man is a questioning and thinking being.

As a living being of flesh and blood, and evidently belonging to material reality which science has learned so much about in recent years, man is able to take up a position regarding reality and reflect on himself and on his place in reality. This is at one and the same time the greatness and the misery of being human. Greatness because he knows he is infinitely above the unconscious world around him; misery because he cannot stop himself from asking questions, even though he knows he cannot find answers to the essential ·questions of what being is, what consciousness is, what time and space are, what life itself is, what finiteness and death are, to questions about his origin, meaning, and destiny.

In his consciousness of being, man is also aware that he is in a certain place and at a certain time. Primitive man thought his habitat was the central point of the earth. He knew that he found himself at the point of transition from the past to the future. He therefore knew where he was. He imagined the proportions of the world around him. He knew the recent past, and of the coming future his knowledge was very small and limited. He had an immediate, non-reflexive consciousness he fitted into the world. He had a clearly defined, fixed place, both as regards space and time. To this self-evident consciousness of place corresponds the biblical picture of man and the world, and hence the space and time consciousness of conventional Christianity.

Modern natural sciences have robbed conventional Christianity of this conventional consciousness of place. As far as his dimensions are concerned man finds himself somewhere between a world of smaller and a world of larger dimensions. With the help of the light-microscope, science was able to penetrate even further into the microcosm. This research had to be halted with the cells. Through the invention of the electron microscope it is now possible to magnify by several million times, and the limits have not yet been reached.[16]

Something similar has taken place with regard to the macrocosm. Geology and paleontology have discovered that the earth has not only existed for millions of years, but also that it was populated by living beings. Even mankind, which appeared as the last among the living beings, comprises a time span of several hundreds of thousands of years. The discoveries of modern astronomy correspond to this enormous prolongation of the primitive imagination of time and duration. What the light-microscope did for biology, the light-telescope did for astron-

[16] R. Teunissen, *Het Leven van Plant, Dier, en Mens* (Elsevier, Amsterdam, 1965), p. 13.

omy. By increasing the size of the light-telescope it became evident that the galaxy of the Milky Way, to which our sun and its planets belong, consists of more than a billion stars. And there are thousands of such Milky Way galaxies, separated from each other by immeasurable distances. What the electron microscope did for biology, the modern radio-telescope did for astronomy. While the light-telescope had been able to span distances of millions of light years, modern astronomy has in recent years penetrated distances of billions of light years.[17] The farthest limits have not yet been reached. Discoveries are made of new agglomerations of worlds, of worlds in *statu nascendi*, and of clashing world-complexes in a state of decline.

Until recently we were quite ignorant of the extent and the age of the cosmos. The Milky Way galaxy with its billion stars appeared to be an immeasurably extensive universe. Now we know that the extent and life-span of this galaxy are of little significance when compared to the practically infinite extent and life-span of the total cosmic reality.

Compared to the achievements of the modern science of astronomy, the earlier shocks of the transition from the geocentric to the heliocentric world picture are of little or no significance. The same can be said of the motions of the heavenly bodies and the speed with which they move. The earth rotates around its axis in only twenty-four hours; the earth revolves around the sun in only one year, the earth going through its course with a speed of about nineteen miles a second. All this is nothing compared to the speed with which our solar system moves in the direction of the star Vega which also belongs to the Milky Way galaxy. It means nothing compared to the speed with which the entire Milky Way galaxy rotates around its axis and to the speed with which the whole galaxy is moving to unknown distances.

Our own solar system is at the edge of a super Milky Way galaxy. With a speed of about 2,500,000 miles per hour it rotates around the axis of the Milky Way galaxy. If the movements of the solar system are added to the movements of the Milky Way, and if the movements of the Milky Way are integrated into the movements of other galaxies, we must conclude that our earth undergoes a change of place by millions of miles in an hour, and by many thousands of miles in a second. Every time I finish

[17] Nigel Calder, *Radio Astronomy* (London, 1958).

writing a sentence I find myself at a place in the universe which is removed by tens of thousands of miles from the place where I was when I began the sentence. The same applies to the reader when he reads the sentence.

Where in space do we find ourselves? Nowhere! What significance are the seventy or eighty years of a man's life when compared to the age of the universe? No significance whatever! What is the significance of a journey of a few thousand miles on this earth in comparison to the billions of miles we cover with our planet during our lives? None whatsoever! All our distances, our durations and our speeds are insignificant when compared to the distances, time, and speeds of the cosmos. The conclusion to be drawn from all this is that modern astronomy has presented us with a mysterious "problem of placelessness" as Guardini has called it.

When in 1934 Guardini published his brilliant study on Pascal, the discoveries of radio astronomy had not yet been made. Yet what he then said about the loss of place and constancy can be properly applied to our present condition: "The moral oppression of vastness and infinity . . . becomes so intolerable that the last element of stability disappears. . . . Man no longer has any place; he is not at home anywhere. He neither knows what kind of being he is nor why he is here . . . Existence lacks all foundation . . . Man has become placeless. He is suspended just anywhere. In spite of his qualities he is merely somebody. His measure of reality is purely relative . . . Hence, faced with the world, man is filled with fear and anxiety; before the powers of the universe he is filled with terror." [18]

Following Guardini's reflections on the problem of placelessness, Fortman in *As Seeing the Invisible* describes the religious situation which arose through the loss of place: "Modern man knows that place does not exist outside the universe and that there are no vacant places in the universe. Hence the question arises of where there is place left for God. The stronger the immensity of the universe speaks, the more it hides God from us (in contrast to the former awareness that the heavens proclaim the grandeur of God)." [19] In our modern awareness we have lost our place in the

[18] Romano Guardini, *Christliches Bewusstsein* (Kösel Verlag, Munich, 1950), pp. 53ff.
[19] *Op. cit.*, p. 299.

universe. God too has lost his place. We no longer know where God is, where we are to look for him and find him. The modern question is: "God, where are you?"

This presents us with a religious problem which we cannot go into here. It is the purpose of this chapter to trace the causes of the undermining of conventional Christianity. In this connection we have thus far dealt with the radical changes in man's image of the world caused by natural science. We shall also have to consider in what aspects the image of man has changed, too. In doing so we shall limit ourselves mainly to the consequences of the rise and development of modern psychology and the sciences associated with it.

*Psychology*

Psychology literally means the science of the soul. Even among Greek philosophers and the Christian Church Fathers we meet reflections about the soul of man. These were based on the primitive vision of dualism between body and soul, and on the conviction that what was lower in man was to be blamed on the body and that what really mattered was the striving for the perfection of the soul. In conventional Christianity this was understood as "saving of one's soul." During the Middle Ages psychology was caught in the web of Aristotle's speculative psychology and of Augustine's theological psychology based on the bible. In conventional Christianity the current conceptions of the soul are still for a good part based on this prescientific psychology.

The founder of scientific psychology is Wilhelm Wundt (1832-1920). He was the first to see the close connection between somatic and psychic functions. He was also the first to base psychology on well-planned and methodically executed experiments. He spoke of physiological and experimental psychology. At the beginning of the twentieth century there were different schools of psychologists whose approach to the soul followed their own proper method. In Germany intentional psychology prevailed, in England evolutional psychology, in America functional psychology, and in France pathological psychology. It cannot be said however that at that time the development of psychology constituted a shock to conventional Christianity.

One reason for this is that until a short time ago man was inclined to be more interested in the phenomena of nature which surrounded him than in the phenomena of his own existence—in the hidden causes and motives at the root of his existence. The remarkable transition of interest from nature to man, and the subsequent rise of modern anthropological sciences, is characteristic of our own time.

In his theological anthropology Karl Barth speaks in this connection of a more or less morbid narcissim by which man threatens to turn gradually into an introvert. In any case, it would seem that, apart from professional psychologists, many of those interested in psychology are slightly disturbed and unbalanced, hoping through reading psychological publications to find a solution to their personal psychological difficulties. As a result the consequences and implications of modern psychology have not yet reached the general public and have yet to cause a shock in the circles of conventional Christianity. It is quite likely that the development of scientific psychology took place too gradually to be able to cause a sudden and severe shock.

In fact, however, the rise and development of modern psychology in our century constitutes a greater danger to conventional Christianity than any other shock thus far indicated. Even the definitive breakthrough of the notion of evolution will in the long run not entail consequences which are as farreaching as the radical transition in the vision of man brought about by modern psychology. Here, as in evolution, a sharp distinction must be made between factual and lasting achievements on the one hand and provisional, passing hypotheses and theories on the other.

Just as the rise of the doctrine of evolution is connected mainly with the name of Darwin, the name of Freud stands out in the rise of modern psychology. The development of psychology runs from Freud through Adler to Jung. Medical science has formed a solemn pact with modern psychology in today's psychiatry and neurology. The psychically disturbed person today is considered and treated in a manner essentially different than that of a short time ago. Modern psychology has, for example, given us a really new vision of sexual phenomena. Only in recent days has it begun to be the common property of the general public by means of the stage, film, television, and literature.

When we can ask ourselves how modern psychology will in

the long run make a considerable contribution to the further undermining of conventional Christianity, we shall find several answers.

In the first place, it seems that modern psychology, assisted by the achievements of neurology and pathological psychology, has put an end to the age-old dualism of body and soul. Professional psychologists are increasingly convinced that man is a unity. Man does not *have* a body; he does not *have* a soul; he is at one and the same time body and soul in an inseparable intertwining of both. Human existence has a somatic-physiological and a spiritual-psychological side, and both sides suppose and influence each other continuously. It is inconceivable to have a living body without a soul, just as it is to have a living soul without a body.

It is obvious that this vision of the connection between body and soul will necessarily have consequences on the conventional conception of the immortality of the soul, of an afterlife of the soul in heaven, purgatory, or hell, of the invisible contact which is supposed to exist between the deceased and the living believers. In particular among Protestant theologians there has been a growing conviction that the entire man dies, body and soul and that the resurrection on the last day will be a resurrection for the entire man, body and soul—an entirely new beginning. In that understanding, however, one cannot disregard the question of where the continuity lies between the old man who died and the new man who rose.

Although it has become apparent to me that the greatest majority of psychologists have definitively discarded the dualism of body and soul, and although professionals have emphatically insisted that generally little value is attached to the insights of Jung in this area, I think that in order to be complete I should draw attention to Jung's point of view.

In particular I should like to point to Jung's "psychological commentary" contained in the English edition of the Tibetan *Book of the Dead*. As a result of an ever growing rationalization process of spirit and mentality, Western man inevitably stops with the uncritical assumption that everything psychological is subjective and personal.[20] With regard to Indian notions about *karma* and reincarnation Jung warns: "We know desperately lit-

[20] W. Y. Evans-Wentz, *The Tibetan Book of the Dead* (Oxford University Press, London, 1957), p. xliii.

tle about the possibilities of continued existence of the individual soul after death, so little that we cannot even conceive how anyone could prove anything at all in this respect." [21] After extensive argumentation in support of his viewpoint concerning the independence and timelessness of the soul (in which Jung notes in passing that the Catholic Church is alone in the Western world to care for the souls of the dead), Jung concludes that "every serious-minded reader must ask himself whether these wise old *lamas* might not, after all, have caught a glimpse of the fourth dimension and twitched the veil from the greatest of life's secrets." [22] This, therefore, is a warning on Jung's part.

Regarding the relation between soul and body it should also be observed that psychology in the widest sense does not limit itself to man but concerns itself with all living beings, if only because of the fact that all are capable of sense perceptions.

Sense perception belongs to the unsolved and perhaps unsolvable riddles of the world of living beings. Sense impressions are conducted through the nervous system to a place in the brain where, on the basis of the corresponding stimulus, hearing, sight, feeling, taste, or smell, comes about. How this is possible is an inscrutable puzzle.

As far as man is concerned, psychology does not occupy itself with the study of an immortal soul which inhabits the body, but with man as a physiologico-psychologically determined ego. As such man—and man only—is conscious that he is. Man does not only have sense perceptions; he is conscious of perceiving and reflects on reality. He gives meaning to things, he makes value judgments, he decides, he acts consciously, he is responsible for his actions, he is aware of beauty. Usually man has at least an idea of whoever or whatever is at the basis of the mysterious fact of human existence, and he desires to know and be in community with him or it. It is therefore possible to speak of experiences and behavior which are typical of being human. Psychology occupies itself with the methodical study of these experiences and behavior. This leads to our second point.

Modern psychology brought a new vision to the relation between body and soul. It has also supplied an essentially new insight into the hidden and until recently scarcely suspected causes

[21] *Loc. cit.*
[22] *Op. cit.*, p. 50.

and motives which in many instances are at the basis of psychic experiences and behavior. What is involved here is the part which the wide and complicated field of the unconscious plays in the genesis of psychic experiences, situations, and possibly disturbances, and also in the formation of various reactions, judgments, attitudes, decisions, and behavior.

We all knew that the knowledge consciously acquired in the course of our lives is only partly available in our consciousness. The major part is stored in the unconscious storage chambers of what we call memory. In a manner which we do not understand, we can with greater or lesser trouble recall to the conscious a part of our unconscious knowledge. Under certain circumstances, facts and events can come back to us even without a willed effort. It then becomes evident that what we thought we forgot forever had remained present somewhere.

The wide area of the unconscious contains, however, infinitely more than the knowledge we consciously acquired. Throughout our lives, without willing it and unconsciously, we gather pleasant and unpleasant, favorable and harmful impressions which are not only carefully stored and stacked away but which also —without our knowing it—continue to act in our unconscious life. At a given moment and under certain circumstances they may lead to experiences or actions in our conscious life which we are either pleased or afraid of without really seeing how it is possible that we experience or do this or that.

We also experience the world of the unconscious as an energetically living and acting reality in our existence when some problem interests us strongly and when we continue to occupy ourselves with it in our sleep. Sometimes we have a clear notion of its solution when we wake up. Also at one time or another everyone has had the feeling that sense perceptions are not always caused by outside stimuli. They seem to arise in the conscious without the senses, such as voices, phenomena of light, visions. If these perceptions have no basis in reality outside ourselves we speak of hallucinations. We are inclined to think that hallucinations, as well as dreams, are false illusions, and we tend to look at them as abnormal. But they have their root in the world of the unconscious, which is a real part of our existence. Why should hallucinations and dreams be abnormal and unhealthy?

In our dream life particularly, all sorts of secrets, hidden desires and strivings, unconscious psychic situations, processes and workings, come to expression in our consciousness in some symbolic manner (insofar as we remember our dreams). The methodical study and analysis of the dream life led Sigmund Freud to write *The Interpretation of Dreams*. When this appeared in 1900 it began an entirely new stage in the history of psychology. The discovery of the part played by the unconscious in man's existence was a positive and lasting achievement of the greatest significance. It had farreaching consequences for understanding and judging all that takes place in man's life from the psychological point of view. Modern psychology provides a really new vision of the forms and content of a person's life. A well-trained psychologist reads a biography with completely different eyes than someone who still lives in the pre-psychology phase of culture. In particular, modern psychology provides a totally new understanding and judgment of the sexual, emotional, ethical, moral, and religious existence of man.

The transition brought about by modern psychology in all these respects has only recently begun to penetrate the awareness of the public at large. Not only are people beginning to be aware of the fact that in all the respects just mentioned we have been wrong in our explanations and judgments of the facts, but they are also beginning to realize that the unconscious is highly susceptible to artificial influences such as hypnosis, suggestions, injections, and medication. A well-known psychologist assured me that the bible does not contain any "miracle" that cannot be reproduced by modern psychological means.

At any rate it is certain that because of the rise and discoveries of modern psychology a totally new light has been thrown on many stories from the bible, as well as on experiences of the mystics, the behavior of saints, the action and preaching of prophets and reformers, the real motives for religious action, and the manner in which men judge and encounter one another. All this acquires a totally new sense and meaning if we see and try to understand it in the light of modern psychology. There is no facet of conventional Christianity, particularly in the area of religious images, devotional practices, pious experiences, moral behavior, and the manner in which Christians usually judge and treat one another, which has not come to be seen in a new light.

And as a result they must be judged in the light of the discoveries of modern psychology.

In the third place modern psychology has direct consequences of a purely theological nature. One of the principal foundations on which faith is based is—at least among many groups of Roman Catholics and Protestants—the religious experience. In the Twenties Emil Brunner wrote a book called *Mysticism and the Word*. This book states that it is illusory to base faith on mystical, religious, or any other emotional experiences. On this point Karl Barth agreed with him. On the one hand Barth rejects the religious experience as a foundation of the faith, and on the other he rejects any psychological approach to the bible, revelation, and faith, in order to protect the faith against dangerous psychologisms. We shall return to this in the seventh chapter. First we shall have to consider another most serious shock which conventional Christianity has suffered. The focal point of the shock lies in modern biblical science. The shock was the result of the discovery that all conventional Christianity is based on a conception —in many ways fictitious—concerning the manner in which the various books of the bible originated and the influences which played a part in their origin. This applies particularly to the four gospels. The absolute authority attributed to the bible for centuries has appeared in an entirely new light.

The chapter which follows has a rather unsatisfactory title, chosen for the lack of a better one: "Bible and Culture." Contrary to what the reader might possibly suspect, this chapter does not deal with the mutual relation between the bible and culture. It was chosen for purely technical reasons. The chapter deals with two independent complex causes that contributed to the undermining of conventional Christianity. These are the results of modern biblical science, and, quite independently of the former, the profound changes which are coming about in our modern culture.

# 4. Bible and Culture

Although the most obvious results of the scientific study and examination of the bible are accepted in practically all Christian Churches today, it cannot be said that the problems created within conventional Christianity by biblical science have found completely satisfactory solutions. There still exists a serious discrepancy between the understandable efforts of the Churches to save the traditional content of the faith, based on a literal understanding of the bible on the one hand and the definitive achievements of biblical science on the other.

In the first place we must examine what these definitive achievements are and in what respect they have undermined conventional Christianity. It will become clear that the application of the achievements could not possibly be limited to the explanation of the bible. The facts discovered inevitably raise the question of the historical reliability of biblical stories, the question of what we really know with certainty about Jesus of Nazareth, and the question about the origin and nature of earliest Christianity.

Only in this century did the results of scientific research begin to play a part in the complicated and manifold problem which faces the Church. Yet the antecedents of modern biblical science go back to the seventeenth century. The principal discoveries concerning the origin and structure of the bible and the acceptance of the new vision of the bible in scientific circles date from the second part of the last century. Any other science would have immediately acknowledged and accepted facts ascertained with such great certainty. But the science of theology constantly experiences a restraining influence which is the unfortunate aspect of the concern of the Churches to preserve their particular traditions and to safeguard the ancient treasure of faith.

It is impossible to present a brief review of all the findings of modern biblical research. One of the main discoveries revealed that the books of the Old Testament are compilations by one or more unknown final editors who gathered and ordered all sorts of material borrowed from oral tradition or from written sources.

The editor(s) then used this material of different origins to compose the books of the bible as we now know them. Inevitably this discovery led to an entirely new vision of the history of the people of Israel, of the origin and development of the moral and ceremonial legislation and of the cult, and to a new vision of the place of the prophetic in the religious history of the Israelitic-Jewish people.

Building on the research, theories, and writings of men such as Astruc (1750), Eichhorn (1775), Gerdes (1800), De Wette (1810), Ewald (1850), Graf (1865), and Kuenen (1870), it was ultimately Julius Wellhausen who was able to conclude the struggle for the recognition of the new vision of the origin and construction of the Old Testament, and for an acceptance of the consequences which this entailed. There still are orthodox circles and fundamentalist sects who violently resist what they consider to be an attack on the bible and on the Christian faith. But it is safe to say that theologians of most Churches have gradually accepted the general content of the modern vision of the bible. However, this acceptance forced the theologians to face an entire complex of problems which are still being discussed.

Wellhausen's *Prolegomena zur Geschichte Israels,* published in 1878, was translated into English in 1885. In England W. Robertson Smith, S. R. Driver, J. Skinner, and others succeeded in introducing the new vision of the bible into wider circles. The most serious shock came to conventional Christianity when the principles and methods of modern biblical research began to be applied to the New Testament. In the following pages we shall restrict ourselves to the discussion which touched upon the core of the understanding of the Gospel and the Christian faith.

In 1905 Wellhausen's *Introduction to the First Three Gospels* appeared. In this book he continued to build on suggestions of his predecessors. He also subjected these suggestions to profound criticism, particularly that of Baur who had posited the untenable theory that all four gospels dated from the second century. Ultimately Wellhausen concluded that the Gospel according to Mark was the oldest one. He maintained that this gospel was known in its entirety to the final editors of the first and the third gospels. The other two evangelists supposedly also used a collection of *logia* (words of Jesus). Since Wellhausen, this course is usually referred to as Q (*Quelle*). The authors are also said to have used some of their own material. Concerning the theory that the final edition of the first and third gospels are from the hands of Matthew and Luke respectively, many researchers since Wellhausen consider this doubtful, if not improbable. At any rate it is clear that as far as style and content are concerned, there is a close connection between the first three gospels.

With some reflection no one can fail to be struck by the fact that the fourth gospel is in all respects unique. The language, construction and content of the narratives ascribed to Jesus in this Gospel differ so remarkably from the narratives and parables of Jesus mentioned in the first three (synoptic) gospels that it is hard to believe the synoptic and the Johannine narratives originate from the same person—Jesus of Nazareth. The fourth gospel originated toward the end of the first century. It is improbable that it was written by the disciple and apostle John, but possibly by one of his converts. It may rely partly on the oral tradition of John.

As far as the letters of Paul are concerned, precise comparisons in terminology, style, mentality, and content have awakened serious doubt in the genuineness of these letters—in the genuineness of the tradition which ascribes the letters to the apostle Paul. The letter to the Hebrews is no longer ascribed to Paul by any bible researcher. As for the other letters it is difficult to arrive at a generally satisfactory conclusion. The oldest of them—the letter to the Galatians—dates from about 48 A.D. The letters to Timothy and Titus, considered to be the latest writings of the New Testament, date from the beginning of the second century and can hardly come from Paul. The book of Revelation is certainly not from the same writer as the Gospel of John and the Johannine letters. In the ancient Christian Church it was long considered to be spurious, and the reformers of the sixteenth century were at a loss what to do with it. In any case it is addressed to the persecuted Christians in Asia Minor with the intention of strengthening them and consoling them while awaiting the imminent return of Christ.

## The New Testament

This last observation leads us to many difficult problems which have arisen in connection with the new discoveries and insights concerning the origin, historical reliability, and religo-theological meaning of the New Testament. Once the researchers started critically comparing and interpreting the content of the New Testament they fell from one descrepancy and riddle into another. The problems of the New Testament have gradually become so manifold and so complicated that the religious historian C. J. Bleeker of Amsterdam correctly observed that if the message of the bible is considered to be an absolutely authoritative message, one must necessarily ask what this authoritative message consists of. In that event numerous difficult questions inevitably arise relating both to the foundations and the content of Christian belief.[1]

A first problem that confronted theologians from Albert Schweitzer to Rudolf Bultmann was the eschatological problem concerning the last things—the return of Christ, the resurrection of the dead, and the last judgment. What can be found about these in the New Testament; what did Jesus say about them according to the synoptic Gospels; what do we find about them in the letters of Paul to the Corinthians and the Thessalonians; what in the second letter ascribed to Peter; what in the final book of the bible? What is the total impression these create? What can we do with it in the light of the modern image of the world, of the course of human history, and in the light of the new visions of the future on the basis of evolution such as we find for example in Teilhard de Chardin? This is not the right place to go into these questions, but it is certain that even on this latter point alone the current conceptions of conventional Christianity have been severely undermined.

## Jesus of Nazareth

A second and certainly the most serious problem closely connected with the new vision of the New Testament is one of research into the life of Jesus. What do we actually know of Jesus of Nazareth? [2]

Questions about the life of Jesus of Nazareth, and finally even

---

[1] C. J. Bleeker, *Christ in Modern Athens* (Brill, Leiden, 1965), p. 111.
[2] A. F. J. Klijn, *Wat weten wij van Jezus van Nazareth?* (Boekencentrum, The Hague, 1962).

the questions about the historicity of Jesus, necessarily had to arise as soon as it became clear that the four gospels are not biography in the usual sense of the word. They are not the writings of one writer (the respective evangelists to which they were ascribed on the basis of tradition) but are compilations in which older historical traditions are mingled with later visions and interpretations. It was obvious that scholars who considered themselves scarcely (if at all) bound to the traditional consideration of the bible would apply also New Testament writings to the strict norms of modern literary and historical research.

The scientific approach to the life of Jesus dates from as early as the eighteenth century. Undoubtedly it stems from the rationalist spirit of the Enlightenment. However, this does not mean that it has not brought facts to light which are of lasting significance for a correct understanding of the biblical data. Hermann Samuel Reimarus, the first to occupy himself with the facts concerning the life of Jesus and the origin of Christianity, in order to prevent theological and Church quarrels and disputes, shared his findings with only a small closed circle. After his death Lessing published seven fragments (c. 1775) which gave the impetus to the debate. A beginning was made to research the life of Jesus, a study which was to occupy the entire nineteenth century. Of the fragments of Reimarus, only the final two were concerned with the historical Christ—the fragment about the stories of the resurrection and the fragment about Jesus and his disciples.

The harvest of a century-long research into the life of Jesus was reaped by Albert Schweitzer and was gathered together in his book *From Reimarus to Wrede* which appeared in 1906 and which in 1913 was published in a revised and expanded form under the title *History of the Research into the Life of Jesus*. In the meantime, in 1911, Schweitzer published a book relating the history of the research into Paul since the Reformation. Later another important book appeared dealing with the mysticism of Paul. Meanwhile Schweitzer studied medicine, and after his graduation in 1913 he founded his hospital in Lambaréné.

Two stages of development can be distinguished in the nineteenth century research into the life of Jesus. In the first stage the researchers proceeded from the historicity of the data. As rationalists they were scandalized at the miracle stories and at the miraculous character of the birth and resurrection stories. Therefore they attempted to interpret them so that they would be intellectually acceptable.

The second stage was introduced by the publication of the work of D. F. Strauss entitled *The Life of Jesus* (1833). After that time, efforts to make the stories acceptable were relegated to the background. In close connection with the discoveries about the origin of the New Testament writings, the question arose more and more frequently whether and in how far the gospel stories are historically trustworthy and acceptable.

Nineteenth century research into the life of Jesus concluded that it is impossible to compose a "modern" biography of Jesus from the different and often contradictory data of the four gospels if the biography is to correspond to present historical norms. Rather, the historical figure of Jesus disappears for the researcher, and as a result some extreme bible researchers have even asked themselves whether Jesus has existed in actual fact. This question has been considered from all angles, but as far as I know it has been determined that the historicity of Jesus cannot be called into doubt.

Meanwhile, however, it remains unanswered whether and in how far we are able to ascertain from the gospels who Jesus was, what he preached and did, what happened to him, and how early Christianity arose. The images of Jesus presented by research into the life of Jesus have not been able to stand up to the test of continued scientific critique. Schweitzer states that the research has had negative results. It has turned out to be impossible to present Jesus of Nazareth as an historical figure in the midst of many other historical figures mankind has produced. It is not a historically justified image of Jesus which is at the basis of belief in Jesus Christ and which awakens faith, but the power which emanated from Jesus' appearance for the past twenty centuries in all corners of the earth. "To our world Jesus means something because a mighty spiritual power emanated from him which still flows forth in our own time. This fact is neither destroyed nor confirmed by historical knowledge." [3]

The conclusion of Albert Schweitzer can conveniently be considered as the bridge from nineteenth to twentieth century re-

---

[3] Albert Schweitzer, *Geschichte der Leben Jesu Forschung* (Mohr, Tübingen, 1921), p. 632. English text: *The Quest of the Historical Jesus*, trans. by W. Montgomery (Macmillan, New York, 1950).

search about the Jesus of the gospels and about the origin of Christianity. Briefly summarized its results are the following:

It is extremely difficult, if not impossible, to determine the historical core of the stories about Jesus of Nazareth and the words he spoke. Practically all New Testament scholars agree that the gospels do contain historically reliable elements. But opinions are considerably divided when it comes to the exact determination of the degree of historicity. In connection with the publication of *Honest to God*, the sensational book by the Anglican bishop of Woolwich, the archbishop of Canterbury spoke of Bultmann's historical skepticism which was said to have affected Bishop Robinson. It is remarkable that others judged Robinson's reserved attitude toward Bultmann to be a remnant of an antiquated conservatism. A mitigated judgment of what the research has actually rendered can be found in Klijn's book which we referred to already and in a somewhat more extensive work of Günther Bornkamm, entitled *Jesus of Nazareth*.[4]

In the second place all researchers agree that the gospels do not contain historiography in the usual sense of the word. The gospels are not biographies. Rather, they are witnesses to the faith of the first and second generation of Christians. They present a historically fixed picture of the faith of the oldest Christian communities rather than the words and deeds of Jesus himself. The core of the community's faith was the belief in the resurrection. The gospels intend to give a picture of who the risen person was during his existence on earth. The picture is constructed from historical and nonhistorical materials. From the differences found in the evangelists it becomes evident that the picture of the synoptics deviates strongly from that of the composer of the fourth gospel. At the same time remarkable differences exist even among the synoptics themselves.

The historicity of the birth and resurrection stories is accepted by only few bible researchers. This not so much because of the miraculous character of what is narrated, but because of the contradictions in the manner of presentation. It is impossible to give a satisfactory explanation for the contradictions by considering the different stories as complementary.

According to the passage in Luke 2, 39, Mary and Joseph returned to Nazareth after having fulfilled all the prescriptions of

[4] Cf. note 2 above.

the Law of the Lord; according to Matthew 2, they were still in Bethlehem when the magi from the East arrived after a long journey, and they took refuge in Egypt because of the impending murder of the innocents (about which nothing is known in the history of that time). Something similar occurs in the stories about the resurrection. According to Matthew 28, 7, and according to Mark 16, 7, the angels at the tomb ordered the woman to tell the apostles that they were to go to Galilee, and that they would see the Lord there. According to Matthew 28, 10, this order was confirmed by Jesus himself when he appeared to the women. The evangelists Luke and John, however, state that the disciples remained in Jerusalem and that Jesus appeared to them there in the evening of the first day of the week while the doors of the place where the disciples were staying were closed for fear of the Jews. According to John this apparition was repeated a week later. Apparitions in Galilee are mentioned only in Matthew 28, 16-20 and John 21. From the preceding verses it is clear that we are dealing here with later additions. The disciples received the missionary command in Galilee according to the end of the Gospel of Matthew, whereas at the end of the Gospel of Mark the event took place in Jerusalem. The Gospel of Luke gives the impression that prior to the ascension the disciples did not leave Jerusalem, whereas the Gospel of John, in chapter 21, gives the impression that after the death of Jesus the disciples returned to Galilee to resume their task as fishermen on the lake of Tiberias.

Difficulties of a similar nature also occur when we ask how Jesus died. According to Matthew and Mark Jesus died with the words "My God, my God, why have you forsaken me?" According to Luke he died with the words "Father into your hands I commend my spirit" (citations respectively from Psalms 51 and 31), and according to John with the words "It is consummated." These three different presentations do not complement each other but give three different visions of Jesus' death, three different interpretations of the same event—or at least three different traditions. Evidently it is not a question of the exact representation of what happened but a testimony of faith concerning the sense and meaning of the death of Jesus.

These few examples can be multiplied by many others of a similar nature. They are mentioned here to give some idea of the nature of the problems discovered and raised by modern bible research. For the time being there can be no question of unanimity concerning the manner of solving them.

Research into the sources and the origin of the gospels has given an entirely new vision of the question of their historical reliability. This new vision has given impetus to research into the question of who Jesus was or was not, of what he thought and did, and what he experienced. This leads us to a third main problem, which concerns the content of the Gospel that Jesus proclaimed and the immediately connected question of how the New Testament Gospel concerning Jesus should be read. What does the New Testament proclaim about Jesus and his heavenly Father? What is the meaning of the expressions Son of God and Son of Man? What is meant by the Kingdom of God? What sense and meaning does the New Testament attribute to the coming of Jesus into the world, to his action in word and deed, to his suffering, his death on the cross, and to his resurrection? In short what does it mean when the Christian believes in Christ and is baptized in his name? According to the bible and the New Testament, what is the essence of Christianity?

## Bultmann

It is impossible to give a brief resumé of all that has been said about this since von Harnack (*The Essence of Christianity*, 1899-1900). The discussion about these questions is still in full swing. In the past ten or twenty years the discussion has concentrated increasingly on the exegetico-theological work of Rudolf Bultmann, and in particular on the treatise he published during the second world war under the title of *New Testament and Mythology*, with the subtitle: *The Problem of Demythologization of the New Testament Proclamation*.

In this book, published anew in the first volume of *Kerygma and Myth*, Bultmann tries to establish a bridge between modern bible research and the exegesis based on it and present-day theology. This is nothing new. Numerous dogmatic works exist, especially among the reformed who work exclusively from scripture, which are based on a certain exegesis of sacred scripture, just as there are other exegetical works which are meant to demonstrate the truth of a certain doctrine or theology. In Bultmann neither of this occurs. It is true, however, that, though being an exegete, he transgresses the limits of bible research and enters the area of theology.

But he does this in an entirely new fashion. Some provisional observations must be made in this connection—provisional because in doing so we are running ahead to a completely separate cause of the undermining of conventional Christianity to be dealt with in subsequent chapters. What we have in mind is the transition from the classic essentialist to the modern existentialist way of thinking. Bultmann is convinced that modern theology must be existentialist. In our own time there is no longer an abstract-speculative questioning into the essence and nature of man, but a concrete-analytic questioning into his existence—into that which is concretely proper to being-human and only to being-human, that which makes man man.

We are dealing with a totally new way of thinking which contains a completely new approach to reflection on all human problems, in particular the problems of faith and theology. It is quite true that in the Reformation Luther had an approach to an understanding of the bible that was more existential than essential, but in general Reformation theology had a predominantly essentialist character.

This transition in modern thought also shows a second aspect which utilizes logical positivism and linguistic analysis. Words, images, and expressions which have been used for centuries and which occupy an important place in the Bible, in creeds, and in conventional proclamations have in our century gradually changed meaning as a result of changes in our manner of perception and thinking. They call forth different associations than they did before. It is not at all certain that preaching cast in conventional terminology still affects the hearer. It is also questionable whether the person who reads the bible really reads what was meant there. One of the principal problems of modern exegesis is to determine what precisely is meant by biblical terms and to decide what words they should be replaced with if the bible is to continue saying to modern man what it is intended to say.

In short, one of the most urgent and actual problems is how we are to interpret the bible, in particular the New Testament, in such a manner that today's man understands the message which comes to man from God through the bible. What is the originally intended content of the biblical message, the biblical proclamation, the *kerygma*, and how is this message to be interpreted and portrayed if modern man is to understand it according to the original intention?

It was this problem with which Bultmann occupied himself throughout his life. The main contributions of Bultmann toward a clarification and solution of these questions in this area have been collected in four volumes entitled *Belief and Understanding*.[5] These volumes contain the most profound, most lucid, and most useful analysis of the problems with which modern exegesis of the bible is faced.

Because it is necessary to limit ourselves we must omit certain critical questions such as whether Bultmann understood and interpreted the early Heidegger correctly, whether it was right for him to pass over the reversal which took place in the later Heidegger, whether Bultmann became stagnated in an old fashioned, rationalistic conception of natural science and in an antiquated liberalism, and whether he was acquainted with what experts nowadays understand by myth and mythology. There are a number of interesting and necessary questions here.

But we are limiting ourselves to the main point. This concerns principally what Bultmann has called "demythologizing." While this is not a fortunate term, it cannot be replaced by another. It is not a fortunate term because the expression "demythologizing of the New Testament" can easily, though erroneously, be taken to mean that all myths should be removed from the New Testament. This is not Bultmann's intention.

What Bultmann means to say is that the message which reaches us in the New Testament inevitably finds expression in the bible in forms which could be understood in the time of the writers. The picture of the world and of man of that time was permeated with what Bultmann calls a "mythological" way of thinking. The same applies to the causes which were then attributed to certain events, to what was considered possible, and to the conceptions which people formed. As a result of the changes in the world-picture and the picture of man which occurred in the past few centuries, as a result of the mechanization of the world-picture, as a result

[5] R. Bultmann, *Glauben und Verstehen*, 4 vols. (Mohr, Tübingen, 1933-1965).

of the idea of evolution, and as a result of the achievements of psychology and the other modern sciences, man has acquired a totally new vision of causality and of the connection between things and events, of what is possible or impossible, and especially of what has meaning and not.

Modern man has once and for all left the old, mythological way of thinking in favor of a new scientifically founded manner of thought. Moreover he no longer thinks in an essentialist but in an existentialist way about man and all that belongs to the domain of man. Since the message of the New Testament, the *kerygma*, is expressed in a mythological form no longer understood by anyone, it is absolutely necessary in the interest of modern man that the message be interpreted in contemporary form. As far as Bultmann is concerned this is quite evidently an existentialist manner of approach and interpretation. If there is question here of "myth and *kerygma*" it does not mean that myth and *kerygma* are, as it were, two different components of the New Testament, the myth of which would have to be removed in order to save the *kerygma*. Such an idea of Bultmann's intention can only obfuscate the discussion. What does matter is of course *kerygma*. In earlier times *kerygma* could not be proclaimed in forms other than myth. But in our own times *kerygma* must be interpreted and proclaimed in the form of human existence as conceived in our time, otherwise the New Testament proclamation remains unintelligible. What Bultmann therefore basically intends is (as Macquarrie formulated it in his scholarly and balanced book about *The Scope of Demythologizing*) nothing but the translation of mythological into existential statements.[6] This is indeed a most necessary and meritorious undertaking.

But we are immediately faced with serious difficulties. In spite of the careful, well considered, and sober manner in which Bultmann worked at the execution of his plan, he has had to endure sharp criticism which varied from total rejection by the right wing to total rejection by the left wing. The extreme right wing fears that Bultmann is on a completely wrong road because demythologizing affects and endangers the *kerygma* in all respects. The extreme left wing rejects Bultmann's effort to save

[6] John Macquarrie, *The Scope of Demythologizing* (S.C.M. Press, London, 1960), p. 226 cf. also: S. M. Ogden, *Christ without Myth* (Harper and Row, New York, 1961).

the *kerygma* and believes that Bultmann should have attempted to diminish both the mythological form and the *kerygma*. On the one side there is the desire to preserve conventional Christianity as it has always been. On the other side there is a belief that not only conventional Christianity but the biblical message as such is out of date.

The actual problem which Bultmann—in my opinion quite *ad rem*—has raised is whether and in how far the translation from one form into another influences, affects, and possibly even undermines the *kerygma* itself. This is the actual and inevitable problem. No theologian can or may withdraw himself from reflection on this problem, particularly because of pastoral reasons. This does not necessarily mean that a person must and can agree with Bultmann on all points. Numerous questions have arisen which are either directly or indirectly connected with Bultmann's demythologizing. These are not questions which proceed from unbelief. Nor are they artificial, arbitrary, and unnecessary questions. They simply are questions with which any Christian who is not playing hide-and-seek is necessarily faced because of the many different causes dealt with in the preceding chapter, and which have in various respects undermined conventional Christianity.

The fact that exegetes and theologians only partly agree with Bultmann's diagnosis and therapy, and that they think differently about related questions of detail, does not mean that the problem Bultmann raised and which is under constant discussion is not urgent and actual. For a collection of the principal contributions to the discussion we would refer the reader to the nine volumes of *Kerygma and Myth*. Karl Barth's judgment can be found in number 34 of *Theological Studies*, entitled "*Rudolf Bultmann; An Attempt to Understand Him.*" Apart from the limitation and content of the *kerygma*, the historicity of the gospel stories is also discussed, as is the question of whether the interpretation of the *kerygma* in contemporary form must necessarily have an existentialist character.

The present development of bible research bypasses Bultmann on important points. In recent days there is renewed examination of the life of Jesus. The general opinion continues to be that the gospels are not of a biographical nature, but the historical core of them is being enlarged again within more clearly delineated lines.

As Klijn has remarked:"The possibility remains that on the basis of the gospels a picture can be formed of Jesus' person and work." [7] Research is opening up into the mysteriousness of Jesus' appearance. Jesus is a historical figure of flesh and blood who belongs to this world. "And yet, right in the midst of the world, he is irreversibly other. This is where the secret of his efficacy and of his rejection lies." [8] The greatest riddle for Jesus' disciples and for the early Christian community was the fact of his death. All evangelists are quite specific in the stories of his capture, the double condemnation, the way of the cross and the death on the cross. What is involved here is the puzzle of a Messiah who dies on the cross. The solution of this puzzle was considered by the disciples and the first Christians to lie in the resurrection. Whatever a person might think of the marvelous and contrasting stories of the resurrection, one thing is historically certain: the disciples firmly believed in the resurrection of Jesus. This belief united them; it had a community-forming effect, and the belief of the apostles in the resurrection was from the very beginning the foundation of the Gospel and of the entire Christian faith. This is clear from the ten discourses in the Acts of the Apostles and from the fifteenth chapter of the first letter of Paul to the Corinthians.

## The Early Christian Community

In the meantime, however, another problem is coming to the fore. On the one hand the picture of the historical Jesus is beginning to get a sharper focus, and on the other hand bible researchers are beginning to form a more distinct picture of the early Christian community. In contrast to Bultmann and his school, some scholars are again inclining toward the opinion that there is a certain continuity between the first disciples and the early community. The belief concerning Jesus which arose in the early community and which acquired a fixed form cannot have been separate from the picture of Jesus which the disciples—who went about with him for several years—had kept in their memory.

[7] A. F. J. Klijn, *op. cit.*, p. 16.
[8] G. Bornkamm, *Jesus von Nazareth* (Kohlhammer, Stuttgart, 1960), p. 51. English trans.: *Jesus of Nazareth* (Harper & Bros., New York, 1961).

Yet other factors must also have played a part. Researchers in more recent years are again paying attention to the religious environment in which the early community arose and developed. One reason for this lies in the 1947 discoveries of the Dead Sea scrolls which are part of an ancient library in Qumran. Several translations have already been made of the Qumran texts, and the deciphering and research are still in full progress.[9] Much has been written about whether or not the early Christian community was influenced by the world of thought expressed in the Qumran documents.

Here one could go two ways. One might start from a fixed conventional Christianity considered to be safe from attack and maintain that too much of the primitive Christian heritage is absent from the Qumran texts to be able to speak of any relationship. From that position one can try to reason away their striking similarities with ancient Christianity by explaining them differently.

On the other hand, one could start with what at first sight appear to be striking similarities and utilize them as much as possible to describe the origin and the nature of early Christianity. Archibald Robertson, for example, states: "The similarities between the customs of the Dead Sea sects and those of the early communities are too numerous to think they happened by chance; the common sharing of goods, the community meal, the blessing of bread and wine, the apocalyptic expectation of the final victory of the 'Son of Light' over the 'sons of darkness,' even the name 'New Covenant' by which the sect was known to its members." [10] Might not certain notions which even today are commonplace in conventional Christianity have their origin somewhere else than in Jesus of Nazareth? And what is the relation between the teaching of Paul and that of the twelve apostles? How did the Church with its ministries and sacraments develop from the early Christian community? It does not seem that the all-too-simplistic notions about these questions in conventional Christianity, whether Roman Catholic or Protestant, will be confirmed by the historical investigation into the origin of Christianity.

[9] T. H. Gaster (intr.), *The Dead Sea Scriptures in English Translation* (Doubleday, New York, 1956).

[10] A. Robertson, *Die Ursprünge des Christentums* (Günther, Stuttgart, 1965), p. 240.

The urgent question that presents itself here is whether facts and events justify the position that the Church, in its growth and development, remained true to the spirit of Jesus' preaching and to the actual meaning of Jesus' command to his disciples, or whether the teaching, the morality, the ecclesiastical exercise of authority, the sacramental practice, and piety have undergone foreign influences of non-Christian origin, thus straying farther and farther away from the spirit and intention of their origin. A well-founded and true-to-reality answer to this question is of the utmost importance for ecumenism, in particular for relations between Christians and non-Christians. The restoration of unity among Christians and all questions of a religious or ecclesiastical nature will have to be approached and answered, not from tradition and convention alone, but from the word, the command, and the intention of Jesus Christ himself as we learn to know him from the Gospels with the aid of unprejudiced bible research.

## The Rising World Culture

We are now switching to an entirely different group of causes by which conventional Christianity has been undermined. Once we ascertain that the world culture now in a process of becoming contributes to the undermining of conventional Christianity, we see that it is not a matter of severe jolts but rather a gradual cultural process which threatens the continued existence of a number of conventional forms of Christianity. Whether this should be applauded or rejected is a question that does not matter in the context of this chapter. What we are doing here is merely ascertaining facts and their consequences.

If this book dealt with the Christian message as something static, complete in itself, unchangeable, and therefore having the same meaning for all times and cultures, there would be no sense in investigating the influence of the development of culture on the core of the message. However, this book does not deal with the Christian message, but with conventional Christianity. To what degree the core of the Christian message shows itself to its full advantage in conventional Christianity is an important question, but this is not the place for it. We are dealing now with the undermining of conventional Christianity and with the accumulation of causes which contributed to it. We cannot pass over the changes which Western culture has undergone in the course of this century, nor can we disregard the future character of the still nascent world culture.

A Christian can hardly consider the Gospel message as a product of culture. Conventional Christianity, on the other hand, is largely a product of culture. Its forms of expression, conceptions, and customs, its entire spirit and mentality are rooted in the world of Greco-Roman-Germanic civilization, and are so grown together with Western civilization that profound changes in the general pattern of culture necessarily influence the tenability of conventional Christianity.

The shocks we have indicated in this and the previous chapter are shocks of a cultural nature. Since the rise of the modern natural and anthropological sciences a primitive, naive, and simplistic attitude toward reality has gradually had to make place for a reflexive, critical, and analyzing attitude with a growing sense of the meaning of facts, connections, and processes. The way which modern man approaches, studies, understands, appreciates, and experiences reality has radically changed in a brief span of time.

This rapid development, which more and more evidently is directed toward an entirely new and still nascent world culture, has for a long time been exercising its influence on every area of human existence. Conventional Christianity alone has resisted this influence. An American study has shown that even in the field of political and social relations the percentage of diehards is largest among conventional Christians.[11] Conventionality and prejudice go hand in hand. No conventionality, however, is more stubborn than religious conventionality. As a consequence, the chasm between conventional Christianity and the nascent world culture is imperceptibly but steadily widening, and the tension between the two has gradually become greater and more critical. It is one of the great assets of the Second Vatican Council and of parallel developments in world Protestantism to have seen this clearly.

If we wish to examine the relation between conventional Chris-

---

[11] G. W. Allport, *The Nature of Prejudice* (Anchor Books, New York, 1958), p. 420: "Among those (out of 400 students) who report that religion was a marked or moderate factor, we find the degree of prejudice far higher than among those who report that religion was a slight or nonexistent factor in their training."

tianity and the nascent world culture, it is obvious that we must first enquire into the characteristics of this nascent world culture. I think I am right if I say that these characteristics can be listed under three denominators which perhaps can be best indicated with the words democracy, technology, and secularization.

## Democracy

Literally democracy means "government by the people." It could be understood as a situation where the "common" people rule without paying attention to the knowledge, advice, warnings, and just wishes of the "better" people. If this were the case the situation would have arisen by means of a revolution of the people against those who alone are able to give direction. This, however, is not what I mean by democracy.

Democracy is a valuable good of culture which must be striven for and to which the development of civilization is directed as to a final goal. The democracy intended here is a democracy in the process of becoming. It supposes level of development in the population where all normal adults are capable of judging given situations, of acquiring sufficient insight into questions which arise, and of exercising a constructive influence on the decisions made by competent authorities.

In a real democracy it is impossible for a small group of governing men to issue commands which must be accepted unconditionally by the mass of the population, and obeyed without reflection. In a developed society such a situation would be nothing less than a spiritual form of slavery contrary to human dignity. Despite the birth pangs that accompany the evolution of the future world culture, it is clear that new culture is conceivable only if it is characterized by democracy in the sense we have just described it. In the nations of the "free world," the principles of democracy were definitively accepted in the course of the past century, even though its functioning is often still defective on many points.

Conventional Christianity has not been favorably inclined toward democracy in Church matters. This applies not only to the Roman Catholic Church but to the reformation national Churches as well, even though the later no longer make a distinction between the clergy and laity. Anyone familiar with the reformed Churches knows that it is sometimes just as difficult to deal with a synodal as a curial dictatorship. The forms and methods may differ, but the reformation Churches also expect members to accept conformity to the will of ecclesiastical authority. Because of the nature of conventionality, conventional Christianity fears any undermining of the teaching and discipline current in this or that particular Church. It therefore depends on principles and, if necessary, on strict disciplinary measures.

A too-democratic spirit is highly dangerous for the quiet and unchangeable continued existence of conventional Christianity. Yet the spirit of democracy has entered into the Churches. At least on two points this constitutes a serious threat to the conventional forms of Christianity. In the first place a democratic mentality undermines old forms of the exercise of authority. In the second place the sense of community proper to democracy breaks down the walls of separation which the Churches have constructed among themselves in self-defense.

## Technology

The word "technology" derives from the root of the Greek verb for "to produce" and the corresponding noun *techne* which means proficiency, skill, handiwork, artifact, and also invention. When we hear the word technology in our Western culture we think not so much of handiwork but of all the instruments which result from scientific discoveries and inventions. Technology is the practical fruit of the achievements of modern natural science and tangible proof that the principles and methods of these sciences are correct. Technology has brought about such radical changes in the manner of living and in man's relation to nature that our's has been called the age of technology.

The word technology makes us think of modern industry with its variety of ingenious machines, computers, and robots, of the modern means of transportation, from the steamboat and motorboat, automobile and train to the latest inventions in the field of aeronautics and astronautics. We think of modern means of communication, from the telephone and wireless, the phonograph and radio, television and tape recorders, to the application of technology in the area of agriculture, horticulture, fruit-growing, livestock breeding, the fishing industry, and in the area of nutrition and pharmacy, and finally of the numerous applications in the medical field.

In a wider sense, we can also include efforts to classify people, to register them, to insure them, and to support them through a fiscal system that excludes risk and inequality as much as possible. This technical culture is spreading all over the world. Men everywhere live, eat and drink, travel and dress in the same way, independently of how well off they are. It is unmistakable that a process of increasing equalization is going on. Moreover, practically all of life is regulated by the competent authorities. Our life can no longer be conceived of without bureaucracy and uniform education systems.

No one is foolish enough to deny that all this demands an effort to liberate people all over the world from the yoke of poverty, sickness, insecurity, worry, suffering, difficulty, and misery. But at the same time there is the constant threat of total annihilation by the use of the latest discoveries in physics and chemistry in the manner of waging war.

If religion were a matter of purely religio-philosophic truths based on the correct application of the laws of logic, the development of technology could have little influence on religion. But religion is a matter of the total man in his relation to God. Man is dependent on ideas which fit into his level of culture. He needs symbolic stories and actions which fit into his pattern of living, which are related to his conception and evaluation of life, and which are closely related to the manner in which man sees and experiences himself and the world he lives in.

It is clear that man not only forms and influences his environment, but that he is also influenced and formed by it. Not only is man busy changing the pattern of nature into a pattern of culture, but people of nature are becoming people of culture; not only is our time a time of technology, but man too has become technical man. Even a person who knows nothing of technology lives in a technological world and is constantly using the possibilities and results of technology. Without noticing it we are beginning to think technologically; we are beginning to see ourselves and others more and more as numbers and to treat people as things. We are beginning to be more impersonal.

Added to this is the fact that we are increasingly forced to protect nature against an ever expanding culture. In spite of our best efforts we are becoming more and more estranged from nature, even on our tourist holidays. Modern man is becoming increasingly businesslike, calculating, sober; he is financially and statistically oriented even in religious matters. Just as God has been entirely excluded from the scientific explanation of natural and cultural phenomena, so has God come to stand more and more outside the practice of human living in work and recreation. As long as no uncontrollable disasters—such as mortal illnesses, economic collapses, or atomic wars—threaten, we men of our time can get along quite well without God. In fact, as a result of the increased tempo of life we scarcely have time to think of God.

As far as religious questions, theological debates, and ecclesiastical worries of previous generations are concerned, the present generation is thoroughly tired of them. It is not so much indifference toward the question of existence or the relation to God by which modern man is being increasingly estranged from conventional Christianity, it concerns the ever increasing distance between conventional religious practice and contemporary manner of living and thinking. This is the principal cause of religious indifference and the emptiness of the church buildings.

## Secularization

Secularization points to one of the most evident characteristics of the nascent world culture. As a result of modern education, press, radio and television, film, paperback books, and modern world literature a growing number of people fall under the influence of world culture cast in a totally new framework, and which is still in the process of becoming. They see how in a very short period of time age-old religious notions and practices, views of world and life, human relations, and social forms are disappearing to make place for a culture based on technology.

Men's thinking and striving are becoming world-centered. This earth and this world human life is the span between birth and death. Modern man finds it most difficult to conceive of a world outside this one, of an existence after death in another world.

Hence even among Christians who are still "convinced" Christians there are fewer who make efforts to despise worldly things in order to obtain heavenly things. Prayer, meditation, and contemplation, are disappearing from daily life. There simply is no time left for them. Moreover, an effort at transition from modern life to a life more heavenly than worldly creates a strange and uncomfortable feeling of unreality in an increasing number of people.

This secularizing process is taking place all over the world and in all world religions. It undermines age-old images of faith, forms of piety and cult and attitudes toward the world and toward fellow men. The process takes place in the hidden, unconscious life of man. When talking with Christians who follow the old manners about the increasing "indifference" and about "empty church buildings," it always strikes me how little awareness they have of what is taking place in the world. Few really see the inevitability of what takes place. People hope for improvement by arousing interest in old questions and tried paths, either by better prepared sermons, by renewing religious services, and in particular by more lively and attractive singing during the services. These are excellent in themselves. But the question is whether the servants of Gospel and Church are sufficiently aware that all conventional Christianity—all the way down the line, in all its forms of expression and appearance which derive from a disappearing culture—has come to be a debated matter.

The secularization inherent in the rise and development of the new world culture faces "Christianity" with the choice of radical renewal in all respects or complete collapse, together with the dying culture from which it has derived its forms of thought and living.

A number of new religious problems are closely related to this fact. The religious element in man's existence relates to questions which daily life asks of man by reason of its very actuality and nature. These questions depend on the level and character of the civilization man has reached. A certain pattern of culture involves a certain type of religious questions. The conventionality of religion can, because of its stubbornness, result in religious answers and religious forms of expression and practice which continue to exist for centuries while the existential questions they correspond to are no longer asked and have been replaced by completely new questions which conventional Christianity does not supply answers for. In that case religion has become obsolete.

Conventional Christianity has now arrived at such a situation. The official religion in its conventional shape no longer answers questions of daily life in a form modern man can understand. Paul Tillich pointed this out as early as 1951 in the first part of his *Systematic Theology*:

"It is not an exaggeration to say that today man experiences his present situation in terms of disruption, conflict, self-destruction, meaninglessness, and despair in all realms of life . . . The question arising out of this experience is not, as in the Reformation, the question of a merciful God and the forgiveness of sins . . . It is the question of a reality in which the self-estrangement of our existence is overcome, a reality of reconciliation and reunion, of creativity, meaning and hope." [12]

Modern man no longer asks how he must come to terms with sin, but how he must come to terms with the enigmatic character of existence in which he finds himself. Undoubtedly the theologian will be able to find a connection between the way modern man experiences his existence and the way the bible speaks of sin. But modern man no longer understands the word "sin" in its full seriousness and depth because he interprets and explains his existence in the light of all kinds of scientific achievements in a way which scarcely leaves any place for the biblical awareness of sin. This is closely connected with the process of secularization taking place in all of humanity.

For a long time, and not without great concern, many have seen that continuing secularization threatens Christianity in its conventional forms. But it took a long time before it became evident that secularization inevitably belongs to the nascent world culture, and that it is a positive asset in the clarification of the Christian message. A remarkable example of this is the change of Bonhoeffer's vision of secularization.


*Bonhoeffer*

In his design of a Christian ethic, published posthumously by Eberhard Bethge in 1949, and based on notes from the first years

[12] Paul Tillich, *Systematic Theology* (Chicago, 1951), Vol. I, p. 46.

of the war prior to his imprisonment, Bonhoeffer states, with a view to the process of secularization:

"Western civilization is about to deny its historical heritage as such. Western civilization is inimical to Christ. That is the peculiar situation of our time and it is real decadence." [13]

From the context it becomes apparent that Bonhoeffer saw the process of secularization as a process of decadence; he saw the secularized world as a world which opposes itself to Christ and to the Church, defender of the Christian heritage against the onslaughts of a godless world.

We remember hearing similar condemnations of the evil world in prewar sermons, articles, and books. This tone can also be found in the chapter on "Church and World" in my own book *The Christian Dilemma*. A radical change took place in Bonhoeffer's vision of secularization during his imprisonment under the nazi regime, an imprisonment which was to end in his execution. In his posthumously published letters from prison [14] he no longer considered the secularization as having started in the sixteenth or seventeenth century but as early as the thirteenth century. Once this position is adopted one could suppose the process of secularization to have begun with the first awakening of the Greek spirit.

Of greater importance, however, is the change in the vision of the nature and role of secularization. In the letters from prison, secularization is explained naturally and as a necessary development that must be accepted by the Christian. In Bonhoeffer's view, the Church has failed to understand this. The Church has closed itself up and has turned its back upon the world. In its self-satisfied and condemnatory attitude the Church has opposed itself to the world. It is not the world but the Church which is to be blamed for the separation between the two. It is not the Church's task to adopt a hostile attitude to the world and condemn it. The Church's task is to say in the spirit of love: "Your concern is God's concern. Whether you realize it or not, everything taking place in our age shows that God is busy with the world. Not only the Church of Christians but the entire world, all of humanity, occupy a place in God's plan."

[13] Dietrich Bonhoeffer, *Ethik* (Kaiser Verlag, Munich, 1963), p. 115.
[14] Dietrich Bonhoeffer, *Widerstand und Ergebung* (Kaiser Verlag, Munich, 1962), p. 215.

Bonhoeffer's view of the world and the process of secularization is now beginning to be common among Christians. Ecumenism is no longer merely a hope for a united Christianity; it comprises the whole world and all humanity. God excludes no one from the *oekumene*. He calls every person in the need, anxiety, and worry of his human existence whether the person realizes it or not. God is concerned with the lot of every man and of all mankind. Continuing secularization is God's work. Christianity is involved in it as much as the rest of mankind. It is the Christian's duty and mission to make a positive contribution, in the spirit and intention of Christ, to the nascent world culture —not by an antithetical and proud attitude over and above the world, but by humble service to the world, in collaboration with all men.

Bonhoeffer was one of the first to realize clearly that the relation between Church and world can and may no longer be seen through the eyes of conventional Christianity; he realized that conventional Christianity had been undermined and come to an end. He discovered the end of conventional Christianity as the necessary result of the process of secularization and the coming of age of mankind now going on in our century. The totally new complex questions with which Christianity is faced can be summarized under this one aspect: "Jesus Christ's preoccupation with the world-come-of-age." [15]

For Bonhoeffer the future of Christianity and world culture does not need the God of conventional Christianity or of any religion whatever, but the God of the bible—the God and Father of Jesus Christ of whom the bible gives testimony, even if in a human, history-bound and therefore imperfect manner. As a result we can find in Boenhoeffer's letters from prison the first use of the expression "Christianity without religion." [16] In conventional Christianity biblical terms have acquired a tonality and content no longer intelligible to modern man. What is required is a secular reinterpretation of such concepts as penance, faith, justification, rebirth, sanctification, and so on.[17] There must be a secular interpretation of the Gospel.[18] There must be a seculariza-

15 *Op. cit.*, p. 231.
16 *Op. cit.*, p. 182.
17 *Op. cit.*, p. 185.
18 An attempt has been made by Paul van Buren in *The Secular Meaning of the Gospel Based on an Analysis of Its Language* (S.C.M. Press, London,

tion of Christianity. Secularization is not a danger which must be attacked (such as in Mascall's well-known work *The Seculariza-tion of Christianity*); [19] it is a task with a positive sense and significance.

## Summary

The general revolution in the thought and action of mankind which we are now experiencing has completely undermined conventional Christianity and has placed the questions which man as man necessarily asks in a completely new light. The consequences cannot be fully seen as yet. But two facts are certain. The first is that there are numerous questions, especially of an ecclesiastical nature, which could arise only in a climate of thought which has gone for good. To take an arbitrary example, if a person were still to busy himself with questions about transsubstantiation or consubstantiation, or whether ordinations in certain cases are valid or not, he would be entirely immune to the changes of thought now taking place in mankind. He would be positing problems which fit only into a world of thought which has outlived itself. He would be continuing to interest himself in conventional questions which in fact are obsolete.

The second fact is that, while retaining the fundamental data and values which of their very nature are irreplaceable, we must make a completely new beginning with our reflection and shaping of forms. For the Christian—this means to cite Bonhoeffer once more—that he ask himself "What do Christianity and Christ mean for us today? The time is past when we could say everything to man by means of words—be they theological or pious words; gone also is the time of inwardness and conscience, even the time of religion as such. We are proceeding toward a time which is completely without religion; man as he is can simply no

---

1963). For the application of linguistic analysis to religious concepts, cf. Ian Ramsey, *Religious Language* (S.C.M. Press, London, 1957), and John A. Hutchison, *Language and Religion, Studies in Sign, Symbol, and Meaning* (Westminster Press, Philadelphia, 1963).

[19] E. L. Mascall, *The Secularisation of Christianity* (Darton, Longmans and Todd, London, 1965). This is mainly a criticism of Robinson's *Honest to God*, from a Thomistic-Scholastic viewpoint. Cf. also Cobb, *Living Options in Protestant Theology* (Philadelphia, 1962), pp. 33ff: the Thomism of Mascall.

longer be religious." [20] For mankind this does not mean that the question of God has completely disappeared. On the contrary, consciously and unconsciously, openly and under camouflage, mankind today is moved by the question of God as he never was before. Neither classical philosophy nor the old answers of the various religions can satisfy modern man. The question of God has once again become a really open question, a question to which no ready-made answer can be given. All other questions of a religious, theological, and ecclesiastical nature center around this question.

If at the end of this chapter we look back for a moment at what has been done so far, it becomes obvious that the reader—possibly with some concern—asks himself what remains of conventional Christianity as it exists now. Only one answer is possible to this question: not very much. The subsequent chapters will confirm this answer. The question of what will happen will be the subject of the final chapter.

The old conceptions, theories, norms, and practices of conventional Christianity are finished. In all respects we are at a new beginning. The reconstruction will be the task of all men, Protestant and Roman Catholic, conservative and liberal, Christian and non-Christian, believers and non-believers, together. As Christians we are faced with this dilemma: either there will be no more Christianity or a Christianity renewed and reborn in its very foundations. This, and not the mostly obsolete antithesis between Rome and the Reformation, is the actual "Christian Dilemma."

The varied problems of the given situation have centered more and more around the question of God. This will be dealt with in the following chapters. Today's man asks what the real meaning and content is when we speak of God. Who is God; where is God; how and where can we find him? Do we really have to do with God in our human existence? Does God concern himself with us? Is he not a silent God? Has he really revealed himself to us? How do we know this with certainty? What is belief in God and how do we arrive at it? Does Christ have something to do with this? If so, then what about non-Christian religions? What can and may we still believe? What must we do in our contacts with those of other faiths or those who do not believe? If the

[20] Bonhoeffer, *op. cit.*, p. 178.

Christian faith is really based on God's revelation, then how are we to interpret and practice this faith? How should the Christian, without self-exaltation, exert himself in the service of mankind? What should be the relation between the Christian Churches? What task does the Church have to fulfill in the interest of the nascent world? What contribution do Christians have to make to the coming, new world culture still in a process of becoming?

These questions are involved. But all these questions, including those about Christ and the Church, center around the one question which occupies all men consciously or unconsciously: the question of God.

# 5. Philosophy and the Problem of God

T he last few pages of the preceding chapter were intended to be a provisional balance sheet and orientation. Ultimately the entire problem which resulted from the undermining and disappearance of conventional Christianity centers around the problem of God. When we concentrate on this fact we also have a necessary limitation in mind.

The rise, development, and application of modern science, the change, which the climate of thought and manner of living are still undergoing as a result, the nascent world culture characterized by democracy, technology, and secularization, are all asking numerous new questions about religion, Christianity, Church, and faith. There is a voluminous and rapidly growing amount of literature which cannot be completely known and commanded by any one person. But even apart from such a possibility we should run the danger of losing ourselves in too vast an expanse if we were to try to tackle in even a slightly sufficient manner all aspects of the present spiritual and religious situation and the problems connected with it. We must therefore necessarily limit ourselves to what is most important. In this chapter we shall occupy ourselves with existing problems insofar as they ultimately concern the problem of God.

We shall have to take up again the matter of the undermining of conventional Christianity with which we ended the previous chapter. In the two preceding chapters we limited ourselves to what could be called the *realia*, the facts, connections, possibilities which have come to light through the sciences, and the applications and concrete changes in the pattern of life which resulted.

Here, however, we shall have to consider a totally different complex of shocks which have contributed to the undermining of conventional Christianity. In contrast to the *realia* of the previous chapters, we could here speak of the *noumena*—what is going on in the human spirit. There are profound changes in manner of thought and mentality, in the way in which the spiritual aspect of being human is functioning. We purposely speak of the "spiritual," and not of the "intellectual" or "rational" aspect. While these latter do play an important role, man as spiritual being is more than a rational animal.

Especially in the past couple of hundred years the thought of man and the entire manner in which his spirit functions and in which he exists precisely as man have undergone profound changes, if not revolutions. In this connection, too, a great number of questions concerning religion, Christianity, Church, and faith could be asked. All conventional Christianity in all its aspects and articulations has lost its firm basis as a result of them. There is such confusion that one can scarcely see the woods for the trees. It is therefore all the more necessary to limit ourselves to the ultimately most important question: the question of God.

It is obvious that the development of the sciences with resulting changes in patterns of life are not independent from the revolutions taking place in the spiritual existence of man. The causes of the undermining of conventional Christianity have also given impetus to the general revolution in the thought and action of mankind which we are now experiencing.

Equally obvious is the fact that the functioning of the human spirit has undergone profound changes in the past two centuries, and earlier as well. Even from the very beginning man has been a changeable and developing being both materially and spiritually. While it is true that the gradual development of nature and culture was accompanied by ups and downs, still the stage of culture in which man finds himself now is a link in a process of evolution thousands of years in duration and still going on. All aspects of being-human are involved in this process and are related to each other. One might speak of "an evolution of religious consciousness." [1] This evolution, however, is closely connected with the evolution of the human spirit in general, and this in turn cannot be separated from the material and social evolution which man experiences on earth.[2]

[1] K. A. Hidding, *De evolutie van het godsdienstig bewustzijn* (Aula Books, No. 184, Utrecht-Antwerp, 1965).

[2] Harvey Cox, *The Secular City* (Macmillan, New York, 1965); H. Kraemer, *World Cultures and World Religions* (Lutterworth, London, 1963).

In this connection we can discern many periods of culture of long duration in which it would appear that a spiritual development suddenly took place, putting a definitive end to an obsolete period of culture and introducing a fresh one. All indications are that for the first time in human history mankind in its totality finds itself in a period of total reorientation and renewal which forms the transition from an old, decaying civilization to a new, still nascent world culture.

The crisis which mankind all over the world finds itself in today is a crisis of hitherto unknown proportions, depth, and significance. It is radical. It reaches everyone and everything. The new mankind which will be born of this crisis will be a different and new mankind in thought and action. The way of thinking, the way of experiencing existence and all reality, and therefore the religious aspect of being-human, are in our time subject to a radical revolution. This applies to the nature, the approach and the answer to the question of God. Here we shall limit ourselves to the shocks which conventional Christianity had to endure during the past couple of hundred years.

## Cultural Evolution

First, however, a few observations must be made in order somehow to bridge the gap between the past and the present.

Modern philosophers who occupy themselves with the characterizations of the nascent world culture against the background of the past generally distinguish three main stages in the evolution of mankind. Harvey Cox, who in a somewhat one-sided manner approaches the distinction between these stages purely sociologically, calls the first stage the period of "tribal man" —man as he is entirely concerned with the tribal group he belongs to.[3] The second stage is that of the "town man" who has become "himself" and who, by searching into himself, by thinking, speaking, writing, and acting, distinguishes himself from the world outside and from his fellow man as something individual. The third stage, which has now arrived and is the stage of the future, is that of "technopolitan man"—the big city man who is growing into a world citizen, because the entire world is in a process of becoming one large world city, one large *technopolis*.

[3] Cox, *op. cit.*, pp. 7; 60ff.

In each of the three stages religion has a certain place. The first stage is religious pure and simple. Religious matters are purely a tribal concern, while at the same time they dominate all expressions of life. The second stage is characterized by an individualization of the religious element and by a certain tension between the religious and other aspects of culture. The third stage, of which we are now experiencing the beginning, is, as a stage of culture, without ·religion.

The first stage is the stage of the primitive community man, the second is that of the individualist citizen, the third is that of the profane, pragmatic, and cosmopolitan world-man. To any of these three types of man belongs a certain type of religiousness, a certain attitude toward the question of God, a certain manner in which the question is posited, approached, and answered. In this respect we find ourselves at a completely new beginning.

From a spatial point of view the three stages occur next to each other. There still are some peoples entirely in the first stage, although their number is decreasing so rapidly that soon we shall no longer be able to find a primitive tribal culture on earth. On the other hand, only very few areas exist where the modern world culture has come to full flowering. In most countries all three stages are still found next to each other. In any nation, even in any one person, elements from the most different stages of culture can continue to exist side by side in lesser or greater harmony, and often in a noticeable tension. "We are all tribal, town, and technopolitan to some degree, but technopolitan culture is the wave of the future." [4]

Since the forms of religious thought, belief, and action are to a high degree culturally determined, a large part of the religious problems and conflicts which occur in our time, both in Churches and in individual believers, must be explained against the background of the extraordinary cultural situation which we find ourselves in at present. On further examination conflicts often appear to be more related to forms of expression than to the nature of belief in God.

The stages of culture which mankind has gone through can of course also be considered from a less one-sided sociological point of view; for example, they can be approached against the background of the development of thought or against the background

[4] Cox, *op. cit.*, p. 6.

of the evolution of religious consciousness.[5] It then becomes obvious that everything is interconnected. All aspects of culture, both material and spiritual, mutually influence each other. Whether the modern world citizen will be religious or not is just as much determined by his technopolitan pattern of living as the religiousness of primitive tribal man was determined by his cultural environment.

It can, for example, be said that tribal man did not distinguish himself from the reality of which he was a part. He experienced his reality by participating in it. His religiousness was exclusively communitarian—a participation in the religiousness of the tribe, the community. Even in Christianity there are still many who experience their being-Christian in this primitive fashion.

Town man, the citizen of Western civilization, is no longer merely a participating man. He sees objects and distinguishes himself as subject from the objectively given reality outside himself. He considers reality and reflects on it. His thinking is no longer exclusively perceptive, but understanding, conceptive. He asks about nature and essence. He thinks ontologically even when he reflects on himself and on God. Western man examines, searches for connections, establishes relations. He has gradually become more scientific and critical, and therefore more individualistic. It is clear that religious problems and conflicts are inevitable when a Church or an individual becomes stagnated in a previous stage of development while others are accepting a newer stage.

In our time we find ourselves in the transition from town man to technopolitan man. The inclination to reflect on the nature of things is gradually declining among the younger generation. Reality is accepted as it is presented by science in all its various forms. Man is in a mutual relationship with reality which has been transformed and, as it were, re-created by a continually detailed and perfected technology. Together with the pattern of life, thought also undergoes a radical transition. It stops being essentialist and ontological and becomes more and more existentialist and functional. One necessary result is that modern man has become less receptive to the manner in which classical philosophy and theology, based on Plato and Aristotle, have posited, approached, and answered the question of God.

[5] Hidding, *op. cit.*, p. 52.

Like all great world religions, Christianity has in many respects been culturally influenced and determined. In some forms of expression the phenomenologist of religion easily recognizes the influence and effects of primitive culture. An important field of research concerns the influence which the primitive culture of our Germanic ancestors has had on conceptions, interpretations, and practices which arose in the Church in the course of the Middle Ages. In fact from the very beginning Christianity has been subjected to the influence of very different cultures that succeeded each other. Christian faith and practice were, for a good part, conceived and explained by "converts" according to their spiritual and religious origins.

Language played an important part in this. Language is closely connected with culture. The words which concern the spiritual and religious aspect of a culture can be understood only from within that culture. Usually they are connected with imponderables and awaken certain associations which are lost or replaced by others as soon as they are translated into a language of another culture. Whenever the Christian proclamation used a new language, the content of the proclamation was open to the danger that the new language might not be able to reproduce the originally intended content in its purity. New words might imperceptibly give it a slightly different sense and meaning. In recent years many researchers have been occupied with the relation between language, logic, and religion.[6]

The language of Jesus and his disciples and the early Christian community of Jerusalem was Aramaic. This, as the older Hebrew, was a semitic language in which practically all of the Old Testament was written. It is not possible to penetrate the most real sense and intention of the Old Testament without a proper knowledge of Hebrew. Hebrew is the language form in which Jewish thought, a typically semitic way of thought, can be expressed in words. Any translation into a non-semitic language loses something of the deepest sense. Arabic, the language in which the Koran, the holy book of Islam, is written, stands closer to the language which Jesus spoke than does the language of the New Testament.

The language of the New Testament is Greek. For anyone who would approach the sense and intention of the preaching of

[6] *Cf.* note 18 of chapter four.

Jesus and the earliest Christian proclamation, this is where the first difficulty lies. The words of Jesus, the earliest stories about his life, originally handed on in Aramaic, and the witness of faith of the earliest Christians are no longer available to us in the original language, but exclusively in Greek translation.

Translation is always a hazardous enterprise, especially when the respective languages belong to two different worlds of language and culture. Even the best chosen word of translation frequently awakens some accidental associations which were absent in the original. This difficulty is all the greater when a person tries to translate terms which have a philosophical or religious meaning into a language which belongs to a totally different world of thought.

Every language is connected to a certain manner of thought, understanding, and approach. In the religious realm this applies in the first place to the names used to speak of the supreme being. Certain religious emotional values are connected with names. The names *Yahweh* and *Allah* do not say exactly the same as *Theos*, *Deus* and *Dieu*, or the names God and *Gott*. This applies to names and to every religious notion. The words *amath*, *aletheia*, *veritas*, and truth, though synonyms, do not say exactly the same thing. Even if a word of the same language is used by speakers who belong to different schools of thought it does not have the same meaning. Words such as truth, faith, justice have a different meaning when used by a Christian than when used by a non-Christian. They have a different meaning when used by a Roman Catholic and a reformed Christian. If it is hard enough to indicate to people of one's own language what one precisely means, it is all the more difficult to proclaim the Christian faith in a language of a people that has not yet arrived at "Christian" thought and faith.

The Christian faith originated in the semitic world of thought; and has, in its expansion over the world, had to successively pass through different worlds of language, thought, and culture, and has had to adjust itself to them. It was not only a question of language but of thinking and culture. Christian theology in particular is of Greek origin. In the Church of the West the approach and answer to the question of God has for a thousand years been determined by the intellectualism of the Greek mind and the moralism and legalism of the Roman mind.

This brings us to two difficulties. The first is whether we can be certain that the Gospel and the Christian faith as they have come to us by way of the Greco-Roman world really correspond to the actual meaning of Jesus, of the early Christians, and of the bible. In ever-growing circles, Christians are asking themselves whether they should not return from the God of official Christianity to the God of the bible. Bonhoeffer left his conviction that we must become "religion-less" before being able to encounter and learn to know anew the God of the bible—the God and Father of Jesus Christ.

The second difficulty is whether the Greco-Roman form which Christianity adopted in antiquity and in the Western Middle Ages is in the long run tenable and "digestible" for people who belong to an essentially different world of language, thought, and culture. The Reformation was a warning in this direction.

Aside from being a protest against late medieval devotions and "magic" conceptions of ordinations and other sacramental actions which arose under the influence of the primitive thought of the newly converted Germanic peoples, the Reformation was a reaction to the intellectualism of the scholastics, to the legalism of moral theology, and to the mechanical formalism of the liturgy. The Germanic mind could no longer bear this. The Reformation was a first effort to renew Christian faith and life in the spirit of the Gospel and in biblical testimony in general. This return to the sources, however, had to be bought at the price of a disruption which Christianity has not been able to overcome after four and a half centuries. Moreover, reformed Christianity has largely slid back to a sort of Protestant neo-scholasticism and to a confessionalism and church formalism which *mutatis mutandis* is no more evangelical and biblical than the former Roman Church. In our own days a competition has arisen between Roman Catholic and reformed Christians to return to a church proclamation and practice in an authentically biblical and evangelical sense, and to a corresponding evangelical understanding of faith and life. Many cherish the hope that this common purpose will lead to a greater mutual respect, to real reconciliation, and finally to a complete restoration of the ecclesial and sacramental communion which was lost.

## The Problem of God

If we concentrate on the problem or question of God, this is not to be understood as a question of whether God exists or not. Nor is this question under discussion in our time. A believing Christian does not ask that question. He believes that a person who asks that question seriously is no longer a believer. If the question were thus posited, the believing Christian would not consider himself involved in it. In this chapter, however, the problem is the question of God in the widest sense: how contemporary man inquires about God, what moves him when he asks about God, what stops him, what bothers him, and how he is involved when his fellow man asks or does not ask about God. These are only a few arbitrary indications of what we mean when we say that the crisis which resulted from the undermining of conventional Christianity is centered particularly around the problem of God.

Christian faith in God has always been understood by the Christian as an answer to the way in which God has revealed himself in Jesus Christ. Without this revelation belief in God in a Christian sense would be impossible. At the same time, the Christian has always been convinced that faith in the Christian sense is not a human achievement but a gift of God. To be able to believe in God man must be moved to faith by God himself. In this sense it is not necessary to prove God's existence on philosophical grounds. Many Christians—especially in the reformed Churches —may even be of the opinion that God cannot be proved, that it is not permissible to reason about God as if he were an object of human speculation or research. For them, even the manner in which a person speaks of God makes it clear whether the person really believes in the living God or in an idol of his own making. There is such a thing as a "godless talk" about God. The present destruction of conventional concepts of God must, in this light, be seen at least partially as a rejection of idols.

This, however, does not change the fact that from the very beginning, when Christianity was introduced into the Greek world of thought, the apologetes felt the need to found belief in God not only biblico-evangelically, but rationally. They intended to prepare the way for those who did not yet believe, that they too might arrive at faith in God as revealed in Christ. Also, they wanted to show that the Christian faith of revelation was not in contradiction to a rational belief in God, but was its completion.

Thus Christian theology has from the very beginning asked about God and witnessed him in two ways: from human reason and from divine revelation. From the very beginning Christian theology knew the distinction between natural theology and theology of revelation. The subject of the first was the rational teaching of God while that of the second was the revealed teaching of God. The first was considered, if not as the foundation, certainly as a support of the second. Medieval scholasticism built the two into an imposing unity. It was a reflection of the Christian faith in God in terms and categories of Greek philosophy, particularly of Plato and Aristotle. Since that time the ontological argument of Anselm and the aristotelian-thomistic proofs of the existence of God have always belonged to the inventory of conventional Christianity.

In spite of the fact that Luther, Calvin and other reformers spoke in favor of an authentically biblio-evangelical foundation for the *kerygma*, faith and the life of faith, of theology and of church practice, natural theology was never quite discredited even in reformed Christianity. The manner in which Lutheran, reformed, and Anglican theology posited, approached, and answered the question of God has, until Karl Barth's complete rejection of it, always had a philosophical structure. This has been particularly so since the beginning of the Enlightenment and the Copernican revolution which Immanuel Kant brought about in Western philosophy by his three "critiques." In nineteenth century Protestant theology the question of God was again dealt with in the framework of philosophy or in reaction to it.

Consequently, it is because of the development of German philosophy over the past two centuries that belief in the God of conventional Christianity has endured severe shocks.

## The Enlightenment

In the first phase of the Enlightenment around the turn of the seventeenth century the God-problem was not yet noticeable. On the contrary, if ever stubborn efforts were made to prove clearly and distinctly "that God exists" by means of old proofs and with the aid of the discoveries of the natural sciences, it was at that time of transition. In his book about the rise and development of the Enlightenment as it affected theology, Wolfgang Philipp lists a great number of titles of contemporary works that were dedicated to one or another aspect of what was called physico-theology.[7] One author would write a book about petino-theology (bird theology), another about rana-theology (frog theology), another about locusta-theology (locust theology), while others could devote an entire book to ichthyo-theology (fish theology), chorto-theology (grass theology), hydro-theology, astro-theology, chino-theology (snow theology), or bronto-theology (thunder theology). These are only a few arbitrary examples. In each of these books the existence of God, his greatness, his wisdom, and his providence were proved on the basis of one of the many "wonders of nature." Johannes Timm proved in his book that God exists on the basis of man's spine; Gottfried van Hahn proved it on the basis of the anatomy of man's hand; Johann Wucherer on the basis of the anatomy of man's brain. Voluminous works in the area of physico-theology appeared in Holland by Bernhard Nieuwentyts, in France by J. F. Vallade, in England by William Derham, and in the United States by Jonathan Edwards. All this was strictly serious. Complete titles, together with name of author, place and date of publication can be found in the bibliography of Phillips' book mentioned earlier.

*Immanuel Kant*

In his precritical period Immanuel Kant also devoted writings to similar physico-theological argumentation to prove the existence of God. In 1775 his *General Natural History and Theory of Heaven* appeared. According to its preface the intention was to prove that Kant's system was in agreement with religion, and that "after the dispersion of the fog the glory of the supreme being bursts forth brightly." [8] Kant's writing about the only possible basis for proving God's existence, which appeared in 1763, is a clear indication of the direction of his three great "critiques" which

[7] Wolfgang Philipp, *Das Werden der Aufklärung in theologie-geschichtlicher Sicht* (Vandenhoeck & Ruprecht, Göttingen, 1957), pp. 21ff.

[8] Ed. Vorländer of Kant's *Die Religion innerhalb der Grenzen der blossen Vernunft* (Leipzig, 1922), Introduction, p. XIII.

were to cause such a revolution in philosophy. Already in this book Kant makes a clear distinction between faith in God and proof of God: "It is obviously necessary that a person convince himself that God's exists; yet it is not equally necessary that he prove it." [9]

In the 'seventies of the eighteenth century Kant was continually working on the elaboration of his critiques. *The Critique of Pure Reason* appeared in 1781, *The Critique of Practical Reason* in 1788, and *The Critique of Judgment* in 1790. The word "critique" was not intended by Kant to mean "rejection" but "examination"—an examination into the positive possibilities and into the limits of the human power of thinking; an examination into what reason is capable and incapable of, and into the categories which make thought possible and determine it and which form the basis of the objective validity of thought. To disqualify Kant's thought as subjectivism is to radically misunderstand Kant's theory of knowing. It is precisely the intention of Kant's main works to supply human knowing with an objective and unimpeachable basis by methodical and unprejudiced examination of the power of knowing. In his *Religion within the Limits of Pure Reason,* which appeared in 1793, Kant applied the principles of his theory of human knowing to the natural knowledge of God.

Kant's *Critique of Knowing* was the first, catastrophic shock which undermined the confidence of conventional Christianity, Roman Catholic and Protestant, in the validity and tenability of the old, current proofs of the existence of God.

The radical revolution brought about in the area of philosophy by Kant's theory of knowing is generally considered as a "Copernican" revolution, analogical to the revolution in the cosmic world picture caused by Copernicus. The revolution caused in our century by Karl Barth in evangelical theology could likewise be called a "Copernican" revolution. Whether these revolutions should be evaluated positively or negatively is a question which in the framework of this chapter must be left out of consideration.

At any rate it is certain that—at least outside the limits of the Roman Catholic world—Kant's fundamental critique of knowing is considered to be the beginning of an entirely new era in the

[9] *Op. cit.,* p. 15.

history of Western thought. Even in the most recent edition of the encyclopedia *Religion in the Course of History and at Present*, the lasting significance of Kant's discovery is summarized as follows:

"Kant's critical system, like that of the Platonic doctrine of ideas, was epoch-making. In this system all the problems of modern philosophy under discussion in different countries and schools until then were overcome according to common principles and raised to a higher level of reflection. Present philosophical awareness, its problems, its method, and its language have their origin in the thought of Kant. In particular newer schools of philosophy were based on following or criticizing Kant." [10] The acknowledgment of the positive and lasting significance of Kant's critique of knowing does not, in contemporary philosophic thought, mean that Kant has said the last word, nor that his system should be permitted to be absolutized as a kind of new *philosophia perennis*. But it is no longer possible to eliminate Kant from the development of Western thought. In the contemporary approach to the question about God, Kant is always present behind the scene. The cause of this is that by his critique of the conventional proofs of God's existence Kant "made any foundation of the idea of God on experience in this world impossible." [11]

In very brief summary, Kant's critique of the classical proofs of the existence of God comes to the following:

The ontological proof of God's existence which bases the argument for the existence of God on the concept of God is an unwarranted leap from the order of ideas to the order of existence.

The cosmological proof of the existence of God applies the principle of causality, valid in the realm of phenomena that can be perceived by the senses, to a realm where it is not valid. It is inadmissable to conclude from causality, insofar as it is applicable within our world, to a cause which lies outside our world.

The teleological proof of the existence of God, concluding to God's existence from the admirable order of things, is based on a one-sided reflection on reality and on an arbitrary choice of the facts that are supposed to show the order. In the experience of total reality too many bewildering facts and events can just as

---

[10] *Die Religion in Geschichte und Gegenwart* (Mohr, Tübingen, 1957-1962), Vol. III, col. 1127.
[11] *Op. cit.*, Vol. II, col. 1729.

soon be considered chaotic and unreasonable, so that a person cannot base his argument exclusively and naively on the admirable order and meaning of all that exists.

It is quite obvious that Kant's critique of the proofs of the existence of God was a serious blow to the "natural" knowledge of God. The reason why theologians of the first phase of the Enlightenment attached such great importance to "natural" proofs of God's existence lay in their skepticism of a knowledge of God that had been "revealed" in a special way. All man's knowledge was for them natural knowledge which becomes man's property through sense perception and rational thought. Kant's critique wiped out the foundation of their natural knowledge of God. What this meant for the question of God became obvious when Johann Gottlieb Fichte's work *An Essay toward a Critique of All Revelation* was published in 1792 and was highly praised by Kant. This book contains an acute and consistent application of Kant's theory of knowledge to the existing conventional notion of revelation. It does not have to take second place to Kant's own effort to draw the consequences for the question of God from his newly acquired principles concerning the critique of knowing, published in Kant's *Religion within the Limits of Pure Reason.*

### Kant and Fichte

Kant and Fichte transferred the foundation for the knowledge of God from the experience of the world without, to the experience of being-human. In passing it should be noted that this transfer paved the way—through the early religio-philosophical writings of Schelling and particularly of Kierkegaard—for the existential approach to the question of God as it is today.

According to Kant and Fichte neither nature nor history provide proofs by which God could become "revealed." No matter how logically some proofs of God's revealing action in nature or history are constructed, they are in reality fictitious proofs. Kant, Fichte and all the Enlightenment rejected proofs of God's action through miracles because miracles were said to be contrary to the achievements of science. Nor did Kant and Fichte acknowledge the factual basis of an unusual and special revelation not subject to demonstration and verification which must be accepted and believed by man purely on the authority of a heteronomous power held to be infallible, whether it be the bible, the Church, the pope, a council, a confession or any other. Man is a rational, autonomous being, and it cannot be expected, much less demanded, of him that he hold something to be true on the authority of another if this is contrary to his own understanding or conscience.

The only road to belief in God that remains open in Kant and Fichte is that which begins with the conscience. The categorical imperative, the "thou shalt" of the moral conscience is a general human experience. Conscience is just as much as inalienable characteristic—an "existential" as it would be called today—of being-human as is the capacity to think and will. A totally conscience-less man would no longer be a human being, just as a completely unrational and will-less man would no longer be man. The fact that man is man and not something else, and that this being-human either stands or falls with a certain given manner of being, is something that cannot be denied.

This fact of the categorical imperative cannot be rationally explained. But neither can it be reasoned away. It is true that man has a moral consciousness and that as man he must act according to this consciousness. This moral consciousness is not the same as a purely rational judgment about good or evil. When man comes into conflict with this moral consciousness by discarding the command of conscience, he feels guilty, whether he wills it or not. This is so, but it is not subject to explanation. For this reason Kant and Fichte do not construct a proof of God's existence from conscience based on "pure" reason; the "proof" of God's existence is based on "practical" reason.

In Kant and Fichte, religion and ethics coincide. The necessity of moral action leads practical reason to accept God, the immortality of man, and human freedom not as conclusions of pure rational thinking, but as postulates of moral action. For them, without these postulates moral action would be meaningless. During his existence man could live under the command of the moral law without being aware of the sense and meaning of obedience to the moral law, which under certain circumstances can be an extremely difficult obedience. For Kant and Fichte, religion lies in the acceptance of the moral precepts as precepts from God.

The moral sense of responsibility, proper to any man as man, supposes that a person believes God (which does not precisely mean "belief in" God) when it presents itself in the conscience as a sense of responsibility toward "God" or whatever the Highest Judge might be named. It seems, therefore, that Kant and Fichte leave room for a proof of God's existence from the conscience based on "practical" not on "pure" reason.

We are still trying to build a bridge from the old conventional Christianity to the contemporary problem of God. It is clear that within our scope we cannot go further into the philosophy of religion of Kant, Fichte, Schelling, and Hegel, though we must not omit to mention at least Schelling's *Readings in the Philosophy of Myth and Revelation*.[12] A few words must be said about the approach to the problem of God in nineteenth century Protestant theology. In this connection Friedrich Daniel Ernst Schleiermacher (1768-1834) who stood at the beginning of a new development has sometimes been referred to as the "Church Father" of the nineteenth century.

## Schleiermacher

Since Kant, the question of God has been posited, approached, and answered from the way in which man experiences and lives his human existence. This is not bottomless subjectivism because man reflectively considers his own existence as an objectively given reality to be accepted as it is. It is this objectively given reality of his existence (i.e. that which makes a man to be a man) which is nearest to him.

Since in Kant the categorical imperative is the *a priori* given that determines both the moral character of human action and the relation between God and man, ethics and religion fall, as it were, under one common denominator. A separate religious *a priori* which the religious aspect of being-human rests on is lacking in Kant. The great significance of Schleiermacher is that he did not base belief in God on a purely moral *a priori*, but on a specifically religious one.

This specific religious *a priori* consists, according to Schleiermacher, in pure and simple feeling of dependence. Just as the

12 A new edition is being prepared by Frommann Verlag, Stuttgart, 4 vols.

categorical imperative, which cannot be further explained, belongs to being-human and determines the necessary moral character of man, so is the necessary religious character of man determined by the fact that man cannot have more than a pure and simple feeling of dependence. This belongs to being-human as such. Man is just as certainly and necessarily aware of this feeling of dependence as he is of the categorical imperative. The categorical imperative is not denied by Schleiermacher. But for him the categorical imperative is the given *a priori* on which man's moral character rests, while the pure and simple feeling of dependence is the undeniably given *a priori* on which the religious character of being-human rests.

This feeling of dependence is called "pure and simple" because it cannot be further explained from experiences which might show that man is in many respects a being who depends on many different factors. It is not a conclusion from experience; it precedes experience. Nor is it an emotional feeling. It is awareness—an immediate, non-deducible knowing. In my being-human I am as man determined *von anderswoher* (by a reality which surpasses being-human). It is proper to man as man that he not only has a thinking and moral consciousness, but that he also has an awareness of pure, absolute dependence, a religious awareness. Religious awareness is the basis on which an encounter between God and man is eventually possible.

In the second part of the eighteenth century the Enlightenment gradually developed a skeptical attitude toward natural as well as revealed religion. The enlightened intellectuals looked with disdain upon religion as a matter which had been overcome once and for all. To account for religion in general and for Christianity in particular, Schleiermacher published in 1799 five *Discourses about Religion for the Educated and for Their Despisers*, a work which he continued to revise with each subsequent edition. In 1821 and 1822 he published the three volumes of *The Christian Faith, Composed According to the Principles of the Evangelical Church*.

We cannot go further into Schleiermacher's teaching of the faith. But as a proof of the fact that Schleiermacher's foundation of the faith was not individualist and subjectivist we might point to the necessary role he assigned to the Church, the communion of all true believers, as the place where belief in Christ arises, develops, and is preserved. Schleiermacher was the rediscoverer of the significance of the Church and its need for unity. He could be considered the founder of the ecumenical effort among evangelical Christians.

In an edition of Schleiermacher's *Discourses* of 1888, an interesting introduction can be found that touches upon the relation between Schleiermacher and Kant.[13] With Kant, whose writings he had studied profoundly, Schleiermacher agreed that no man can be made to be religious by way of logic. However, he differed from Kant in that he assigned its place to piety. To quote a few passages from the introduction: "It is quite understandable that Schleiermacher, in his pronounced opposition to rationalism and in his high esteem for religious living, rejected the theoretical props which Kant constructed for it in order to give piety its own proper place." [14] This, however, did not mean returning to the old proofs of God's existence: "Piety and religious faith never allow for a demonstration of reason and cannot be forced on man by logic; on the contrary, they rest on the immediately perceived or inwardly experienced communion of the soul with God." [15]

Protestant theologians of the nineteenth and the early twentieth century have in the long run found Kant's conception of God and religion too rationalistic and theistic. They continued to search for a better foundation of belief in God, more in accordance with the nature of faith and piety. But since Kant the convictions that a "proven" God is not really God, and that "proof" is contrary to true respect and awe of God, can be considered inalienable achievements of Protestant theology.

It is quite true that toward the end of the nineteenth century there was a revival of Kantian idealism in Germany and that in England the monistic idealism of Hegel had quite a following among theologians. But in general it can be said that Schleiermacher's notion of religion and Christianity, of knowledge of God and divine revelation, dominated nineteenth century theology and the pre-war years of the early twentieth century.

The most outstanding theologian who continued in the footsteps of Schleiermacher, making a name for himself in England

13 Ed. Lommatzsch, Gotha, 1888.
14 *Op. cit.*, p. 13.
15 *Op. cit.*, p. 30.

and the United States, was Rudolf Otto, who died in 1937. In 1917 he published his principal work, *The Sacred*, which went through more than thirty editions and was translated into several languages. His affinity with Schleiermacher led him to prepare a new edition of the *Discourses*. This affinity can also be seen in Otto's great interest in mysticism, liturgy, and ecumenism.

Starting from Kant's theory of knowing, and deeply convinced of the definitive end of the pre-Kantian, intellectualist metaphysics and its proofs of the existence of God, Otto tried to give a further and more detailed definition of the religious *a priori* proper to man as man. He formulated this *a priori* as "the Sacred." From Christian and non-Christian sources he tried to show how man, precisely because of the nature of his being-human, is open to intuitive impressions and all sorts of experiences concerning the mystery hidden behind reality. Every human who is really "human" has the awareness of the sacred. It is this capacity that enables man to break through the wall which separates the world of ideas from the world of the intellectually unknowable *Ding-an-sich* and have a real experience of the Sacred, the totally Other which cannot be contained in concepts and words but which precisely for this reason is all the more awe-inspiring.

## Religious Experience

The theology of Rudolf Otto was about to conquer the Protestant world far outside the borders of Germany when in about 1920 (and practically simultaneously with Karl Barth's sensational commentary on Paul's letter to the Romans) Emil Brunner published in Switzerland his book *Mysticism and the Word*. Like Barth's commentary, this book jolted all who read it and whose religious conviction was in one way or another based on religious experience. For more than ten years Barth and Brunner were named in one breath as the two Swiss theologians who together had caused a radical revolution—a new Copernican revolution —in Protestant theology, and in particular in the foundation of belief in God.

Both men had arrived at the insight that any foundation of the faith on any human capacity of any kind would come under attack from philosophy, natural science, and psychology. Therefore belief in God could be "saved" only if any foundation of this belief on something human would be considered a hazardous enterprise, a building on quicksand.

Belief in God cannot possibly find a sufficient ground in reason, in nature, in history, in the esthetic, moral, religious, or any other experience. For an absolutely unshakeable certainty of faith man is entirely and exclusively dependent on God himself, on God's revealing action witnessed by God's word in sacred scripture and as the word speaks to man and moves him to faith. Any other foundation of belief in God, any deduction of belief in God *von anderswoher* will result in one or another form of pseudo-faith, pseudo-piety, pseudo-religion, in illusion. This is the conviction of Barth, Brunner and their followers.

Among a large portion of Protestants, at least in Europe, the trust in reason as a safe foundation of a religious conviction of faith had become undermined since Kant. Now, by the appearance of Barth and Brunner, the trust in religious experience as the basis of faith was also seriously shaken. According to Barth and Brunner belief in God has no other foundation than the word of God. Anyone looking for another foundation and justification will necessarily fall victim to the many different shocks which have in the course of the past few centuries successively undermined the faith of conventional Christianity. In other words, whoever still, after everything that philosophy and science have yielded, tries to base his faith on something other than God's word must, according to Barth and Brunner and their school, necessarily fall into unbelief.

Faith rests on revelation from God. Revelation has found its definitive incarnation in Jesus Christ. To this fact (that the Word of God became flesh in Jesus Christ) sacred scripture testifies. On this biblical testimony the proclamation of the Church is founded. The Church proclaims the word of God to anyone who is willing to hear it. The Church draws from sacred scripture alone and from no other source whatever. The word of God thus proclaimed is the only possible and viable basis for belief in God which is not an illusion but a true and unassailable belief.

How a person can know that the proclaimed word of God will not turn out to be another unreliable word of man is a question that arises from unbelief. Belief in God's word is aroused by God himself, by the Holy Spirit. Belief in God is a gift of grace from

God through the Holy Spirit. A person who really believes no longer asks for human arguments. If anyone does, it is a manifestation that he does not believe in God.

After the Second World War the theological discussion in the Protestant field has seen some remarkable transitions. Karl Barth's influence since 1945 declined everywhere. Brunner knew a brief revival in the United States, but at present he is practically outside the discussion. Among Germans, Rudolf Bultmann's theology was, up to about 1960, the focus of attention. It would seem that in more recent years a certain fatigue or disappointment has developed due to the fact that neither Barth nor Bultmann was able to provide a satisfactory and lasting solution to the pending problems. More attention has been given to Paul Tillich whose writings are beginning to appear in German.[16]

In the meantime, one has the impression that the theological discussion in Europe has come to a standstill. Barth, Brunner, Bultmann, and Tillich are all from the same age. Tillich died at the age of 78, and Brunner at the age of 76. Their names were prominent in the Protestant world for almost half a century. But where are the young theologians who can speak in our time in contemporary terms which will be heard everywhere and stimulate the discussion, just as the leaders of the past fifty years? Who will take their place? It seems that theologians in Europe are not capable of doing more than drawing up a balance sheet, unless Niftrik is correct when he expresses the opinion that a change in the theological atmosphere can be detected as a result of the publication of Moltmann's *Theology of Hope*.[17]

The most remarkable transition in the theological discussion since the Second World War is that from the German to the English language, and in particular the transition from Europe to the United States. If it is true that the culture of the "free world" is determined more and more by the United States, it would seem that world Protestantism of the future will be dominated by the development it is experiencing now in the United States.

Besides the two Niebuhrs, Paul Tillich has since the war been considered the principal theologian of America. Whereas in Germany Tillich would seem to be coming to the fore only now, he

---

[16] Paul Tillich, *Gesammelte Werke* (Evangelisches Verlagswerk, Stuttgart 1960), 19 vols.

[17] J. Moltmann, *Theologie der Hoffnung* (Kaiser Verlag, Munich, 1964).

passed his peak in the United States even before his death. His influence is now being replaced by a number of younger theologians, among whom John Cobb can be said to take first place.

Partly due to the newest developments in philosophy and science, much has recently happened in the thought and life of Christianity, in Church practice, and in the relationship to the world outside the Church. And much is still taking place; far-reaching changes occur in an ever-increasing tempo so that almost unnoticed we find ourselves in a new, hitherto unknown religious situation, of which the Second Vatican Council with its inheritance of still unsolved problems is one of the symptoms.

The present situation is characterized both by a serious effort toward adaptation, if not toward complete renewal, and by a sensible religious insecurity and unrest. One of the most vexing problems centers around revelation and the operation of the Holy Spirit. This concerns the question of the factuality of revelation, All religions have recourse to revelation. But on what do we base our conviction that the word of sacred scripture derives from God himself, not from writers? What is the nature, the sense, and the meaning of revelation, supposing that the latter is a fact? How can one psychologically determine that certain religious expressions and convictions did not arise in the "usual" manner, but through the operation of a force "from without"? In this connection, one is inclined to reflect on a passage in Dietrich Boenhoeffer's letters from prison where he ventures the suggestion that soon not only all physical but also all psychical phenomena can be "explained" without the intervention of a divine cause.[18] These and similar problems increasingly occupy the attention of the religiously educated youth, especially in America. The difference and the relation between belief in God and atheism is a particular issue. There is growing awareness that there are kinds of belief in God that remind one of atheism and kinds of atheism which point to a genuine belief in God.

In his book about phenomenology and atheism, Luypen suggests a criterion for judgment: "Whoever maintains that nothing else exists or can exist other than that which he sees as he sees the world is an atheist. Whoever maintains that he sees God, just as he sees the world, is also an atheist. This therefore means that

18 D. Bonhoeffer, *Widerstand und Ergebung* (Kaiser Verlag, Munich, 1962), p. 216.

both the denial and the acknowledgment of God can be atheism." [19] It might well be that the atheism of many atheists is a revolt against pesudo-gods. It might well be that the breakdown of conventional Christianity, which some people are so concerned about, will turn out to have been a destruction of idols. It is quite conceivable "that not all those who say God does not exist are atheists. A good atheism is possible, an atheism which consists in the rejection of pseudo-gods, of those gods of which it is matter-of-factly said that they exist." [20] The problem of God is closely connected with the problem of being, with ontology, with the question what "being" precisely means.

## Existentialism

The manner in which an answer is sought to the question of God is a result of a new Copernican revolution in philosophical thought, to which Kant's undermining of the classical metaphysics was merely a prelude. This revolution is so profound that the consequences cannot yet be fully seen. Further development is still in the process and is creating an entirely new climate of thought, a new mentality. This is especially noticeable in the younger generation. The old manner of approaching the problem of God has become quite unintelligible. One can no longer think and speak about God in the way which the older generation of believers—and the official Church also—frequently still do.

The classical essentialist notion of God and man has had to make way for the existentialist, the static for the dynamic, the objective for the personal, the dualist (supernature-nature; spirit-matter; object-subject) for the monist, the objective for the functional. All these aspects of the thought-revolution are closely related to each other.

At the origin of this revolution we find the Danish thinker Sören Kierkegaard (1813-1855), who was discovered only after the First World War. We are also reminded of the phenomenological philosopher Edmund Husserl (1859-1938). Thinking man does not stand outside reality. He is part of it. His existence

[19] W. Luypen, *Fenomenologie en Atheisme* (Spectrum, Utrecht, Antwerp, 1963), p. 9.
[20] *Op. cit.,* p. 10.

functions in an immediate relation to all that is, and all that is acquires sense and meaning only in and through the thought of man. Man does not live in two or more worlds. Nor is he himself something apart. Nor do God and reality stand separate from one another, as if God is there beyond and reality here. Reality is *one*. Man is oriented to total Reality by thinking, and total Reality becomes clarified, is "revealed" in human thought, in human consciousness. The inscrutable mystery of being-human lies in this, that man alone is, by his thought, aware of being, and that being, as it were, "lights up" in the thought of man. Thinking and being, though they can be distinguished, are inseparably related to each other. There is a unity of thought and being.

From within this new world of thought, the philosopher who has contributed most to a revolution in theological thought is Martin Heidegger (born in 1889). Heidegger, Barth, Brunner, Bultmann, and Tillich are contemporaries. Simultaneously with Bultmann and Tillich, Heidegger lectured for some years at the University of Marburg. Heidegger soon acquired fame by his book *Being and Time*, which appeared in 1927.[21] By its analysis of human existence, the book laid the foundation for French existentialism. It also exercised great influence on the theological thought of Rudolf Bultmann. (And in this connection the question could be asked whether and in how far Bultmann understood Heidegger's meaning correctly.) [22] Paul Tillich's thought, too, was strongly stimulated by Heidegger's analysis of human existence, but Tillich continued to build on it in a more original manner.[23] Heidegger's post-war writings indicate an important transition in his thought which he himself described as *the reversal*. It is common to speak of the early and the later Heidegger. Karl Barth's successor in Basel, Heinrich Ott, was strongly influenced by the thought of the later Heidegger.[24] He also belonged to the discussion group of European and American theologians who

[21] Martin Heidegger, *Sein und Zeit* (Max Niemeyer Verlag, Tübingen, 1963). English text: *Being and Time*, trans. by J. Macquarrie and E. Robinson, (SCM Press, London, 1962).

[22] Cf. for example: J. M. de Jong, *Kerygma* (Van Gorcum, Assen, 1958).

[23] Kegley-Bretall, *The Theology of Paul Tillich* (Macmillan, New York, 1961), p. 14. Cf. also Tillich's *Systematic Theology*, Vol. I, p. 210.

[24] Heinrich Ott, *Denken und Sein, Der Weg Martin Heideggers und der Weg der Theologie* (Ev. Verlag Zollikon, Zurich, 1959). Cf. Robinson-Cobb, *The Later Heidegger and Theology* (Harper and Row, New York, 1963).

together published a book about the significance of the later Heidegger for theology. Another member of this discussion group was the theologian John Cobb whom we mentioned earlier. However, the latter did not base his natural theology on Heidegger, but on the American philosopher of nature Alfred Whitehead.[25]

This leads us to our own day. After the preceding historical consideration, intended to build a bridge between the past and the present, the following three chapters will be devoted to a more detailed treatment of the manner in which the problem of God is approached in our time. Both clarity and the available space demand that a selection be made. Passing over such important thinkers as Karl Jaspers and Gabriel Marcel, we shall have to limit ourselves to the purely philosophical approach of Heidegger, the purely theological approach of Barth, and the philosophico-theological approach of Tillich, which Tillich himself characterized as the correlative approach.

Among all living beings on earth man is the only being that thinks and reflects. Man, precisely insofar as he is genuinely "man," cannot help but reflect on existence and on the manner in which he experiences and lives reality. He also considers what everything is based on, where it has its origin and its final goal, how being acquires its meaning. In one way or another, man thinks about "God." Even if Barth were correct in saying that all thinking and speaking about God without Jesus Christ is thinking and speaking about a pseudo-god, an idol, the fact would still remain that man reflects about "God" and that he continues to do so after he has encountered God in Jesus Christ. For this reason we must begin by reflecting on human existence and on the question of whether and in how far this thought, proper to man alone, has to do with God. From what follows it will become clear why we have selected the thought of Martin Heidegger.

[25] John Cobb, *A Christian Natural Theology* (Westminster Press, Philadelphia, 1965).

# 6. Existence and Existents

**M**artin Heidegger was born in 1889 in a suburb of Basel and was baptized in the Roman Catholic parish church where his father was a sexton. While he was a pupil at the minor seminary he began to show an interest in philosophy. He later gave up the idea of joining the priesthood. In 1909 he went to study philosophy and theology at the University of Freiburg im Briesgau. He graduated in 1914 as doctor of philosophy with a dissertation entitled *The Theory of Judgment in Psychologism*. In his dissertation Heidegger defended the objectivity of human thought against the subjectivist psychologism of his day. The question "what is thought, where does it lead, and what sense does it have" is one of the core questions on which Heidegger reflected and wrote for more than half a century. He still has not yet achieved his final goal, something said to his advantage. In this connection one is led to think of a citation from one of Hölderlin's poems with which he was later to conclude his *Introduction to Metaphysics* "For the mindful, God abhors untimely growth." [1]

In 1916, the same year in which Edmund Husserl became professor at Freiburg, Heidegger established himself there as a private tutor. It was Husserl's hope to discover a philosophical method which, based exclusively on irrefutable facts, might achieve absolutely and objectively established truth with the certainty that natural science did in its own field. Almost from the first Heidegger came under the influence of Husserl and in 1920 became his assistant.

In 1923 Heidegger was named ordinary professor in Marburg, an appointment of great significance for his furher development. It was here that he befriended Rudolf Bultmann. This put him in touch with the theology of the early Karl Barth, and through

[1] Martin Heidegger, *Einführung in die Metaphysik* (Niemeyer, Tübingen, 1958), p. 157. English text: *Introduction to Metaphysics*, tr. R. Manheim (New Haven, Yale, 1958).

him with the writings of Luther and Kierkegaard. He also had a friendly relationship with Karl Jaspers. At this time Heidegger stopped being a practicing Catholic. His thought was beginning a new and independent phase of thinking, the first fruit of which was *Being and Time* appearing in 1927. Many contemporaries instantly considered Heidegger as the leading thinker of this century. As early as 1928 he was appointed the successor of Husserl in Freiburg, where he remained until his emeritus retirement in 1959. His inaugural address dealt with the question *What Is Metaphysics?* [2] The address went through several printings and is generally considered the best introduction to Heidegger's thought. At any rate it throws much light on many of the most difficult passages in *Being and Time*.

*What Is Metaphysics* was supposed to have consisted of two parts. The second part, however, never appeared because Heidegger was unable to find a satisfying answer to the extremely difficult problem raised in the first part. The answer cannot be given by *one* thinker at a time chosen by himself. It is dependent on the development of philosophic thought in the future.

It gradually became clear to Heidegger that his approach left something to be desired. In the early 'forties a transition occurred in Heidegger's thought which is usually referred to as "the reversal." The transition by no means denied Heidegger's past for his new thought continued to build on the positive values of the past. Even though the analysis of human existence presented in *Being and Time* is of great importance, the real question on which Heidegger concentrated more and more was not the question of human existence as such but the question about the inscrutable mystery of being and the question about the relation between the mysterious power of man that we call "thought" and the mysterious being which causes given beings to really "be" instead of "not to be." In this connection reference should be made to an epilogue which Heidegger wrote in 1943 for the fourth edition of his 1928 inaugural address and to an introduction he attached to its fifth edition in 1949.

The introduction dealt with the nature of a metaphysics that was to be overcome. According to Heidegger, Greek and all

[2] Martin Heidegger, *Was ist Metaphysik?* (Klostermann, Frankfort a/M., 1960). English text: *What Is Metaphysics?*, tr. Walter Kaufmann, in *Existentialism from Dostoievski to Sartre* (Meridian, New York, 1957), pp. 207-221.

classical Western philosophy have gradually lost sight of the secret of being and have thus become more and more tied up with beings, with all the disastrous consequences attached to this, particularly in regard to the question of God.

Meanwhile, in 1955 a writing entitled *The Line* appeared, which was published again in 1959 under the title *The Question of Being*.[3] Even after his emeritus retirement he continued giving lectures. He has been in close contact with Heinrich Ott, Karl Barth's successor in Basel, and has personally attended several of Ott's workshops on his most recent writings. The topic of these writings is mainly the mutual relation between the questions of being, thought, and speech. In particular the question about the nature of language has come more and more to the fore. This is obviously of great importance for that theology which above all seeks to be a theology of the word. It has also increased the significance of the later Heidegger for all theology, as seen in the attention which several European and American theologians have paid in the past few years to Heidegger's most recent publications.[4]

Heidegger has recently begun to occupy himself with the important questions of the origin and essence of technicity and the consequences which the increasing and necessary technologizing of mankind and world will have on culture in general and on the question of God in particular.

There is an acute danger, he feels, of a degeneration of man's power of thought and speech and of an increasing devaluation of the word. Technical man is lapsing into an oblivion of being contrary to the nature of being-human, and he gradually gets farther away from a real understanding of being, which, religiously expressed, means a regression from a real questioning about God. This can be prevented only by a genuine "reversal." Heidegger repeatedly tried to illustrate his point of view and vision by referring to Nietzsche. In 1961 he published in two volumes, under the title of *Nietzsche*, his lectures and writings on Nietzsche.[5] The collection *On the Road to Language*, published

[3] Martin Heidegger, *Zur Seinsfrage* (Klostermann, Frankfort a/M., 1959). English text: *The Question of Being*, tr. W. Kluback, (J. T. Wilde, Twayne, N.Y., 1959).

[4] Cf. note 24 of chapter five.

[5] Martin Heidegger, *Nietzsche* (Neske, Pfullingen, 1961). Cf. Martin Heidegger, *Holzwege* (Klostermann, Frankfort a/M., 1963). English text: *The Age of the World View*, tr. Marjorie Grene, *Measure*, II, 1951. According

in 1959, is also important for our subject.[6] We also refer the reader to the reading list at the end of the book.

Heidegger has been exposed to criticism from several sides, criticism which concerns among other things Heidegger's etymology and the use he makes of classical texts. But this is not the place to treat such criticism.

Whatever the judgment about Heidegger, it is of great importance to know that a thinker has appeared in our age who is convinced that the way of thinking of classical metaphysics is a dead-end street and to know that there are theologians following Heidegger who have arrived at the conviction that the road of classical metaphysics does not end in belief in God, but if followed consistently, ends in atheism. If Heidegger is right, then Western thought finds itself on a downward slope, having reached its nadir in Nietzsche's nihilism, in an empiricism pure and simple, and in the ever-increasing technologization of man by which he is more and more reduced to a thing.

## The Reversal

It is obvious that Heidegger does not opt for this latter development. In fact, he searches for a way out and thinks he has found it in his "reversal." There is no such thing as a logical and practical way out which can be adopted or rejected; one has to wait for this way out which will present itself in due time to the person who has begun again to think authentically: "It may be that we have already arrived in the shadow of this coming reversal. When and how the time will come for it to come to pass no one knows. Nor is it necessary to know. A knowledge of this kind would indeed be the most pernicious thing for man to have, for his essence is to be the-one-who-is-waiting for the essence of being, and while thinking he protects it. Only when man waits as

---

to Heidegger, Nietzsche was the first to indicate, in *Die fröhliche Wissenschaft* of 1882, the fact that Western philosophy and theology end in the "death of God." This is not a personal, atheistic opinion of Nietzsche, but what is meant is a situation in which Western man finds himself without as yet realizing this, and which is becoming apparent only in our time, to anyone who wishes to see it (*Holzwege*, p. 193).

[6] Martin Heidegger, *Unterwegs zur Sprache* (Neske, Pfullingen, 1960).

the keeper of the being of truth and of truth itself can he expect the arrival of the common fortune of Being, without lapsing into the pure will-to-know." [7]

Every word is important in the above citation. Heidegger stands before us in the full greatness of his ingenious vision of the future. It is quite true that Heidegger places great demands on the intelligence of his readers. But the person who is not discouraged and who tries to follow Heidegger's thought until its full import becomes clear must realize the significance that Heidegger's "reversal" may have for the theology of the question of God.

If Heidegger's vision rests on reality and not on illusion, the question arises for the believer whether it is in the nature of fatally decaying Western thought that we find the most profound cause both of the collapse of conventional Christianity and the origins of the contemporary problem of faith in connection with the question of God. What is involved here are fundamental questions of theological thought which today's theologians are only beginning to discover. It will more and more be a matter of retesting age-old, standing concepts and terms which in classical theology (both Roman Catholic and reformed) were all too easily and matter-of-factly considered as useful material to explain belief in God.

What is concerned here is the conquest and purification of a schematic, mechanical, conceptualization based on purely formal logic and typically Western. It is beginning to be questioned whether this conceptualization is appropriate to the belief in God with which theology should be dealing. For centuries, theology has—at least according to theologians who follow Heidegger —made use of a structure of thought, a system of concepts and terminology by which, without noticing or willing it, it has laid the foundation for the contemporary problem of faith and for modern atheism. In this view, the origin of the problem does not lie in the rationalism of the Enlightenment, or in what has been called scientism, the empiricism of natural science; the origin of this rationalism and empiricism goes back even as far as the first principles of classical Greco-Western thought.

[7] Martin Heidegger, *Die Technik und die Kehre* (Neske, Pfullingen, 1962), pp. 40ff.

## Philosophy and Theology

Before going further into Heidegger's thought we must emphasize that Heidegger does not tire of constantly warning against an intermingling and obfuscating of the basic concern of philosophy on the one hand and the basic concern of theology on the other.

For Heidegger it is not at all obvious that Christian theology and Western philosophy have anything in common, not because he is an atheist as a superficial critic might think, but precisely because he has such a vision of the development of Western philosophy throughout the ages that it puzzles him how theologians have been able to expect comfort from this philosophy. It cannot be denied that Heidegger and Barth meet on this point, though from entirely opposite directions. As a result, Heidegger is fully sympathetic to the angry protest of Luther against the intellectualism of medieval scholasticism and also to Kierkegaard's protest against the intellectualism of Hegel. The theological thought of conventional Christianity welcomed from the very beginning Platonic-Aristotelian thought as a Trojan horse and consequently has fallen victim in a mortal combat. According to Heidegger, it is here that the principal cause is to be found for the dangerous impasse in which Christian belief and thought find themselves at the moment: "A Christian philosophy is a round square and a misunderstanding. There is, to be sure, a thinking and questioning elaboration of the world of Christian experience, i.e., of faith. That is theology. Only an era which no longer fully believes in the true greatness of the task of theology arrives at the disastrous notion that theology can win out or be replaced and made more palatable to the needs and tastes of the time by a supposed refreshing with the aid of philosophy. For the original Christian faith, philosophy is foolishness." [8]

The security of faith is completely *sui generis;* it has its own way, not dependent on any philosophy, of "standing in the truth." For him who stands in the truth through faith the question that philosophy deals with is pure foolishness: "What is being asked in our (philosophic) question is foolishness for faith." [9]

8 Martin Heidegger, *Einführung in die Metaphysik,* p. 6.
9 *Loc. cit.*

This applies all the more if it is true that Greco-Western philosophy has lost sight of the real question of philosophy—the question of being—and has become more and more involved in existents. A Christian theology which should be firmly anchored only in revelation as the bible understands it, can, according to Heidegger, expect nothing but disaster from thought that has decayed into logic and from the traditional physics based on that thought. For this reason Heidegger reminds theologians of the words of Paul: "Has not God turned the wisdom of this world into foolishness? In God's wisdom the world with all its wisdom has not succeeded in finding God; therefore it has pleased God to save those who believe through the foolishness of the proclamation." [10]

Heidegger, for his part, keeps philosophy separate from theology. It can therefore hardly be his intention that theologians from now on should base their systems on his "system" instead of that of earlier philosophers. There is no place for a system in Heidegger; in his current of thought there cannot be a fundamental theology which would base Christian theology on one philosophy or another instead of Hebrew and the Old Testament.

But this does not mean that Heidegger's thought is of no significance to theology. Heidegger's thought could lead theology from the impasse in which it now finds itself as a result of its being tied to Greco-Western philosophy. He deprives philosophy of the capacity to argue rationally against Christian revelation by showing that philosophy, judged from genuine, authentic thought, is itself highly subject to attack. Just as metaphysical and scientific thought does not, as it were, end up with God, founding a basis for belief in God, likewise is it incapable of supplying proofs against belief in God. Western logic, metaphysics, and science have become estranged from thought in the real sense. They do not reach questions which really count for man because of his being-human. In their own area they are important (as can be seen from the victories and achievements of modern science), but they do not penetrate the real and most profound question: the question about being which is posited to man by his human existence.

If the theologian were to allow himself to be led along Heidegger's path of thought to the one and only question which man posits precisely as man (i.e., from that within him which makes

[10] 1 Cor. 1, 20ff.

him a man, a thinking man), this might mean a great liberation for his thought; it could give him a new vision of the sense of revelation and faith and of the entirely proper character of man's reflection on the faith. Heidegger himself does not take this up; he is not a theologian but a philosopher. But it could have great significance if the theologian were to get acquainted with Heidegger's manner of thought.

## Heidegger's Manner of Thought

What does the original character of Heidegger's manner of thought consist of? In the first place it is characterized by the awareness of standing at a beginning: "The most thoughtworthy thing in our thoughtworthy times is that we have not yet begun to think." [11]

Thought begins only when man has an awareness of the infinite difference between existence and existents and consequently between reflection on existence and reflection on existents between the thought which makes man a man and the thought which binds him to, and threatens to make him equal to things, between authentic thought and technical thought. Western thought found itself on the road of technical thought long before there was question of technology in the present sense of the word. Western thought went in the direction of technical thought by reflecting only on existents while forgetting existence.

A second characteristic of Heidegger's thought lies in his sharp distinction between authentic and unauthentic thought. Thought begins and ends with questions, which means that it is never finished. Thought begins with a questioning that is inherent to being-human as such. Only this thought, which man cannot rid himself of precisely because and insofar as he is really man, is thought in the real sense, original and authentic thought. Authentic questioning and thought have nothing in common with curiosity, desire of knowledge, desire for exploration or practical usefulness.

It is clear that hundreds of questions can arise in man which are truly born from a real urge to know but which are not connected

[11] Martin Heidegger, *Was heisst Denken?* (Niemeyer, Tübingen, 1961), p. 3.

with the question man asks because, precisely as man, he cannot fail to do so. Practically all questions of a logical, mathematical, scientific, and philosophical nature are questions which man asks because he finds them interesting or because for practical reasons he is interested in knowing the right answer. It is about these questions that he reflects. But his reflection is not yet authentic thought. Rather, these unauthentic questions occupy men so much that they rarely or never arrive at the authentic question which lies hidden in the inscrutable secret of being-human itself. All through the day men ask questions about all sorts of things, but all these questions concern existents and the mutual relation between existents. That these existents, including man himself, are is accepted as an obvious datum of experience which no one doubts. It is true that most men look with amazement at the wonders of nature, at everything that arouses admiration and stimulates curiosity. But this amazement about all sorts of astonishing phenomena is not the wonder that sets authentic thought in motion. This is the thought which is born from wonderment about existence itself, the wonderment about the fact that after all there is something and not nothing, the wonderment over the fact that I exist, over the fact that I know this, so that in my self-awareness I can say to myself: "I am; I know that I am, and I know that I know that I am." Wonderment about being itself is the authentic wonderment from which authentic questions and authentic thought are born.

A third characteristic of Heidegger's thought lies in its open, dynamic, unsystematic, and never-ending character. According to Heidegger it is a strictly necessary characteristic of authentic thought. If wonderment about being itself is at the beginning of philosophy in the real sense, this "beginning" is not meant in the sense of a first step to which, through philosophizing along the path of logical reasoning, new steps are continuously added until the beginning is finally lost sight of and the end of the path of thought comes into view in the form of a conclusion that holds true once and for all. Such a logical process on a path which leads from a beginning to an end by way of premises to a final conclusion belongs to unauthentic thought. Authentic thought knows no end, no conclusion and no closed system of conclusions which come to a perfect ending. If anyone were to identify such a system with truth, he is talking of truth in an unauthentic sense. Chances are that a person who knows so well that his system is the truth has not even arrived at the beginning of any notion or question of truth in an authentic sense.

## Wonder

When Heidegger, following Plato, states that wonder is the beginning of philosophy, meaning the beginning and stimulus of authentic thought, it is a matter of a lasting beginning, a fundamental beginning, a beginning that continues to be a beginning, never left behind to end finally in a definitive answer. The wonder which Heidegger has in mind is not wonder about the many varied beings in their amazing richness of forms; it is the wonder about being itself. This wonder is and remains the beginning and principle of all thought that is thought in the authentic sense. The more authentic thought progresses, the more wonder grows. What is concerned here is thought that does not solve, but deepens the secret of being about which man wonders; thought that does not end up in an answer. It always remains a questioning, and must remain so if man would continue to be a thinking man, authentically man. It may well be that in many areas a questioning or thinking that intends to find an answer has a right to exist, but it can never be questioning or thought in the authentic sense.

Thought in the authentic sense therefore is a questioning thought, a thinking questioning which never ends. If it were possible to supply an answer to questioning, then wonder would make way for understanding. In this case, too, questioning and thinking would stop and man precisely as man would cease to ask and think. He would no longer precisely be "man." A philosopher who thinks he is able to find the answer to any question would thereby manifest that he has not yet arrived at the wonder about being and at authentic thought. He would no longer be "man" but a think-machine. As Heidegger states it: "Why are there beings at all and not non-being? That is the question. Presumably this is not a pleasing question. Why are there beings at all and not non-being? This is obviously the first of all questions, though not in the sense of a chronological order of questions.

Individuals and peoples pose many questions in their historical passage through time. They examine, explore and test many things before they come upon the question of why there are beings at all and not non-being. Many never arrive at the question, if by this we mean to form the question, to ask it, to get into the very situation of the question instead of hearing and reading the formulated interrogation." [12]

The latter is very important. The wonder, the questioning and thinking which are concerned here is a situation, a situation to which, despite questions and answers, there is no end, a situation that continues precisely insofar as man is and remains authentically human. The full awareness of being and of being-human, consists precisely in remaining in the situation of this question for life. Authentic thought and questioning is nothing else than being aware of being in a situation of continuous wonder about "being" by which beings are. The question why there are beings at all and not rather non-being can be taken from a manual and learned by heart. But this does not necessarily mean that the question is understood and actually asked. Whoever does really understand and ask the question is aware that for man this is the one and authentic existential question compared to which all other questions are inauthentic questions.

## Authentic and Inauthentic Thought

All questioning and answering separated from this one and authentic question about "being" will in the long run end in philosophical nihilism and theological atheism. The great and lasting significance of Heidegger therefore lies in this, that he reinvites both philosophers and theologians to reflect on the one question which matters for man precisely as man, the one question from which all other questions ultimately derive their real sense: the question about the mystery of "being" that causes beings to be.

Meanwhile it is interesting to note that Friedrich Schelling also indicated this question is the most actual question: "It is precisely man who leads me to the final, desperate question: Why is there anything at all? Why is there not nothing?" [13]

---

[12] Martin Heidegger, *Einführung in die Metaphysik*, p. 1.

[13] Friedrich Schelling, *Philosophie der Offenbarung*, 1958, photo mech. print (Darmstadt, 1966), Vol. I, p. 7.

While inauthentic thought seeks an answer for any question and is satisfied only when the answer has been found, authentic thought does not concern itself with an answer, a knowing, an increase of knowledge. The entire concept of "increase" does not belong to authentic thought. With authentic thought it is not a matter of quantitative range and content but of depth and intensity, just as in "believing" in the biblical sense it is not a matter of content and range but of firmness and strength. Authentic thought is a recollection, an indwelling. It tends to "being" which dwells as the concealed ground in all beings. The immense, inscrutable mystery of being-human lies in this, that "being" which dwells in all beings in a concealed and unconscious manner, "lights up" in man's thought and finds expression in dialogue which is really authentic.

## Truth

After this general consideration of the character of Heidegger's thought we can now present a further description of Heidegger's way of thinking. We are now clear about the starting-point which lies in the question about the "being" of beings. Authentic thought consists of dwelling on this question. How does this come to pass and what does it end up with?

In his first major writing, *Being and Time*, Heidegger proceeds from the fact that man (and among all beings man alone) is conscious of his being. No other can give an answer to the question of what it means to be. Therefore the question must be asked of man. In order to find an answer Heidegger proceeds from a very detailed analysis of what makes man to be precisely man in contradistinction to all that is not man. Influenced by Kierkegaard among others, he began with human existence. Although this analysis was meant to be only a starting-point, it made Heidegger the founder of modern existentialism. He himself, however, always continued to dwell on the ontological question, the question about "being." Actually, since the "reversal" of the forties, Heidegger can no longer be called an existentialist.

In man's thought "being" lights up; it comes forth from its concealment in beings into non-concealment. This word is the literal meaning of the Greek word *aletheia* which means "truth."

Quite independent of the question of whether those philologists who criticize Heidegger's etymologies and word-interpretations are right or not, it is at any rate clear what Heidegger intends to say with his etymology. He intends to say that the Greek word for "truth" expresses better what truth is than the German word *wahrheit* (truth).

Truth is revealment, non-concealment. Of what? Of "being" which gives being to beings and which dwells in beings in a concealed manner without ever coming to light. "Being" lights up in man exclusively. It is this lighting up in man that makes man into man as distinct from the thing. The thing is meaningless unless its being and its being-thus lights up in the thought of man. This thought is expressed in speech. When man speaks he says something about the "being" of beings, he gives beings their sense and meaning, he says that beings are what they are and how they are; he "uncovers" the "being" of beings—in other words he speaks "truth." To speak about beings without reflecting on "being" is nothing but talking. In talk, the word is devaluated; it is deprived of its authentic meaning and destiny. And this is the most thoughtworthy aspect of our thoughtworthy times—that we no longer or do not yet think in the authentic sense but that we only talk and discuss.

Thought begins only when man is aware of the infinite distinction between "being" and beings, of what Heidegger later began to call the ontological difference. As long as man has not yet experienced this difference as a reality, he has not yet awakened to authentic thought and to authentic being-human. The occupation with things is, in that case, halfway between animal and human occupation with beings. He accepts the fact that they are and he uses them. But he does not wonder about the fact that they are and consequently does not ask about the secret of the "being" of beings either. Beings do not yet stimulate him to reflect on the "being" of beings. His inauthentic thought and speech keep him caught up in beings.

## *"Being"*

A warning here is not out of place since we are speaking of thought and speech about "being." We are so caught up in beings that when we speak of "being" we are inclined to think of it also as a being, an existent. We are speaking here of the "being" that makes beings to be. We use the noun form and act as if it were an entity of which we speak. Thus in our Western thought (according to Heidegger a decayed thought) we are inclined in theology to think and speak about God as if he too were an entity. We might observe parenthetically that Heidegger's protest against making an entity of "being" lies, among other things, at the basis of some expressions about God in Robinson's *Honest to God*. If readers of this book had better understood this, then the bishop would have been spared much foolish criticism, even including the accusation of his being an atheist.

In any case, in Heidegger "being" which makes beings to be, must not be conceived of as substantive. Perhaps it would be best to say that "being" dwells in beings. The fact that in our language we cannot express the infinite difference between "being" and "beings" makes one think that Western thought has fallen prey to what Heidegger calls the "forgotten-ness of being." Man is so caught up with beings and with the importance beings have for him that he has forgotten to reflect on "being," thinking authentically. He does not "think" but he "thinks about." He thinks about things, he thinks about man as about a thing; and if he thinks about it at all, he thinks about God as a thing, as a being, an existent about which one thinks and speaks as if one could learn to know it this way.

That man does not reflect on "being" means that he shies away from authentic thought. One of the most critical characteristics of this flight is that man is no longer (or not yet) conscious that he shies away from authentic thought, and he does not want to become conscious of it either. In this way Heidegger arrives from the realm of thought at the realm of acting. Man, increasingly occupied with beings, with things, and forgetting the question about "being" as fully as possible, thus escapes as completely as possible from authentic thought.

## Culture

Man's action is at the basis of the world he produces, of the culture he evokes. Heidegger sees in Western culture and ultimately in the entire nascent world culture a development in which the distance between authentic thought and action is ever on the increase. Man's action threatens to degenerate into an action in thought-less-ness.

Man is busy with many things, but ever more thoughtlessly. He sometimes would like to stop and reflect, but he cannot arrive at reflection. He runs on without having the time, the courage, or the will to ask himself what the end will be. But this end is the "nothing," absolute collapse, unless a stop, a repentance, a "reversal" comes to pass. Thought and action are very closely connected. Philosophy and culture cannot be separated. Only a reversal of the direction in which Western culture has gone, back via all thinkers and systems of thought to the origin of thought, can save philosophy and culture together from disaster.

It would seem, however, that modern man does not want to hear of such a reversal. He goes in the opposite direction. Secretly aware of the threat of non-being, modern man exerts himself to secure and defend himself as much as possible against all the dangers that threaten. And science and technology enable him to do so.

Less and less does modern man concern himself about human existence in an existential sense. What he desires is a safe and secure existence. By technical means he postpones the chance of death to a distant a future. Death must be removed from the cultural picture as radically as possible. The unwillingness to think about "being" will ultimately result in an unwillingness to think of the possibility of non-being.

Thoughtlessly man runs along without wanting to reflect on "being" and non-being. He is in flight both from authentic thought and from existential (i.e., conscious and decisive) action. What fear, Heidegger asks, is greater than the fear of authentic thought which would place man necessarily before an existential decision? Only when inauthentic matters are concerned does man decide. The authentic existential decision which matters for man precisely as man is banished as far as possible beyond his thought horizon.

"Thoughtlessness is an uncanny guest who in today's world comes and goes everywhere." [14] This uncanny guest drives modern, technologized man with irresistible force to complete nihil-

[14] Martin Heidegger, *Gelassenheit* (Neske, Pfullingen, 1955), p. 13. English text: *Discourse on Thinking*, tr. J. M. Anderson, and E. Hans Freund, (Harper and Row, New York, 1966).

ism which means no more and no less than the complete denial of what is deepest and most authentic in being-human. Thus a vision of man's future opens up in which man becomes the victim of a force which he himself has evoked, of a technology which he no longer dominates, but which dominates him. In his "forgotten-ness of Being" man has made himself into a part of a technical apparatus which, with an efficacy that respects nothing, is busy dehumanizing man.

The technical apparatus for Heidegger contains not only tech-nological findings in the actual sense of the word but modern means of communication, statistics and registration, travel facili-ties, systems of insurance and taxation, psychological tests and medical preparations, including the extensive and complicated array of means by which human existence is regulated from cra-dle to grave, controlled, streamlined, safeguarded and insured. The product of this entire organization of existence is technical man who is so totally estranged from "being," from his origin, that he never even considers meditatively thinking about "being" itself. Man labors under the delusion that by his science and technology he has become lord and master of all things. In real-ity, however, he has lost himself and has more and more made himself into a thing.

### The Later Heidegger

What does Heidegger suggest to counter this? In his writings of the past twenty-five years he never tires of trying to make clear, in various ways, what the "reversal" to which he invites men means concretely for man's thought.

What he is concerned with is a reversal on the road which Greco-Western thought has thus far traveled. This road must be traveled again in reverse direction. The thinkers we encounter on this road must be interrogated about what they omitted to say. Finally we arrive at the beginning of the road only to encounter once more Parmenides and Heraclitus, the two pre-Socratics to whom Heidegger assigns an exceptional importance in connec-tion with the origin of authentic thought. Heidegger reinterprets the extant fragments of these original thinkers in a way which, due to the "forgotten-ness of Being," is no longer understood and is therefore a cause for scandal on the part of classical philosophers who are incapable of sharing Heidegger's reversal.

In more recent years especially, the way which Heidegger's thought moves has gradually become more clearly delineated.

Authentic thought is concerned with truth considered as unveiling of "being." "Being" lights up and uncovers itself in man's thought. Man cannot arbitrarily dispose of "being" concealed in beings. He must rely on the uncovering of "being." In this connection one might well use the theological term "revelation." The uncovering of "being" itself overtakes thinking man when and insofar as "being" reveals itself in thought. Heidegger speaks of a "mittence" of "Being," where "being" sends itself unto man when he opens himself to "being," when he asks about "being" by which beings are, instead of asking about beings.[15]

Authentic thought does not consist of reasoning but of experience. The experience occupies man's entire life. It is a dynamic, existential experience which is not subject to man's control. A person who stands at the beginning cannot by reasoning determine beforehand where he shall finish up in the distant future. Truth is a living reality and whoever surrenders to it will encounter surprises. Its end does not come into sight on this earth. Thought continues to wait and look forward even though provisional and prudent "formulations" are possible.

"Thought is a step-by-step experience. It requires patience and endurance for definite formulations do not present themselves immediately." [16]

The history of authentic thought depends on the "mittence of Being." This applies equally to mankind in general and to the individual. The road which Greco-Western thought has traveled is not without meaning or significance. This road of the "forgotten-ness of being" is subject to the "mittence of Being." Being forever clamors more loudly for attention. The reversal will come when the proper moment has arrived. Therefore there still is hope for the future. Man cannot in his "forgotten-ness of being" continue to withdraw himself from the "mittence of Being." He is too much man. Dehumanization takes its revenge

---

[15] Translator's note: For the English expression, which is a neologism, I am indebted to Wm. J. Richardson, S.J., who introduces this expression in his book: *Heidegger; Through Phenomenology to Thought* (preface by M. Heidegger) (M. Nyhoff, The Hague, 1963).

[16] Robinson-Cobb, *The Later Heidegger and Theology*, p. 85.

and calls for a reversal. The moment will come when man begins again to "think meditatively."

In Heidegger this "meditative thinking" has increasingly acquired a poetic form. It is true that he himself never became a poet, but he rediscovered a congenial expression of authentic thought which contemplates being in the poems of Hölderlin.[17]

Finally, Heidegger's thought acquired more and more of an emotional character. Heidegger is convinced that the relation between the words he uses is not accidental. The road of "meditative thought" is a road along which the thinker progresses in the reflection on ʿbeing." Meditative thought becomes ever more a thanking thought. Thought does not present man over and over again with new conclusions. The effect of authentic thought is that thinking man himself changes by it. From a thinking man he becomes ever more a thanking man. Even if in first instance man's destiny consists in this—that in his thought the "being" of beings lights up and unveils itself—his destiny lies ultimately in thankfully being "in the world." The thankfulness for being which is silent in beings finds awareness and expression in thinking man.

In the thankful thought of "being" one becomes aware that "being" is the really great gift. "Being" is granted to beings. What is very special to being-human is that if he opens himself to "being," man in his thanking thought becomes aware of this "having been granted." Thus an emotional relation to "being" arises in man, which Heidegger calls "disposition."[18] "Disposition" is the hidden ground of man's happiness, of man's well-being, of a feeling of harmony with total reality which exists because it has been granted "being," which as a gift lights up in the thought of man. Authentic thought has as a "result" an ever closer relation to and an ever deeper trust in all that is, in the total reality in which man exists.

In his publications after 1960, "disposition" becomes more and more a "releasement."[19] Total reality is because it *is* and because it is *as* it is. "Being" (to be exact, *this* "being") has been granted to it. And thus it is good. "Releasement" is not an apathetic acquiescence in something that cannot be changed. It is a positive

17 Hölderlin, cf. R. G. G., 3rd edition, Vols. 8, 394.
18 Heidegger speaks of *Gestimmtsein* or *Befindlichkeit der Stimmung: Was ist Metaphysik?* p. 31. The reversal meant for him also a reversal in his *Befindlichkeit.*
19 Cf. note 14 of this chapter.

and thankful acceptance of "being" as it lights up in thinking man. "Releasement" means thankful and trusting acceptance of "being," to let "being" be what it is. Heidegger uses the word "resignation" to express the attitude with respect to "being." [20] What he means is a conscious renunciation of the will to know and explain by means of scientific investigation or logical reasoning. Investigation and reasoning may have relative importance in the realm of beings, but they have nothing to contribute to the revealing of the mysterious gift of "being" itself, which can only be thankfully commemorated.

## The Problem of God

Heidegger scarcely spoke of the question of God until very recent times. "Being" itself is not yet "God." Possibly it points in the direction of God and possibly this will eventually become clear to authentic thought. Philosophically, it is an open question for Heidegger. He does not mean that believing thought and speech about God derived from biblical revelation are meaningless. The question arises for the theologian whether Heidegger's thought ends up as the springboard for the Kierkegaardian leap, which for some theologians would be the equivalent of biblical "faith."

Undoubtedly traces can be found in Heidegger's thought on "being" which show a similarity (or, if you will a certain analogy) to Christian thought based on revelation. In both instances it is not man who finds the answer; the answer comes from the other side, from the side of "being" by "revealment," and from the side of God through revelation. In both instances man has taken the wrong road, and the first thing necessary is to call a halt on the road toward nihilism and atheism respectively. What is needed is a reversal and a conversion. In both instances it is a matter of a receptive, humble, and thankful attitude toward a given gift, a granted salvation. Salvation and wholeness are related to each other. In both instances it is a matter of man's becoming whole again, precisely as man, in order to begin again to be man in the original and authentic sense and meaning. It may be that

[20] Heidegger does not consider the *Verzicht* in a sort of defeatism, but positively, as a respect for the constant mystery of total reality; cf. Ott, *op. cit.,* p. 163.

the testimony to God based on the bible is the answer to the open question which is and remains the thought of Heidegger. It may be that Heidegger's meditative thinking and the meditative believing of the people of God are attuned to each other, so that they may meet each other in one act of thought, commemoration, thanking and believing.

## Martin Buber

Before proceeding to the manner in which Barth posits and answers the question of God from revelation, we might say a few words about a philosopher-theologian who can at one and the same time be called a supporter and a critic of Heidegger: Martin Buber. His similarity with Heidegger lies in a common attitude of thought. And when ultimately this attitude entails a different way of thought the cause lies in a different vision of human existence, that which precisely makes man to be man. Buber, and many with him, thinks that in Heidegger's vision of human existence certain limitations and a certain one-sidedness can be detected. This one-sidedness would be the cause of the feeling of dissatisfaction which, according to them, is aroused in many by the "lean harvest" of Heidegger's thought.

Martin Buber (1878-1964) was a philosopher of religion and theologian of Viennese origin and of a liberal Jewish background. From 1923 to 1933 he was professor of Jewish philosophy of religion at the University of Frankfort. He taught at the University of Jerusalem from 1939 to 1951.

The starting point of Buber's criticism of Heidegger is the analysis of human existence as presented in *Being and Time*.[21] If by "existential" we understand an element in human existence which is determining for the being-human of every man, the question can be asked whether in Heidegger's analysis all existentials, without which man is not fully man, are shown to their full advantage. In other words, does not Heidegger's vision of human existence suffer from shortcomings which are critical for a correct understanding of the human situation, of the human "condition," to which, therefore, attention must be called?

[21] Martin Buber, *Das Problem des Menschen* (Schneider, Heidelberg, 1954), p. 94.

For example, it is quite striking that Heidegger seldom or never speaks of the ethical aspect of being-human, that he does not speak of conscience as an ethical awareness which is proper to man as man, that he does not mention charity as an existential aspect of being-human, as a "virtue" which one man may possess and another not. Must not, on the contrary, charity (in the sense of *agape*) be considered the highest form of the exclusively human I-Thou relationship? Ysseling also pointed out this shortcoming in the passage on "thought and ethics" in his Heidegger study.[22]

In his analysis of human existence, Heidegger strongly emphasized the passivity of being-human. It is true that man is the only being that knows that it is, but this "there-being" is a "being" which is "thrown" into existence. Man has not chosen "there-being" himself; it happens to him. This passive aspect of being-human remains intact even if man acknowledges "there-being" thankfully as a gift. Not only the fact of being-there is passively determined but for every man even being such and not other. Race, ethnic group, language, descent, class, environment, character, temperament, talent, health—in all these respects, man's being-such and not other is predetermined. Man is capable of doing something, but his possibilities are limited. How and what a man is depends to a considerable extent on certain *a priori* given circumstances. Within the limits of his being-such, however, man is receptive to, stands open to impressions and influences from without as a result of which he can undergo changes in his being-such. Man is not only passive however; he can also exercise an active influence on the world without and on his fellow man.

It is of the greatest importance to know whether in the mutual influence there is an I-It relationship or an I-Thou relationship. Buber was greatly interested in this fundamental difference. A purely objective relationship between man and man is subhuman. Only the personal relationship, in which it is not a matter of being face-to-face with another object but of a person face-to-face with a person, is fully human. An "I" that confronts an "it" is itself also an "it," a "something," a thing. Man is the one who says "I" only when with this "I" he addresses himself to a

[22] S. Ysseling, *Heidegger, Denken en Danken, Geven en Zijn* (Ned. Boekhandel, Antwerp, 1964).

"thou." When the "thou" in turn addresses himself to the "I" who addressed him as a "thou," there arises a typically human dialogue in which one looks at the other, in which two humans do not treat each other as things but encounter each other as human, speak to each other as human and deal with each other as human.

Buber's book *I-Thou* appeared as early as 1923, in the exceptionally creative 'twenties when the influential writings of Barth, Brunner, Tillich, and Heidegger were published.[23] In 1958 a special edition was issued on the occasion of Buber's eightieth birthday. It contained an epilogue in which Buber again clarifies the implications of the specifically human ability to enter into an I-thou relationship. This ability shows to its full advantage only in a relationship between God and man. It is subhuman to consider God a principle, an idea, a postulate. The relationship between God and man is the personal relationship *par excellence*. It is the most original, the most authentic I-thou relationship, the archetype, of which the human I-thou relationship is the reflection.

The word or name of God points to the one who "whatever else he may be, comes to us humans in creating, revealing, redeeming acts and enters into an immediate relationship, thus enabling us to enter into an immediate relationship with him." [24] Consequently, it is not merely a situation in which "being" lights up in the thought of man and in which man is dependent on a "mittence"; it is a matter of a most personal relationship, the human relationship *par excellence:* the I-thou relationship between God and man in which God is the first to speak and thereby makes possible the fully human dialogue.

### Buber's Criticism of Heidegger

Buber's vision and criticism of Heidegger's theory can be found in a later elaboration of lectures given in Jerusalem in 1938 and published in Germany in 1948 under the title of *The Problem of Man*.[25] Although the lectures Buber gave in America in 1951 make it clear that he had become aware of the reversal in

[23] Martin Buber, *Ich und Du* (Schneider, Heidelberg, 1958). English text: *I and Thou*, tr. R. G. Smith (Charles Scribner's Sons, New York, 1937).
[24] *Op. cit.*, p. 116.
[25] Cf. note 21 of this chapter.

Heidegger's thought during the 'forties, it seems that he maintained his criticism. It must, however, not be forgotten that his criticism is based on Heidegger's analysis of human existence in *Being and Time*. Buber's criticism is aimed at what he sees as a "shutting up" of man within himself. Only man is that one among beings aware of "being" and in whose thought "being" lights up. In Heidegger, being-human consists in a conscious relationship to man's own "being." Buber maintains that by conceiving being-human in this way, Heidegger made man into an unreal abstraction by detaching him, as it were, from the context of real human life. Further, Buber holds that Heidegger also gave man a relationship exclusively to his own "being" and that he lost sight of the fact that being-human is characterized precisely by having a relationship with the "being" of "the other." Since Heidegger does not acknowledge the I-thou relationship as an existential, there cannot be an I-thou relationship between God and man. Thus, it is said, Heidegger from the very beginning blocked the road from being-human to God.

The "there-being" of Heidegger is, according to Buber, a monologist "there-being" which leaves no space for the typically human possibility of a dialogue, and which, as a result, shuts man up within himself as in a prison without windows, without perspective, and condemns man unable to say "thou" to utter solitude. Undoubtedly this criticism fits the existentialism of Heidegger's disciple Sartre. But it is doubtful whether the criticism still applies to the later Heidegger after his reversal of the 'forties. However this may be, it is at any rate clear what Buber opposed: "it is not by a relationship to his own self but only by a relationship to another self that man can become complete. This other self may be equally limited and conditioned as himself but in being together the unlimited and unconditioned are experienced." [26]

According to Buber, Heidegger says man in his human existence cannot encounter God, a view due to Heidegger's consideration of man. The secret of being-human lies above all things in the fact that man is receptive to, and as it were asks for, a relationship to reality outside himself in the form of a personal I-thou relationship.

Man is not shut up within himself. He does not address only himself. He is not engaged in a solitary dialogue with himself. Because

[26] Martin Buber, *Das Problem des Menschen*, p. 102.

of the entirely typical nature of his being-human, man can be addressed. He is really man only in his relationship with his fellow man, not as a thing, but precisely as man. Man is a questioning and responding being. Even before he speaks, man is a question to his fellow man with whom he is confronted, a man who expects an answer from his fellow man. A man who is confronted with his fellow man who is his "neighbor" can close himself to human relationship. But this is always subhuman. It means nonacceptance of the other as man. In such nonacceptance, however, one also denies one's own being-human. Man as man depends on the I-thou relationship, and without this relationship man is not man.

## Buber and the Problem of God

It is here that we find Buber's starting point for the approach and the answer to the question of God. Man experiences his human existence as a questioning existence. It is true that this questioning is directed to the "thou" of his fellow man and that it asks for an answer from fellow man; but his fellow man appears capable of answering many questions, though not the deepest and most actual question. The experience of the human I-thou relationship leads man to the realization that ultimately his questioning is not answered by his fellow man but that over and above the "thou" of his fellow man it points to a higher, absolute Thou, a Thou that does answer the question which man is precisely because of his being-human.

It is not a matter of a subhuman relationship to an absolute "being," to a principle, an idea, or a postulate. It is a matter of a thoroughly human (or if you will, superhuman), a thoroughly personal relationship between man and the highest, the one and only absolute Thou, between man and God, questioning man and God who answers. Man asks precisely because in his being-human he is addressed by God: "Man, where are you?" Man asks for God because God asks for man. Man's questioning supposes the possibility of an answer. If God were not the real living God, the God who really answers, then it would not be an inalienable existential of being-human that man, precisely as man, is a questioning man. If God were not really God who calls man to himself because he has found man, then man would not look for him and ask for him. The questioning about God comes from man's not being like all other beings, but because he is man. Without this questioning, man is not man. In this questioning, however, he is open to God and he looks for an answer, for a revelation on God's part.

Of course, much more could be said about Buber's approach and answer to the question of God. As a conclusion of this chapter we must say at least a few things about two aspects of the question of God in Buber.

In the first place we must emphasize that the encounter between God and man is in no way prepared by or based on proofs of God's existence. Proofs belong in the world of the "it," not in the world of the "thou." God is simply the eternal "thou." Man cannot speak *about* God but only *to* God. Not a single image of God corresponds to the real God. Images of God are idols. Even the name of God may not be pronounced so that we humans might not think we can dispose of God: "It is not true that God can be concluded to from something, something from nature as its originator, or something from history as its ruler, or even from the subject as the self that is thought in it. It is not true that something else is a "given" and that God is deduced from it; but God is the Being that is immediately, most nearly, and lastingly confronting us, that may be properly only addressed, not expressed." [27]

Addressing God therefore, precedes any human thought and speech which is really fully human thought and speech. Only when man says "Thou" to God is his "I" a fully personal and fully human "I." This I-thou relationship stands at the beginning of all authentic thought and speech. It is on the I-thou relationship between God and man that the I-thou relationship to fellow man and to all reality rests. In no respect is God a conclusion. He is complete beginning. He is the giver; man is the receiver. But man receives God not as a something but a someone, a content. He receives him as a Presence, a Presence as Power. And God remains the Hidden One, the Ineffable One, absolutely the First and the Last, the Beginning and the End, the one and eternal "Thou" *par excellence*. To say "Thou" to him is what makes man to be man. It is this that makes man's thought and speech into truly human thought and speech: "We have come near to God but not nearer to unveiling

[27] Martin Buber, *Ich und Du*, p. 73.

being or solving its riddle. We have felt release but not discovered a solution. We cannot approach others with what we have received and say 'This is to be known, this ought to be done.' We can only go and confirm its truth. And even this is not a matter of 'ought to,' we can and we *must*." [28] Of God we cannot know anything, prove anything, say anything. Whoever knows, proves, or says anything "about" God, reduces God from a "Thou" to an "it." He does not speak of God but of an idol. When the atheist rejects all idols this may mean he is on the way to an I-thou encounter with God: "The eternal 'Thou' cannot by its very nature become an "it," for by its nature it cannot be expressed in measure and bounds not even in the measure of the immeasurable, or the bounds of boundless being; by its nature it cannot be grasped as a sum of qualities, not even as an infinite sum of qualities raised to a transcendental level; it can be found neither in nor out of the world; it cannot be experienced; it cannot be thought; we fail to meet him who is when we say 'I believe that he is'—'he' is still a metaphor, but 'Thou' is not." [29]

A God who "occupies" himself with man is not God. "The encounter with God does not come to man in order that he may concern himself with God but in order that he may confirm the truth that there is meaning in the world. All revelation is vocation and mission. But again and again, instead of realization, man reflects the One who reveals; he wishes to occupy himself with God instead of with the world. Only in such reflections he is no longer confronted with a 'thou,' he establishes an It-God in the realm of things, he knows of God as an "it" and speaks of him in this way." [30]

God cannot be "proved." God reveals himself in the I-thou relationship, in man's encounter with the eternal Thou. Revelation, though, does not mean a communication of truths, a communication of revealed content, as if man were coming to know things about God. Nor does revelation mean that God allows man all sorts of religious or mystical experiences. Revelation means only that God moves man to say "Thou," and this is all that man needs to be man. If the question is asked to whom man says "Thou," this means a return from the I-thou relationship to

[28] *Op. cit.*, p. 97.
[29] *Op. cit.*, p. 98.
[30] *Op. cit.*, p. 100.

the I-it relationship. God is not a someone, a "he"; God is exclusively a "Thou."

We have now arrived at a second aspect of the manner in which Buber asks and answers the question of God. If it is true that man is unable to say anything about God as an object of research and science, and that man can only say "Thou" to God, the question must be asked whether God is actually a reality for man. In that case one wonders why modern man states that he does not encounter God anywhere, that God is an absent, a silent God. Perhaps, then, Nietzsche and many moderns are right when they say that God is dead, that God does not exist for them. Could it be that Buber and all those who share his conviction of being with God in an I-thou relationship are victims of an illusion?

Buber is clearly aware that this question presents itself to modern man. Not that Buber doubts for a moment the reality of God. For him God is and remains a living reality despite all modern objections. For him God is the Living Reality *par excellence*. But the question posed by modern thought is of much concern to him. How can modern man think God a projection of man, a figment of the imagination, a fiction, an illusion?

### The Eclipse of God

The above-mentioned aspect of the problem of God was treated by Buber in a small book published in 1953, entitled *The Eclipse of God*.[31] It arose from a series of lectures Buber gave at Columbia, Yale, Princeton and Chicago. In this book Buber proceeds from the evident fact that the "eclipse of God is indeed the character of the historic hour through which the world is passing." [32] This fact poses a problem. It seems that in our time the question of God must be approached and answered in an entirely new manner proper to our time.

At any rate, it concerns a given religious situation. The situation is the result of a development which Western civilization, and in particular Western thought, has gone through in the past few centuries due to the rise of modern science and the Kantian

[31] Martin Buber, *Gottesfinsternis* (Manesse Verlag, Zurich, 1953). English text: *Eclipse of God: Studies in the Relation Between Religion and Philosophy*, tr. M. S. Friedman, et al. (Harper Bros., N.Y. 1952).

[32] *Op. cit.*, p. 31.

revolution in philosophy. The present situation consists in this: modern man is no longer able to "grasp" a Reality which is quite independent of himself, and to enter into a relationship which "exists outside his own consciousness." [33] Even the majority of those who are still "practicing" religion continues to employ certain conventional actions but is no longer aware of the divine Reality to which it originally was related.[34]

Buber characterizes this situation with the expression "eclipse of God." The choice of this word is not arbitrary. Buber's entire vision of the present situation and his personal conviction are summed up in this phrase. Just as in an eclipse of the sun the sun itself has not disappeared but continues to shine forth light and to radiate heat in undiminished glory, so too God is the same as always when he has been eclipsed from the awareness of modern man. God is not absent but the soul does not see him. God is not silent; man does not hear him. God, as the true *vis-à-vis* of man, "lives intact behind the wall of darkness." [35] God's Reality is no problem for Buber. His problem is how it has come about that modern man no longer finds God, no longer sees and hears him, that modern man thinks God dead.

Apparently for modern man something has come between him and God. Buber speaks in this connection of "that-which-steps-in-between." [36] Just as in an eclipse of the sun the moon comes in between the earth and the sun so that man no longer can see the sun from the earth, so for modern man something has come in between him and God.

"In our age the I-it relationship, gigantically swollen, has usurped, practically uncontested, the mastery and the rule. The 'I' of this relationship, an 'I' that possesses all, makes all, succeeds with all, this 'I' that is unable to say 'Thou,' unable to meet a being essentially, is the lord of the hour. This omnipotent selfhood with all the 'it' around it, can naturally acknowledge neither God nor any genuine absolute which manifests itself to men as of non-human origin. It steps in between and shuts off from us the light of heaven." [37]

Apparently for Buber this is a historical phenomenon which is

33 *Op. cit.*, p. 18.
34 *Op. cit.*, p. 17.
35 *Op. cit.*, p. 32.
36 *Op. cit.*, pp. 150ff.
37 *Op. cit.*, p. 152.

the final result of a cultural development. Buber basically agrees
with Heidegger in his diagnosis of the situation we find ourselves
in at present. Both regard the situation as the end of a development, as a historical phenomenon. To quote Buber: "Heidegger
rightly looks upon this hour as an hour of night." [38] Both are
concerned with the question of whether and how a favorable
reversal of the situation is conceivable and capable of execution.

Yet Buber persists in his criticism of Heidegger. The deepest
cause from which the present situation has arisen, according to
Buber, also functions in Heidegger's thought.[39] It is true that
Buber agrees with Heidegger's diagnosis that specifically modern
thought simply cannot endure a God who is not confined to
man's subjectivity, and that man has eliminated a self-subsisting
suprasensual world. But, according to Buber, by the self-
subsisting suprasensual world Heidegger means something in
man—a highest end, a foundation and principle of the existent, an
ideal. "But the living God who approaches and addresses an individual in the situations of real life is not a component part of such
a suprasensual world." [40] For this reason Heidegger has also cut
himself off from an authentic I-thou relationship with the eternal
"Thou," the living God. The primal reality with which, according to Buber, the question about God is concerned remains beyond Heidegger's thought horizon. Only once did it seem that
Heidegger was breaking through to the primal reality outside
man to the eternal "Thou" which alone makes man to be a human
"I" in the I-thou relationship with God. What Buber has in mind
is an interpretation which Heidegger in 1936 gave of one of
Hölderlin's texts: "Since we exist as talk, and can hear from one
another." Heidegger's explanation runs as follows: "The gods can
enter the word only if they themselves address us and place their
demand on us. The word that names the gods is always an answer
to this demand." [41] It is here, according to Buber, that Heidegger
testifies to a dialogue-relationship between a divine and a human
spontaneity. But Heidegger did not reach an authentic I-thou
relationship. Buber attributes this to the fact that Heidegger allied his thought to the demonic events of history which overwhelmed the German nation and, at least for a time, blinded it.

[38] *Op. cit.*, p. 29.
[39] *Op. cit.*, pp. 28ff.; pp. 84ff.
[40] *Op. cit.*, p. 29.
[41] *Op. cit.*, p. 92.

However this may be, we seem at any rate to have reached a stage in the history of mankind in which "the gods are silent." [42] The question mankind is confronted with is the question of whether God is indeed silent or whether man closes his ears, whether God is absent or whether man keeps himself absent. This is the question which concerns every human being, because the answer to this question involves genuine human existence.

## The Search for God

In spite of all the differences of opinion between Heidegger and Buber, both consider the present religious situation in which God is, as it were, dead for man to be historical phenomenon. "That-which-steps-in-between," as the cause of the eclipse of God, is a phenomenon characteristic of our time and can be explained from cultural causes.

It is at this point that every convinced Christian who bows to the testimony of the bible concerning man and his relationship to God will place a large question mark. He will ask himself whether Buber's "that-which-steps-in-between" is really the deepest, fundamental and most actual cause of man's incapacity to reach God. Does not every page of the bible testify to a chasm between God and man which can be bridged only by God? Is it not true that the "that-which-steps-in-between" is called "sin" in the Bible; not sin in the sense of a transgression of the moral law but sin in the sense of a self-oriented disposition, of man's aversion from God? Is it not *per se* peculiar to human existence that every human is, without distinction, at all times, and quite apart from great or small sins, plainly "sinner"? And does not the estrangement from God, the indifference and hostility toward God find expression especially in the fact that man despises words such as "sin," and "sinner"? Is not perhaps this situation of separation a situation of all times for all men without distinction, not just a contemporary situation? Does not the fact of being a sinner consist precisely in this, that man does not and cannot have an I-thou relationship with God unless God on his part restores the ruptured relationship? Perhaps the "searchers for God" of our time have taken a path along which a person cannot find God so

42 K. H. Miskotte, *Als de goden zwijgen* (Holland Publ., Haarlem, 1965).

that it is no wonder they come to the conclusion that God does not exist, that God is dead. Is it so obvious that God *can* be found along paths which man picks at his own discretion? If God himself is the one who alone can rightfully take the initiative in the restoration of the I-thou relationship between God and man, is it not obvious that this restoration is possible only along the ways which God determines and shows, so that all other ways are necessarily dead-end roads, roads which end in the death of God? Is it true that the approach and answer to the question of God concern something else than "revelation" on God's part and belief on the part of man?

These questions, which actually are only one question (that of the reality of revelation and faith), lead us from the realm of thought to that of faith, from the realm of philosophy to that of theology, from Martin Heidegger and Martin Buber to Karl Barth. According to Barth the question of God may and can be posed, approached and answered in only one way. All other ways are illegitimate and end up in nothing, not in God, but in some idol. And all idols together are less than nothing. Barth's theology is undoubtedly characterized by a complete exclusivism. To the children of men only one name is given by which all must be saved, the name of Jesus Christ. There is but one means by which the ruptured relationship between God and man can be restored, the salvific work of Jesus Christ; and there is but one way the question of God can be answered: belief in God's revelation in and through Jesus Christ.

The theological witness of Karl Barth must sound absurd to non-Christians, particularly to religious non-Christians. There are even some Christian theologians who condemn and reject Barth's exclusivism. It looks as if the influence which Barth enjoyed for about half a century is declining. Even in the world of reformed Christianity new answers are sought to the question about God. Barth's place, however, in the struggle for the preservation of belief in God is of such importance that, for the sake of being unprejudiced and open to all sides, we must pay close attention to the manner in which Barth has in our time posed, approached and answered the question of God.

# 7. Revelation and Faith

Karl Barth was born in 1886 in Basel. His father was a New Testament expert in the theological faculty of the University of Basel, the same university where he himself was later to teach his Church dogmatics after 1935.

From 1904 to 1909 Barth studied theology in Bern, Berlin, Tübingen and Marburg. As far as theology was concerned he was especially influenced by von Harnack and Herrmann, while in philosophy it was the neo-Kantians, Cohen and Natrop, who influenced him most. After some hesitation he accepted a post as assistant preacher and shortly thereafter he was ordained pastor in Safenwil (Aargau) in 1911. This was Barth's only post as a preacher. From 1921 on he was professor of dogmatics, first in Göttingen, from 1925 on in Marburg, from 1932 in Bonn, and finally from 1935 in Basel. He has given guest lectures at a large number of universities in Europe and the United States.

## The Theology of Karl Barth

Barth's theology was born from pastoral work. Even after he was made professor he regularly continued to preach. In Safenwil it soon became clear to him that a human, profane-scientific and noncommitted spectator theology based on history, psychology, and philosophy could achieve little in the proclamation of the word and in pastoral care. He saw himself forced back to the testimony of the bible, from the human word to the word of God.

Thus from the practice of preaching and pastoral care Barth gradually developed a distaste for and resistance to nineteenth century neo-Protestant theology, and to the humanized proclamation and easygoing conventionalism of the bourgeois Church based on that theology. Later, in his book about *Protestant Theology of the Nineteenth Century*,[1] he could name only Kohlbrugge, among all the theologians he treated, who, as far as the foundation of the faith was concerned, did not build on human considerations but on God's revealing action.

Between 1918 and 1922 a radical transition took place in Barth's vision of the faith and theological thought. He himself was scarcely able to keep pace with the development. In 1919 he published a rather sensational exegesis of Paul's letter to the Romans. The second edition of 1921 had to be drastically rewritten so that "of the first edition hardly a stone was left on another."[2] It was a real theological revolution, a Copernican transition in the realm of theology.

There were many who, used to the contrast between orthodox and liberal, had great difficulty understanding what Barth had in mind. On the one hand he rejected any belief in God based on reason or religious experience, but on the other hand he opposed any form of confessionalism, apologism and church-ism in which God's word was identified with an authoritative but nevertheless human interpretation. Basically it was a matter of relation between divine and human authority. No human norm, not even that of the Reformation, could be absolutized.

In an article he wrote in 1928 about *Roman Catholicism as a Question to the Protestant Church* [3] Barth asked seriously whether, in view of the situation in which Protestantism found itself, it might not be better to become "Roman" again. But he added immediately that this would be going from bad to worse. Actually Barth's protest was directed against all the official and conventional Christianity of those days, both in its Roman and Protestant forms. Orthodoxy and liberalism, intellectualism and emotional piety, natural religion and mysticism, liturgical and ecumenical movements —none of them escaped. For it was a determined and all-determining choice between "the word of man and the word of God in Christian

[1] Karl Barth, *Die protestantische Theologie im 19ten Jahrhundert* (Zollikon, Zurich, 1947). English text: *Protestant Thought: From Rousseau to Ritschl*, tr. B. Cozens (Harper & Bros. New York, 1959).

[2] Karl Barth, *Der Römerbrief* (Zollikon, Zurich, 1947), p. VI. English text: *The Epistle to the Romans* trans. by Edwyn C. Hoskyns (Oxford Univ. Press, London, 1933).

[3] *Zwischen den Zeiten*, VI, p. 274.

preaching." [4] between "the Gospel and religion," [5] between "God's will and our desire." [6]

The answer to the question of God was at stake. At any rate, who really does ask about God? Is the human questioning about God a questioning about the one, living and true God? Can man of himself ask about God? Is it possible for a legitimate questioning by man about God to be something else than an answer to God's questioning about man, a response to God's speaking to man? Is it not true that God must take the initiative and that man cannot do so? Does this not appear to be true as soon as man is really confronted with God's word?

Does it not appear, then, that all man's questioning and talking about God is presumption? Can man ever profit from a human word about God, an opinion rather than an answer to God's own word, to God's revelation?

It is very important to go into some detail regarding the above questions and the answers Barth gives in his theology. If the manner in which, according to Barth, the question of God must be posed, approached and answered is the only way where God, and not a pseudo-god, is involved—the only way which is permitted and warranted according to God's word—then all other ways in which the question of God has ever been posed and answered would have to be radically condemned as meaningless and hopeless. Barth's idea of the question of God necessarily excludes all other visions. It is necessarily exclusive. It is a matter of illusion or reality. If Barth is right, then any questioning or talking about God which is based on man is illusory; if on the other hand Barth's vision rests on an illusion, then there are other possibilities of asking and answering the question.

Barth's theological principles found their first expression in his *Letter to the Romans* which appeared in 1918. But it soon became clear that Barth had not yet been able to liberate his theological thought from the ties of philosophy. Barth, as Luther before him, was able to speak of a Babylonian captivity, but only as a captivity from which belief in God and theology had to be liberated. As we remarked before, it appeared necessary to rework *The*

---

[4] *Zwischen den Zeiten*, III, p. 119.
[5] Vol. 6, *Theologische Existenz heute* (Ernst Wolf).
[6] Vol. 7, *Theologische Existenz heute* (Karl Barth).

*Letter to the Romans* radically. The definitive text appeared in 1922.

Both *The Letter to the Romans* and a pamphlet *Biblical Questions and Insights,* published in 1920, were bolts from the blue. Even Barth himself was scared by the effects. He began to realize that without intending or knowing it he had sounded the alarm and that he was called to be the spoilsport, in a positive and constructive sense, in the theological activity of those days. He soon succeeded in gathering a circle of associates with whom he founded the periodical *Between the Times.* The circle gradually broke up. Peterson became a Roman Catholic. Bultmann did strive for a liberation of the biblical proclamation from its history-bound character, but Barth did not find he could follow Bultmann on the road toward the demythologization of the Gospel message. In 1933 a conflict arose with Gogarten because of his sympathies toward the national-socialist movement of the "German Christians." [7] The most tragic conflict was that with Brunner, whose name was usually mentioned in one breath with that of Barth.

An impossible situation arose when in 1934 Brunner published a pamphlet entitled *Nature and Grace.* Barth reacted violently with an unconditional *"No."* [8] This conflict concerned the relationship between God and man, the restoration of that relationship, the answer to the question of God.

Both Brunner and Barth were convinced that in these matters there can never be a human initiative. Without a self-revelation on God's part no belief in God is possible for man. The difference of opinion between Barth and Brunner concerned whether, even in the state of sin and unbelief in which man finds himself as man, there is something in man that might serve as a point of contact for God's speaking to man and for the restoration of the ruptured relationship between God and man.

In his pamphlet, Brunner, invoking Calvin, had advocated the possibility ultimately to be turned into reality, of a knowledge of and belief in God on the basis of "natural" arguments and independently of revelation on God's part. The question was whether or not it was possible to acknowledge a natural theology

---

[7] Vol. 14, *Theologische Existenz heute,* (in which Barth defends his standpoint against Gogarten).

[8] Vol. 14, *Theologische Existenz heute,* 1934.

not based on revelation. We shall return to this point in our treatment of Barth's theology.

The conflict between Barth and Brunner led to a definitive break in matters theological. Actually, Brunner later thought that Barth had come close to his own point of view. For that matter, many had the impression, especially after the publication of Barth's anthropology in the third part of his *Church Dogmatics*, that Barth had departed from his exclusive and radical point of view. But Brunner's 1951 article *The New Barth* did not bring about the reconciliation he expected.[9] Barth answered such unfounded suppositions as follows: "Several are seeking to track down the secret of the real or ostensible change of direction which I am supposed to have made some time between 1932 and 1938, or rather later according to other scholars. From my own standpoint, the comparatively simple truth is that, although I still enjoy debate, I have gradually acquired more and more feeling for the affirmations by and with which we can live and die." [10]

From what follows in the present chapter it will become clear that there never was question of a basic change in Barth's viewpoint regarding the question of God. If Barth had given up his exclusivism on this point, it would not be worthwhile to spend so much time on it. In that case Barth's vision would simply have become one among the many viewpoints and we would once more be faced with a choice among many possibilities.

The quite unique character of Barth's viewpoint lies precisely in this, that contrary to the many different ways by which man has attempted to solve the question about God in the course of time, there is only one way that really leads to God—namely, when man disregards himself and bases his belief in God exclusively on God's revelation, showing obedient submission to God's word. In that case there is no sense occupying oneself with natural theology, neither with earlier attempts in that direction nor with recent attempts such as that of John Cobb who tries to construct a natural theology on the basis of Alfred Whitehead's philosophy.[11] Barth's viewpoint regarding the question of God is really new; by its very nature it excludes all other viewpoints. Therefore, for anyone who asks about God or who thinks he is

---

[9] *Zeitschrift für Theologie und Kirche* (1951), Vol. 1, p. 92.
[10] *Kirchliche Dogmatik*, Vol. III, p. IX.
[11] Cf. note 25 of chapter five.

asking about God, the fundamental question is whether or not Barth's basic and exclusive viewpoint (which according to him rests on the biblical testimony concerning God's word) corresponds to reality.

One of the principal aspects of Barth's transition was the complete liberation of theology from the grasp of philosophy. This liberation was a laborious task. It is the general opinion that Barth's book dealing with the ontological argument of Anselm (*Faith Seeking Understanding*, 1931) was the final step in the liberation process.[12]

Meanwhile Barth had begun writing what was to be his major work on dogmatics, which has grown into twelve volumes. As had been the case with his *Letter to the Romans*, Barth had to begin all over again at one point. After the publication of what had been announced as *Christian Dogmatics in Outline* (1927), the work stalled. It appeared that the development of his theological thought had not yet been completed; in 1932 the first volume appeared again. In the foreword Barth wrote: "What else was left me, except to begin at the beginning and, true, to say the same thing over again, but the same thing over again in quite a different way." [13] It was a surprise to many that Barth had also changed the title from *Christian Dogmatics* to *Church Dogmatics*. Some rumors said Barth was on his way to the Roman Church. The foreword to the first edition of the first volume of 1932 gives a full explanation for the change of the title. Barth's doctrine of the Church appeared only in 1953 and 1959, as paragraphs 62 and 72 of *Church Dogmatics* and as part of the doctrine of reconciliation. The first volume of *Church Dogmatics* has the subtitle *The Doctrine of the Word of God*; the second volume is subtitled *The Doctrine of God*. These two volumes contain the most important teaching of Barth concerning the question of God. The third volume, consisting of four parts, has the subtitle *The Doctrine of Creation*, and the fourth volume

---

[12] Karl Barth, *Fides quaerens intellectum, Anselms Beweis der Existenz Gottes* (Kaiser Verlag, Munich, 1931). English text: *Fides Quaerens Intellectum: Anselm's Proof of the Existence of God in the Context of His Theological Scheme* (SCM Press, London, 1958). Cf. Hans-Georg Geyer, *Gedanken über den ontologischen Gottesbeweis, Parrhesia,* (EVZ Verlag, Zurich, 1966), pp. 101ff.

[13] *Kirchliche Dogmatik*, Vol. I¹, p. vi.

which also consists of four parts was subtitled *The Doctrine of Reconciliation*. Neither the planned fifth part of the latter volume, nor the fifth volume about *The Doctrine of Redemption*, has appeared.[14]

Barth's recent thoughts published since 1933 in a series called *Theological Existence Today* and from 1938 on in a series called *Theological Studies* are also important. The former was published in collaboration with Thurneysen, whereas the latter was an independent publication. Barth was surrounded by a school of faithful disciples, although among the leading theologians of the Protestant world he became more and more isolated. Meanwhile his writings found growing sympathy and approval among several Roman Catholic theologians. His influence on the theological thought of a good many theologians is connected with the rise of the new theology in France. The mutual relationship, however, retains a critical character, so that the theology of Barth and the Roman Catholic Church are not nearly as close to each other as might be concluded from Hans Küng's book on *Justification*.[15] At the same time, the Second Vatican Council and its resulting constitutions and decrees show clear indications of the indirect influence of Barth on present theological thought within the Roman Catholic Church, at least on a few points.

### Barth and the Question of God

In what follows in this chapter we shall restrict ourselves to the question of how, according to Barth, the question of God must be posed, approached and answered if we can truly speak of genuine, legitimate and living faith in God—in the one and only, true and living God who is in the mind of man when he "dares" to say "God" and speak of him. What must we do to avoid having pseudo-faith in an idol?

Barth, around 1920, caused anxiety to the world of theology by asking whether it was possible and permissible for man to speak

[14] Barth's *Kirchliche Dogmatik* consists of four main volumes, each of which is divided into two or more parts. English text: *Church Dogmatics* (T. & T. Clark, Edinburgh, 1936-1960; Charles Scribner's Sons, New York).
[15] Hans Küng, *Rechtfertigung* (Einsiedeln, 1957). English text: *Justification* (Thomas Nelson & Sons, New York, 1964).

about God. In doing so, is it not inevitable that we create a god after our own image and likeness? In doing so, do we not necessarily run the risk of falling into idolatry and blasphemy? Is not this the great danger of theology? When the Christian says he believes in God, and when he thinks he can and must account for his faith in God by means of a Christian theology or dogmatics, on what does he base his right and duty to speak and act in that manner? How can man begin to say "God" in a legitimate and warranted manner, to speak to God and to give witness to God? Where can the Christian find the answer to this question?

Of course it does not matter what Barth or anyone else thinks about God. The question is how a human being, a Christian, and therefore Barth also, can know with certainty whether his questioning or speaking about God is not on the wrong road, a dead end, instead of the one and only possible road indicated by God himself. This urgent question is, according to Barth, the real question which stands at the beginning of a genuine faith and a justified theology, a theology which, liberated for this reason by God, rightly claims to be "theology": doctrine about God. This question was a severe shock to conventional Christianity.

Barth's theological labor was a struggle to obtain an absolute and irrefutable answer to the question of God. When can a person rightly say that he believes in God? To believe in God is not the same as believing that there is something or someone like a supreme being. Of what profit is a faith based on "natural" certainties? As a result of the rise of modern sciences and modern thought, these certainties have lost their foundations. But then, *can* a person still believe in God? How can a man be certain that his belief in God is not an illusion? How can a believer be certain that his faith is genuine faith, that he is not believing in a pseudo-god but in the true and living God? Where must man begin in order to arrive at belief in God?

This question about the point of departure is most important in philosophy and theology. Man must begin somewhere. But the difficulty is that in the course of time various points of departure have been conjured up. Even if a person wants to begin as much as possible without prejudice, he must begin by choosing one from among the many points of departure, from that particular point of departure which he holds to be the most obvious, the

best, or possibly the only right one. Yet, no one can simply
"make a choice." If a person makes a choice, he also determines
certain norms by which he makes the choice.

This also applies to the realm of theology. The choice of a
point of departure is determined and regulated by norms which
themselves are based on the theology which should really be the
continuation of the first beginning. But in that case there can be
no question of a point of departure chosen without prejudice.
What is held to be an unprejudiced point of departure turns out
to be an "arbitrary" leap into a certain stream of thought and
belief. Sometimes it happens that a person slowly comes to the
realization that the stream he has jumped into leads nowhere.
Then this experience makes it clear to him that he must get out
of this stream; arriving once again at the banks of the stream he
must choose a new point of departure and risk another leap. But
it remains a leap.

Any choice of a point of departure in science, philosophy and
theology is an *a priori* choice of a certain view of the world or
life, the choice of a certain "faith." No person is an exception to
this. Even the most complete nihilism or atheism is based on a
chosen point of departure. The choice is always a risk. From the
very beginning the choice proves that a person has chosen even
before the choice was made—in other words, the choice of the
point of departure was already determined beforehand when a
person imagines he wants to begin without prejudice. It is thus
with every man, and also with Barth.

Before his transition in the 'twenties Barth realized that the
theological stream he found himself in was in fact a whirlpool of
human contradiction and confusion where the certainty of "believing in God" was endangered on all sides. Barth realized more
and more that the cause of the hopeless situation of theology lay
in the natural, human, and therefore relative and deceptive certainties on which the nineteenth century based its belief in God.

Experience had taught Barth that the point of departure of
nineteenth century Protestant theology was fruitless. Consequently another point of departure must be chosen. But, like
every other choice, this new choice was again a leap, a risk. The
choice itself did not stand at the beginning. It was *a priori* determined by the faith in "a reality of revelation." It was not the

choice that determined what was to follow; what was to follow determined the choice.

Barth arrived at the conviction that man is faced with the dilemma of absolutely no belief in God or a belief in God in no way based on any human certainty but exclusively on God himself, on God's action and speech, on God's revelation.

It is clear that an unprejudiced person who does not believe in God must, if he would really be unprejudiced, leave an opening for the possibility that the fact of his having been unable to find God is to be blamed on his having thought that he had to make himself—his own human existence—as the point of departure, and that he himself had to take the initiative toward a possible belief in God, whereas the initiative is exclusively God's, one in which God himself is the point of departure and the basis of belief in God. It may well be that man, not God, is to be blamed for the impossibility of believing in God. An insight into this probability might cause him to ask whether or not revelation on God's part is real.

Thus far, however, we are still caught in the snares of purely human considerations. Karl Barth vehemently denies his choice of the new point of departure, which lies not in man but in God, rests on human considerations. It rests on an experience of having been confronted with God's revealing action, with God's word. And here all purely human certainty vanishes. Here it is a matter of certainty which God alone grants precisely because he really is God, really deals with man, really addresses man. But here, in the real belief in God made possible and granted by God, there is no question of a human choice; it is divine election. Man cannot decide for himself that he will believe in God. It is not this or that choice which determines the point of departure toward belief in God. The point of departure of man's belief in God lies in God's election. Any form of belief in God which rests on one or another foundation within man is an illusion.

The origin of belief in God lies in God himself. In the relationship between God and man it is God who really acts. God is concerned with men. God reveals himself to man. This revealing action is proclaimed on God's authority, not just anywhere, but "within the space of the Church." It is within the Church that man is, through proclamation, called to "being in the Church" and thus is awakened to faith. This is an event in which God deals with man: "Every event in which God acts consists altogether in the fact that men are visibly aroused by God, set apart and gathered together into being in the visible Church." [16]

The visibility is not the profane visibility which can be ascertained in a natural manner and which is evident to everyone. It is a "visibility of faith." "It is only in faith that this event as *this* event, the being in the Church, is visible as *divine* election and sanctification." [17]

There is here no place for self-assurance and overestimation of self. On the contrary, faith in God is entirely God's work in the sinner who is incapable of finding a way to God by himself. ("Sinner" is used not in the sense of evildoer but in the sense of the separation from God proper to all men.) It is closely connected with the contrast between sin and grace. Sin means unbelief and cannot mean anything else. Grace (God's grace) means faith. Faith is a fruit of God's grace. Certainty of faith in no way finds its basis in any capacity of man but exclusively in that which God has done to man. For this reason it is impossible to speak of different degrees of certainty. Faith is always absolute. As sinner, every man is and remains a complete unbeliever; but as one who has grace, as one who expects everything from God and nothing from himself, he is a complete believer. "He who is roused up and gathered into being in the Church has every cause for full certainty of faith; for security and boasting he has no cause at all." [18]

## The Word of God

God deals with man exclusively by means of his word. The word of God comes to us in sacred scripture. It is the commission of the Church to proclaim the word of God. But the word of God reaches man also as a human word. Here lies the problem of the relation between God's word and the human word both in the biblical witness and in the proclamation of the Church. This is the first problem theology deals with.

As far as theology is concerned, it too is human language about

[16] *K. D.*, I 1, p. 49.
[17] *Loc. cit.*
[18] *Loc. cit.*

God. Theology is a form of science, instruction and inquiry—a human activity. Not all theology, however, is language, instruction and knowledge of God. Much of theology is occupied with gods of human making. One can legitimately speak of theology in the true sense of the word only if it has the proclamation of God's word as a presupposition and reflects on it: "Theology reflects upon proclamation. It confronts it as a court of criticism. It is Church instruction of youth on a higher grade, entrusted with the special purpose of testing the coherence of present-day proclamation with the original and prevailing essence of the Church and of indicating the correct and relevant lines upon which to continue it." [19]

Barth maintains, therefore, that theology is a real science. But, on the other hand, he makes a distinction between true and false theology. True or genuine theology can function only "within the space of the Church." Conversely, the Church cannot do without theology because the Church's proclamation of the word of God is not only word of God but also human word. The function of theology consists in preserving proclamation from becoming purely human word by constantly leading it back to confront it with and test it by God's word in sacred scripture. Consequently theology must also establish the norm which decides how far exegesis of sacred scripture is a purely profane, philological and historical activity, and to what degree it is really of service to proclamation by making God's word capable of being heard and understood.

## The Holy Spirit

None of this is possible without the action of the Holy Spirit. Both exegesis and theology have a pneumatic character. They have nothing whatever in common with the science of religion not with a philosophy of religion, phenomenology of religion, psychology of religion, sociology of religion or with history of religions. A person who occupies himself with such things, says Barth in connection with Heiler's book *Prayer*, is not in touch with the matter itself. According to Barth it is clear that the study of the science of religion is incapable of leading man an

[19] *K. D.*, p. 51.

inch closer to a true and genuine faith in God. The scientist of religion is a disinterested spectator who occupies himself with the interesting phenomenon of "religion." The real theologian realizes in everything he does as a theologian that he is existentially involved in his inquiry and reflection. The theologian performs his task by reason of and on the basis of belief which God has granted him through his obedient listening to God's word. The theologian is not a person who starts with human (natural) certitudes and tries to find a way that leads to faith in God for himself and others. Rather he starts with the faith in God for which God has given him the possibility and freedom and then arrives at legitimate answers to questions connected with exegesis, proclamation, and the Christian faith.

The absolute and radical rejection of any semblance of natural theology is, according to Barth, a matter of life and death. Belief in God and knowledge of God are exclusively the fruit of God's "yes" to man. Any "yes" of man to God based on his own human authority is a self-willed "no" to God, a result of the fact that man as sinner is in rebellion against God even in his pious acknowledgment of God. God's "yes" always resounds in man's "no." It calls man to a radical conversion. For the theologian this means a complete rejection of natural theology. He must not engage in it for a moment, even if he were to do so with the intention of rejecting it later. In his *No* to Brunner, Barth says: "We must learn again to understand revelation as a grace and grace as a revelation and thus in constant decision and conversion turn our backs on any 'correct' or 'incorrect' natural theology." [20] His decision and conversion determine whether or not the theologian really believes in God and interprets God's word. Natural theology is so fatal for a real faith in and witness to God that we must not concern ourselves with it in any manner and for any reason whatever. We must shun natural theology. As far as faith in God is concerned this is a matter of life and death.

"A person who is engaged in real theology can only pass by natural theology as an abyss, and if he does not want to fall into it headlong he must stay away from it." [21] And a little further: "If a person is really serious about rejecting natural theology he does not stare into the eyes of the serpent with the chance of being

[20] Karl Barth, *Nein! Theol. Ex. heute* (Munich, 1934), p. 8.
[21] *Op. cit.*, p. 12.

hypnotized and bitten by it. Instead, when he sees the serpent he immediately takes a stick and beats it to death . . . If he takes an interest in this matter, even for the sake of rejecting it, he is no longer involved in theological matters." [22]

Not only is it impossible for man to find a way to God on his own and to make God, as it were, accessible to him, man is also incapable of understanding God's word in scripture, and, as it were, appropriating God's revelation: "To become hearers and doers of the word of God is to realize a divine possibility, not a possibility inherent in our being-human." [23]

Anyone who thinks he has by his own power and in his own way found God and faith in God is a victim of an illusion. On the other hand, a person who thinks he has tried in vain to find God and belief in God by all sorts of ways can arrive at faith in God only when he allows himself to be recalled from those ways by God's word in scripture, because none of those ways lead to God; thus they must necessarily lead to unbelief if they are consistently followed to the end: "All consolation, all power, all truth of God's being-revealed lies in this, that it is God with whom we are dealing in this being-revealed." [24] "How can man ever and in any way know of himself that which is to be known here?" [25]

The question of God therefore refers us to revelation. Not to that which man of his own authority considers to be revelation, but to the only real revelation which proceeds from God and which cannot be acknowledged and accepted in philosophy or science, in the faith which the Holy Spirit brings about in man through the word.[26]

## Revelation and Faith in Barth's Theology

Revelation is a work, an action of God in which God reveals himself, makes himself known in his relation to man without surrendering his hidden and inscrutable being. God's revealing

[22] *Op. cit.*, p. 13.
[23] *Op. cit.*, p. 52.
[24] *Loc. cit.*
[25] *Op. cit.*, p. 53.
[26] Cf. also Vol. 9, *Theol. Ex. heute: Barth, Offenbarung, Kirche, Theologie* (1934).

action is at one and the same time an unveiling and a veiling. God is and remains the subject of his revealing action. He never becomes the object of man's knowledge of God. It is impossible to distinguish revelation as the action of God from a so-called content of revelation which would contain, independently of God's revealing action, the result of this action. There is no source in which the content of God's revelation is stored and from which it could be drawn without connecting it to God's action.

Man cannot place himself face to face with God in order to appropriate God's revelation to himself and from then on have it at his disposal. Even if the knowledge of God obtained from revelation has the character of a faith-knowledge, this is not to be understood in the sense that it is God who reveals himself and that it is man who believes, as if man were the object of revelation and God the object of faith. God is and remains subject in revelation as well as in faith, while man is the object in both.

It is not as a result of God's revealing action that an I-thou relationship arises in the sense in which Martin Buber would have it. God is the only one who acts, even in man's believing. In man's believing, God's revealing action reaches the goal it is aimed at. In the revealing action which reaches man, God leads man to the act of faith. Even the act of faith is an action of God. The act of faith is not the achievement of man by which he appropriates God to himself, knows God as an object, and in that knowledge disposes, as it were, of God.

For Barth the complete exclusivity of God is all important. Without this exclusivity belief in God would again be based on something in man, and thus belief in God would once more be deprived of the certainty of faith. The conviction of exclusivity dominates Barth's dogmatics from beginning to end; without a correct understanding of it there is no possibility of understanding Barth's theology. Because of the principle of exclusivity in Barth's theology not only the act of faith but also the bible, the Church, and the confession of faith have a new meaning and significance, entirely foreign to conventional Christianity.

God's revealing action takes place in Jesus Christ. Jesus Christ *is* God's action of revealing to man. God's word witnesses to Jesus Christ. It is echoed in sacred scripture and is proclaimed within the space of the Church. The Church is where God's word reverberates and where it finds a hearing through the action of the Holy Spirit in man's believing. As a result of his believing, man is placed within the space of the Church, accepted into the people of God. Baptism and the supper visibly signify and ratify his acceptance.

The converse is not true. A person is not accepted into a clearly visible Church by baptism as if he could say: "From now on I belong to the Church." Nor is the Church a definite ecclesiastical organization which dispenses the faith, hands it out as an objectively given thing with certain dimensions and content. Faith is not quantitative. It cannot be fixed once and for all in ecclesiastical pronouncements or bundled together in a confession or catechism. Faith cannot be conserved and carefully stored. Nor is it possible to live by an implicit faith.

Ecclesiastical pronouncements, fixed in a confession and in an official catechism, are at most warnings, beacons in the sea, originating in some critical period when it was necessary to state what really matters in believing. Such pronouncements must be constantly tested against the direct and living word of God. They definitely must not take the place of God's word. Nor do they guarantee that the Church which "possesses" them always is and remains the "true Church." Church is where God's word is proclaimed and believed. The converse, therefore, that God's word is proclaimed and believed in a certain Church to the exclusion of other Churches, is not true. This would replace God's exclusive revealing action by the action of an ecclesiastical institution.

"Church" can exist where it is least expected; and where on the basis of certain "possessions" the Church pretends to be the "true Church" it is possible that "being-Church" is absent. The expression "within the space of the Church" therefore does not mean, for Barth, that it is in the space of a certain Church community or a certain church building. Church is where God speaks. God's word is in no way bound to a Church, to a confession, or to a catechism.

Believing in God is an action of God in man. It has a highly dialectic and dynamic character. It is an event that is always new, an event in which God continues to speak anew to man as often as he is confronted with God's word, with Jesus Christ. Hearing and believing God's word means being placed within the space of the Church, the people of God. Church as people of God is diametrically opposed to Church as institution. In the Church as people of God, God remains subject, even in man's believing. In the Church as institution, the Church is subject, and God is made into the object of the Church's speaking and acting.

With a view to all that has been said in this book concerning the question of God, it must again be emphasized that for Barth the bible places man before a definite and all-determining decision: either man must exclusively count on God's revealing action and hence reject any self-constructed opinion about God, or he must hold onto his own human insight and self-constructed thought and language about God, thus necessarily remaining in uncertainty, if not in open disbelief.

A real and living faith in God rests exclusively on God's revealing action, on an ever new confrontation with the word of God, with Jesus Christ. God always has the final word. Man does not judge about God, about his existence or non-existence, about his being this way or that. Such a judgment is not man's domain. It is God who judges about man and who frees man in faith, accepts him unconditionally as he is as man; and he does this for every man individually, whoever he may be.

For this reason believing is submitting unconditionally to the judgment which God makes in the word about man. Here too real self-knowledge lies. Man learns to know and understand himself neither by a philosophical analysis of human existence nor by psychology, but only by submitting to the judgment of God's Word. Thus man knows what it means to be man.

The Word of God alone, incarnated in the God-man Jesus Christ, says who God is, and decides who man is. All human objections and all certitudes devised by man no longer have place in believing. A person who really believes in God—who takes God at his Word—foregoes any self-willed language about God. He realizes that it is for God to speak, and not for man. Only God's Word gives him freedom to speak about God. The idea that anyone is obviously free to think and speak about God as he likes is human conceit; it rests on an illusion, and basically it is unbelief. Man's language about God may never be anything other than an answer to the question of God, a witnessing of God's speaking to man. Barth emphasizes here that this is not a matter of supposedly divine inspirations.

God's speaking is an action, an event strictly identical with Jesus Christ. He is God's Word, and God's Word is Jesus Christ. The bible is the book which in the Old as well as the New Testament witnesses to Jesus Christ. The prophets, evangelists, and apostles witness to him. To this extent their witness is also God's word. But it must be distinguished from God's Word in the real sense, because it is God's word in the form of a human word. We "possess" this Word in the form of the written word. The oral proclamation of the present Church witnesses to this Word.

Jesus Christ is the revealed Word of God, the bible is the written word of God, the Church in its language and action is the proclaimed word of God. Proclamation is the real commission given by Jesus Christ to the Church. In its language the Church is aware of its humanity and its responsibility: "She is aware of her exposure to fierce temptation in speaking of God, aware also that she has to account to God for her speaking." [27] The criterion of the proclaimed word is the written word. But both point to Jesus Christ. Jesus Christ is the objective reality of revelation. He is the Word of God's revelation before us. But it must become subjective revelation; the Word of God must become revelation in us. This subjective reality of revelation is the Holy Spirit.

It is obviously impossible within the scope of this chapter to give even an impression of all that Barth has to say in the hundreds of pages of his *Church Dogmatics*. This great work intends to be nothing but a continuous reference to Jesus Christ as "God in his revealing action to man." The only criterion which Barth wants to apply, rejecting any self-opinionated speaking about God, is the criterion of the word written in the bible and proclaimed in the Church. This is the only criterion on earth which decides whether human thought and language about God are legitimate and true.

If it were true that Barth's vision of faith concerning God's revealing action in Jesus Christ, concerning God's Word, concerning the bible and the Church, and concerning the one and only way to genuine belief in God, does not rest on an illusion but only on reality, then not only does he give the answer to the question of God, but also any human thought and language about God which would be in contrast with his vision stands condemned.

27 *K. D.,* I¹, p. 1.

## A Precarious Dilemma

Those engaged in theology and in the science of religion have been presented with a precarious dilemma by Barth. If the answer to the question of God which Barth indicates is the correct and right answer, then it must be absolutely the only answer. But that would rob all other answers of any sense and any future. If a person thinks one or more of these other ways to be appropriate and effective, he thereby makes it clear that he is convinced that Barth's vision rests on illusion. We are here faced with an inevitable choice, because it is *per se* impossible that the viewpoint Barth finds he must adopt—on the basis of the testimony of bible and Church with regard to God and man—might possibly be reconciled with any other viewpoint. It is exclusive. All other viewpoints and possibilities are necessarily excluded. This is not so because Barth knows it better than anyone else, but because Barth is convinced that it is the sole criterion based not on human insight but on God's own Word. Barth points from himself to Jesus Christ and to the written and proclaimed word of bible and Church.

However, an increasing number of theologians is asking whether and in how far Barth has actually understood this written and proclaimed word as it seeks to be understood. Barth himself regards this question as an illegitimate one. He will answer: God's Word gives you the answer. Everyone who hears it and submits to it knows that there is but one answer to the question of God. I do not ask you to affirm this on my own authority. But I do adjure you to affirm this on God's authority, on the authority of God's Word, Jesus Christ. Barth placed all those faced with the question of God before a choice which cannot be taken lightly.

## Barth's Exclusivism

The phenomenologist faces an extremely difficult problem here. He does not have a single method to determine how the choice should be made. It is not a matter of philosophical or scientific decision. It is a matter of a decision of faith. As a believer, the phenomenologist can, as any other believer, either decide for or against. He could decide against, for in all Christian

Churches there are numerous believers who, precisely on the basis of their faith-conviction concerning bible and the Church, refuse to accept Barth's interpretation of the bible, revelation, and the Christian faith. But a scientist cannot decide on this criterion. As a scientist, the phenomenologist can do no more than ascertain that there is apparently a conflict of faith solved by different Christians in different manners.

If Barth were asked about the basis of his decision of faith he would reply that there is no other basis than revelation itself and the testimony of the Holy Spirit which leads the believer to acknowledge revelation to be revelation: "According to sacred scripture, God's revelation is a ground which has no sort of higher or deeper ground above or behind it; it is simply a ground in itself, and therefore as regards man it is an authority from which no appeal to a higher authority is possible . . . God's revelation has its reality and truth wholly and in every respect—ontically and noetically—within itself." [28]

If the question were asked how man can know with certainty that what he thinks he has to acknowledge and accept as revelation from God really *is* God's revelation, Barth answers: "The Spirit guarantees man what the latter cannot guarantee himself, his personal participation in revelation. The act of the Holy Spirit in revelation is the 'Yes' to God's Word, spoken through God himself on our behalf, not only *to* us, but *in* us. This 'yes' spoken by God is the ground of the confidence with which a man may regard the revelation as meant for him. This 'yes' is the mystery of faith, the mystery of knowledge of the Word of God; it is also the mystery of willing obedience, well-pleasing to God. All of it exists for man 'in the Holy Spirit,' to wit—faith, knowledge, obedience." [29] This has nothing to do with sensible emotions or with religious experience. This is a matter of a certainty of faith which is certain of itself because God grants this certainty and works it through the Holy Spirit. Both the believer and the non-believer have nothing more to say here. For just as the believer is unable to prove on natural grounds that his faith is based on reality, so too the non-believer is unable to prove that the faith of the believer is based on an illusion.

[28] *Op. cit.*, p. 321.
[29] *Op. cit.*, p. 475.

An extensive treatment of Barth's concept of revelation can be found in the second part of the first volume of *Church Dogmatics*. Apart from some changed opinions in minor respects, Barth remained true in principle to his vision of the question of faith. This is clear from the various volumes of *Church Dogmatics* which appeared up to 1959, as also from his *Introduction to Evangelical Theology* which appeared in 1962.[30]

In particular, in the second part of volume three of *Church Dogmatics*, which deals with anthropology and which appeared in 1948, Barth retains his conviction—which according to him is based on scripture—that man in his present state can by himself know neither himself nor God. All human sciences together are not able to uncover man to himself. If there is something characteristic of human existence, of the human predicament, then it is that man is only a shadow of the real being-human and that he knows no more than a shadow image of himself. Real man exists and is known only in Jesus Christ, and in the belief in him. Man knows himself only in the light of God's Word. Even the world, the cosmos itself is known to man only if he sees it in the light of God's Word. "There is no scientific world-view. On the contrary, it must essentially renounce all such interpretation. A misunderstanding is always involved when its exponents think they can present the sum of the hypotheses which temporarily mark the bounds of their knowledge as a world-view, as 'the view of exact science,' and when theologians in anxious dismay think they must regard this view as an interpretation of reality always entitled to respect." [31] In other words, theologians concerned with the so-called world-view of natural science evidently do not realize that the real world-view becomes revealed only in God's Word.

This applies *a fortiori* to man. The view of man which the anthropological sciences have yielded and about which some theologians are concerned is not the view of real man. This holds true for the views of both philosophy and science. They really say nothing about real man. They arise "in the dead corner in

---

[30] Karl Barth, *Einführung in die evangelische Theologie* (EVZ. Verlag, Zurich, 1962). English text: *Evangelical Theology: An Introduction*, trans. by Grover Foley, (Holt, Rinehart and Winston), New York, 1963.
[31] *K. D.* III², p. 12.

which man has not yet heard the Word of God or no longer
hears it." [32] "Exact science does not touch upon his reality; it
would therefore be foolish to claim being able to ground, explain,
and describe it." [33]

Self-knowledge is strictly impossible for man except in the
faith which uncovers man to himself in the light of God's Word:
"The man who is not taught by God will never admit that he
cannot teach himself; he will much rather suppose that he is very
capable of self-knowledge, and in so doing will betray the fact
that he is not taught by God. But he who has learned from God
that he is incapable of knowing himself will not refuse to accept
and recognize the positive divine knowledge imparted to him
over and above this." [34]

"Just as certainly as we know nothing of ourselves either about
God or about ourselves, just as certainly do we know who God is
for man, who real man is and how the real relationship is between
God and man; and this is known exclusively by the revealed
Word of God." [35] What God's Word says about real man is the
content of Barth's anthropology. It is impossible to go into this in
detail. But it is clear that Barth remained true to his basic principles in his anthropology.

This applies also to the fourth volume of his *Church Dogmatics*
which deals with the doctrine of reconciliation. The second of
three parts contains the doctrine of sin. One of the numerous
forms in which sin reveals itself is the flight into religiosity.
God's word makes it clear that man as sinner simply refuses to
acknowledge and accept the reality, the presence, and the activity of God in the existence of the man Jesus, He takes refuge in
religion: "Precisely as one who worships a higher being, precisely
as a religious or a pious man, he is able to reject precisely this. It
does not matter what name or form he gives to the higher being
which he worships; he finds that he is tolerated by it, not questioned, not disturbed, not seized." [36] Man wants to be in the
right. But in Jesus Christ man is shown to be in the wrong; only
God is in the right. For that reason Jesus Christ is the great
stumbling-block at which every man is scandalized by nature,

[32] *Op. cit.*, p. 24.
[33] *Op. cit.*, p. 26.
[34] *Op. cit.*, p. 45.
[35] *Loc. cit.*
[36] *K. D.* IV², p. 457.

unless in God's power he surrenders to the word of God. The stupidity of the man who chooses to go his own way without God's revelation is shown in this passage: "Whether great or small, every confidence or trust or self-reliance on what we can, and think we must, say to ourselves when we reason apart from the word of God is stupid. It is stupidity to take an attitude in which we think we can authoritatively tell ourselves what is true and good and beautiful, what is right and necessary and salutary. All thought and speech and actions which we think we can and should base on this information is stupid . . . Where an uncontrolled truth or rule, however clear, possesses man or men in the manner in which they ought to permit themselves to be governed by his living Word, only in knowledge of God himself, there we certainly have to do with a revelation, and in principle even with the whole Revelation-economy of stupidity." [37]

It really is necessary to read the whole lengthy characterization of human stupidity to become fully convinced that there is no truth whatever in the superficial opinion of some people that Barth retracted his initial exclusivism. For Barth, there is no knowledge about God, man, and world, which reflects the real situation as it is, and there is no true belief in God except on the basis of God's revealing action and in the light of God's word.

## What Is a Believer?

In proof of this we think we should briefly mention the answer which Barth gives in his *Introduction to Evangelical Theology* to the question of what it means to "believe." Only the man who is truly, personally, and in existential commitment a believer is able to be an evangelical theologian. Hence the question: when can it rightly be said that a person is a believer?

To be a *believer* means to be a man who has been overwhelmed by faith and who from then on is capable only of believing. Believing is not the fruit of some particular exercise of the mind. It cannot be learned. It overwhelms the man who is confronted with the word of God, who acknowledges God's revealing action in it, and who also acknowledges that this action of God in Jesus Christ is directed to him personally, that it so concerns and touches him that he cannot or may not withdraw himself from it.

[37] *Op. cit.*, p. 464.

This acknowledgment is itself a fruit of God's revealing action. To receive the faith is an entirely unique event in the life of man. It is an encounter between God and man in Jesus Christ by means of the word of God—the Gospel word as it directly addresses man from the bible. God's language and action cannot leave the man who is overwhelmed by it, indifferent. It seizes him, changes him, and appropriates him. It causes a radical reversal in his human existence. It arouses wonder, surprise, and duty. These are the characteristics of a believing existence and of what Barth therefore calls a theological existence. The chapter by that title ends with a delineation of true faith.

Believing is not a weaker form of knowing as if one said: "I am not sure, but I can 'believe' it." Rather, believing is the only knowing of which man can and may be absolutely certain.

Nor is believing something one can do on the authority of another, even if this other were the Church. No human authority has the right to demand faith of a man. At best, human authority can point to the authority of God's word. It is even below man's dignity when, in laying down what are called "truths of faith," human authority demands a sacrifice of intellect from the "believer," when it demands, for instance, that he set aside his powers of intellect. Barth vehemently rejects the notion of an "implicit" faith which one holds on the authority of the Church, possibly without knowing its content: "Such implicit faith and its execution certainly looks like unbelief instead of belief. Surely an 'implicit faith' is a base concept of a base business which should never have been embellished by the name 'faith.' This is like a house of cards which no Christian and no theologian should ever be advised to inhabit." [38]

However this is not the most serious thing that can happen in the realm of false belief. In scholasticism the horrible expression was even used of a *fides creatrix divinitatis in nobis,* a faith that supposedly could divinize man so that from his own divinized disposition he would have the capacity or power to believe in God all by himself. Something like this, says Barth, could be expected of a Hindu but not of a Christian. Faith is not a divine power within us. It is an action of God which comes about in the encounter with God by way of the word that witnesses to him.

[38] *Einf.i/d. Ev. Theol.* p. 110.

Finally, believing does not mean "to believe in a faith"—for example in the faith of the parents, educators, or Church, or one's own faith based on rational or other human grounds—"as if man should believe and confess to believe in the faith of the Church expressing itself in lofty words, or ultimately in his own faith, instead of believing and confessing God the Father, the Son, and the Holy Spirit." [39]

In such a case the relationship of faith is an impersonal matter, a "believing" of "something about God." Faith in the biblical sense of the word is not an objective but a personal matter. It is the Living God who calls and man who responds. It is a relationship of faith brought about by God himself—and not my or your faith, not the Catholic, the Lutheran, the Reformed faith as something independent of believing.

Believing is nothing but a conscious affirming, trusting, obeying, brought about in man through the living power of the Spirit who functions in and through the word of God. Any other so-called "believing in God" has nothing to do with real belief in God for which only God can give man the freedom. Any other believing rests on an illusion; only *this* believing is based on reality, the reality of God's speaking and acting. Hence yet another, final formulation of what Barth considers believing: "In the coming to pass of believing what happens is that the Word of God, in the power of the Spirit who lives in him alone (and thus in the sovereignty proper to him alone), liberates one man among many to affirm this Word as indisputably valid, to place his whole joyful trust in the Word, as God's self-expression of his love, speaks to him, and to become unconditionally obedient to him. No one can do this by himself. A person does this only inasmuch as he is overwhelmed by the powerful Word of God, and, newly created, is aroused to such action." [40] To the very end Barth remained true to himself because he wished to do nothing else than be true only to God's Word.

For a lengthy and basic consideration of the question of God by a person who himself belongs to the "school" of Barth I might refer the reader to Helmut Gollwitzer's book *The Existence of God in the Confession of Faith.*

[39] *Op. cit.*, p. 111.
[40] *Op. cit.*, p. 112.

*Helmut Gollwitzer*

In Gollwitzer too it is a question of either/or. Either a faith in
God which rests on some human activity (on an analysis of being-
human, on religious experience, on reasoning), or a faith which
rests on God's action. In the first case, man believes in a God of
his own making, ultimately in himself; in the second case he
believes in the living God, and in this belief he has a real relationship with God. In the first case his faith is based on human
grounds, in the second it is based on God himself. In the first case
the object-subject relationship is cancelled out. God is a manner
in which being-human is interpreted, not a God of action who
confronts man as the real God, who concerns himself with man
and who makes man to be fully man by addressing him and
moving him to faith and obedience.[41] "God's speaking in the
biblical sense can be understood adequately only when one constantly remembers that it is speaking on the basis of permission
and promise, and on the basis of God's condescending. Here, the
word 'undergoing' (and not the dangerous word 'experiencing')
is in place. Biblical speaking is strictly response—response to previous concrete and contingent 'undergoing' of the one who is
addressed, a response in which the God who calls is acknowledged in this 'undergoing' as he who is." [42]

It is clear that for Gollwitzer as well as for Barth everything
centers on two ideas: "coming-to-pass" and "undergoing": revelation and faith. God is the subject of both; it proceeds from
God; God brings it about, both in his revelation (as coming-to-
pass), and in faith (as undergoing). The bible testifies to both
and the one who really believes in God testifies to both. For the
man who really believes in God, any faith in God based on
anything else is merely an illusion. Or could it possibly be that
the witness to the coming-to-pass and the undergoing is based on
an illusion? It is basically with these two mutually exclusive possibilities that the present theological discussion regarding the
question of God is concerned. Or again, could it be that Tillich is

---

[41] Helmut Gollwitzer, *Die Existenz Gottes im Bekenntnis des Glaubens*
(*Kaiser Verlag, Munich*, 1964), p. 37. English text: *The Existence of God in
the Confession of Faith*, tr. James W. Leitch (Westminster Press, Philadelphia, 1965).
[42] *Op. cit.*, p. 111.

correct when he thinks that there is a third possibility in which the two other possibilities are partly based on illusion and partly on reality?

## Faith and Illusion

Whatever the answer, the present discussion with regard to the question of God is ultimately concerned with the answer to the question of illusion or reality. In this connection, Werner Schilling's book *Faith and Illusion* could be called the counterpart of Gollwitzer's book.

Schilling also occupies himself with the question about a tenable and acceptable foundation of the evangelical faith, about a foundation which is firm because it is based on reality and not on illusion. The present theological situation is, according to Schilling, one of great perplexity. Neither Barth nor the Church has been able to save theology from this situation. This is because Barth's foundation of faith is still somewhat in the air.

According to Schilling the positive significance of Barth's theology lies in the fact that theological discussion and teaching has forcefully and very seriously drawn the attention to God himself, to revelation and Church, and not only to a description of religious consciousness. But according to Schilling the price which Barth had to pay was too high: "There are really no personal grounds for the faith, for is God not also the subject of hearing, besides being the subject of speaking? Faith is taken from the human soul, just as an event is taken from history. Added to this there is also a strong emphasis on the possibility of questioning human existence and the notion of God's judgment. Radical criticism of culture is one of the consequences. Any divine revelation and divine intervention apart from Christ is denied. This in turn results in the necessity of condemning all extra-Christian religions and any belief in a general testimony of himself which God gives in nature, in the life of man and in history. In the long run this leads to a presentation of Christianity as essentially a kind of remedy against all 'religion' which cannot be satisfactorily judged." [43]

[43] Werner Schilling, *Glaube und Illusion, Von gegenwärtiger Theologie und evangelischer Glaubensbegründung* (Ev. Presse, Munich, 1960), p. 24.

It is clear that Schilling not only considers the price too high but that he finds the consequences of Barth's theology absurd and that he is greatly scandalized by them. According to Barth, however, this is the scandal which Jesus spoke of when he said "Happy the man who is not scandalized in me" (Mt. 11, 6). The Gospel contradicts so strongly everything that man by himself had ever imagined about God and himself that it necessarily evokes resistance on the part of man. Believing, according to Barth, occurs precisely when man abandons his resistance to God's word and submits unconditionally (no matter how absurd it may seem) to the judgment of God's word about the human existence and situation.

Therefore the question that counts is not whether we humans think the price too high. The question is whether Barth's interpretation of the bible, and his theological interpretation of God's word coincide with the meaning of the bible. Quite apart from the consequences of Barth's theological viewpoint, and quite apart from prejudiced opinions from others, exegetes should ask themselves whether God's word in sacred scripture says in fact what Barth hears. This exegetical decision must be based not on a preconstructed philosophy of culture and religion but on a complete readiness to allow the bible to say what it wishes to say.

If the bible is not a human word but the full reality of God's word, then a legitimate exegetical decision can be made only in obedience to God's word; in that case an exegetical decision is also a decision of faith. Then it would be unbelief and disobedience to ask whether submission to God's word may have absurd consequences for our beloved opinions about God and religion and about man and culture. Therefore it is not Barth who holds "absurd" opinions. Supposing that Barth's theology leads to absurd consequences; this—Barth would say—is not Barth's fault; it must be attributed to the judgment which God lays down in his word.

Despite Barth's negative criticism of Bultmann,[44] both agree that neither of them will have anything to do with human certainty as the basis of faith. Bultmann is convinced of the *autopisteia* of God's word—or, as Bultmann calls it, the *kerygma*. The

---

[44] Karl Barth, *Rudolf Bultmann, Ein Versuch ihn zu verstehen*, Theologische Studien, Vol. 34 (EVZ Verlag, Zurich, 1952). English text: *Rudolf Bultmann, An Attempt to Understand Him*, in *Kerygma and Myth* Vol. II (S.P.C.K. London, 1962), pp. 83-132.

force of conviction lies in the message itself, and whoever has heard and understood it will no longer ask for human certainty. Bultmann even calls this an application of the teaching of "justification by faith alone" to the knowledge of God. Knowledge of God also comes about only by faith. What many find rather peculiar in Bultmann's vision is that the "by-faith-alone" idea leads Bultmann to derive the demand to demythologize the message as radically as possible in behalf of the people of our time. This demythologization is for him a demand which is not only not contrary to faith, but is contained in it: "Quite like the doctrine of justification, radical demythologization destroys any false certainty and any false desire for certainty on the part of man, whether the certainty is based on his good deeds or on his ascertaining apprehension. The man who wants to believe in God as his God, must know that he has absolutely nothing on which he can base his faith, that he is, as it were, suspended in air, unable to expect a proof of the truth of the Word which speaks to him. For the basis and the object of the faith are identical. Only he who discards all certainty will find it; only he who is prepared to enter into complete darkness." [45] On this point therefore Bultmann stands in principle on the side of Barth and not on that of Schilling.

Of course it is not my intention to protect Barth against Schilling. Certainly he does not need it. My intention is to present as clearly as possibly the problems dealing with the question of God, which has become painful or at least obscure for so many people.

The testimony which, according to Barth, is based on the bible, on God's own word, is too serious, too important, and has consequences that are so far-reaching that an unprejudiced person cannot simply bypass it. Supposing that Barth's much criticized exclusivity was indeed based on God's word, then the answer to the question about God would have been given once and for all, and any other position would be without a future, no matter how "scandalous" this may sound to "natural" man, to man as sinner. Therefore the first question is whether Barth's interpretation of the bible, in the light of the bible itself, is plausible, tenable, and acceptable.

Even if this question were answered in the affirmative, we

[45] *Kerygma und Mythos* (Reich, Hamburg 1952), Vol. 2, p. 207.

still would not be at the end of our questions. On the contrary, the real questions are then only beginning. For then Schilling's objections against Barth are, in the mind of modern man, directed against the bible itself. How can modern man know with certainty that the word of the prophets, evangelists, and apostles is not ultimately a purely human word, however seriously intended? Barth will answer that God himself gives this certainty. Of this he is quite convinced. But could not this conviction also be an illusion?

How is it that thousands of people seriously study the bible, hoping to find answers to their vital questions? how is it that thousands, filled with the desire for salvation, listen to the Church proclamation without hearing the bible say what Barth hears in it? How is it that, for example, Buber, who knows the bible so well, believes in God but not in Jesus as the incarnate Word of God? What is the cause of all this? How is it, furthermore, that the biblical witness is interpreted in such totally different ways in the proclamation of different Churches? How is it that so many are completely unable to discover that it is really God, not man, who speaks through the bible?

Certainly it is not Barth's intention that this last question should be answered on his authority. But in view of the fact that there are many serious objections to Barth's exclusivist viewpoint, where shall we find a norm by which it can be decided whether and in how far Barth's theological testimony is based on reality or illusion?

If we consider what has been happening during the past ten or twenty years in the Christian Churches and in theological reflection, it will become clear that the theological pendulum which had swung to one extreme in the person of Barth is now beginning to proceed in the reverse direction. A reaction against Barth's exclusivism is being felt. It seems that theology is moving in a circle.

Barth's reaction to all nineteenth century theology has turned into a call for the return of Schleiermacher, for religious experience, for mysticism. But there is also a call for an entirely new inquiry into the origin of bible and Christianity. The linguistic and historical bible and dogma research is opening up entirely new ways. An effort is being made to put the bible into new words so that it will be heard in our present secularized world.

An effort is also being made to arrive at an entirely new theology which proceeds from the achievements of philosophy and science of modern times, and which is to that extent a new natural theology. Against this background men are asking about the possibility and eventual reality of revelation on the part of God. Even a theological rejection of any notion of revelation is beginning to rise.

We shall have to examine all of this in the chapters that follow. Before doing this, however, we shall first have to devote a chapter to the manner in which Paul Tillich asked, approached, and answered the question of God. It is not yet clear whether and in how far existential thought is a final phase or a new beginning. Is existential philosophy dead or alive? Is there a reverse side of existentialism? [46] Does Tillich, together with Barth and Bultmann, stand at the end of a theological phase, or is it possible to discover—at least in Tillich—symptoms of a new course toward a more satisfactory solution to the question of God?

At any rate, Paul Tillich was undoubtedly the most influential theologian of the past twenty-five years in the United States. Interest in his thought is only beginning in Germany. For that reason he has an important place in the current of thought with which this book deals. The next chapter will treat of Paul Tillich, and in particular of what he himself calls the correlation between human existence and divine revelation, between philosophy and theology. Tillich is convinced that his method of correlation "explains the contents of the Christian faith through existential questions and theological answers in mutual interdependence." [47]

[46] Fritz Heinemann, *Existenz-Philosophie lebendig oder tot?* (Kohlhammer, Stuttgart, 1954) Jenseits des Existentialismus, id. 1957. English text: *Existentialism and the Modern Predicament* (Harper & Bros., N.Y., 1958).
[47] Paul Tillich, *Systematic Theology*, I (Nisbet, London, 1953), p. 68.

# 8. Existence and Revelation

Paul Tillich was born in 1886 in a German village not far from the Polish border where his father was a Lutheran preacher. Together with Barth, Brunner, and Bultmann, he belongs to a generation of truly great theologians who for almost half a century gave direction to the new theological thought in the realm of world Protestantism.

In 1900 he moved to Berlin where he became a student of theology in 1904. After Berlin he also studied in Tübingen and Halle. From the very first his principal interest lay in the boundary area between theology and philosophy. Both his dissertation for a doctorate in philosophy in 1910 and for his licentiate in theology in 1912 dealt with Schelling's philosophy of religion.[1]

Ordained a Lutheran preacher in 1912, he served as a chaplain for the armed forces during the First World War. Immediately after the war Tillich settled as private tutor in the new branch of the theology of culture at the University of Berlin. For five years he gave lectures dealing with the relation between religion and the fields of politics, art, philosophy, psychoanalysis, and sociology. He saw his task to be one of apologetics. It was his intention to show scientifically that there was place in the rising modern society for a Christian conviction of faith and for a Christian attitude.

Until his death early in 1966, Tillich put his scientific labor at the service of a practical goal. He pointed out very clearly the rapid and profound changes which were taking place in the life of thought and in the life of mankind. He understood well that the age-old conventional forms of Christianity had seen their day. After the publication in 1926 of his book *The Present Religious*

[1] Paul Tillich, *Die religionsgeschichtliche Konstruktion in Schellings positiver Theologie* (Breslau, 1910), and *Mystik und Schuldbewusstzein in Schellings philosophischer Entwicklung* (Halle, 1912).

*Situation*,[2] he closely followed the religious situation and wondered how the Church and individual Christians should answer the increasing number of hitherto unknown questions and difficulties which confront the Christian of today. No ostrich policy and shortsighted defense of conventional opinions can save the religious situation. This can be done only by radically clearing away what has become antiquated and by courageously trying to renew Christianity in all its expressions.

In 1924 Tillich was appointed professor at the theological faculty of Marburg, where he came in contact with Heidegger and Bultmann. With Bultmann he felt the influence of Heidegger's existential thought, although he was able to assimilate this influence into his own thought in his own way. In 1928 he accepted an appointment as professor of philosophy of religion and social philosophy in Dresden. As early as 1933 his religio-socialist views brought him into conflict with Hitler, and he moved with his family to America. This brought an end to his German stage of life and to the long series of his German publications.

In many respects his move to America meant a new beginning. From his autobiographical notes, which are spread over various publications, the religious situation in America captivated him. It never resulted in disappointment and trouble but was always a refreshing stimulus to new thought, discussion, and work. Tillich never regretted his transition from the intellectual climate of Germany to that of America. He was able to establish such a successful synthesis between his German and his American stage of life that since the second world war he was generally acknowledged as the most influential theologian in America.

In America he was received by Reinhold Niebuhr, who later also made an unsuccessful attempt to bring Dietrich Bonhoeffer to safety in the United States. In 1933 Tillich was appointed professor of philosophical theology at the Union Theological Seminary in New York. After his retirement at the age of seventy, he continued to give regular courses at Harvard University, the University of California in Santa Barbara, and the University of Chicago. A person who would like to meet Tillich as a profes-

[2] Paul Tillich, *Die religiöse Lage der Gegenwart* (Ullstein, Leipzig, 1926). Cf. also Karl Jaspers' book, which appeared at about the same time: *Die geistige Situation der Zeit* (Sammlung Göschen, Berlin 1931) No. 1000.

sor in action should read the report of a seminar given in Santa Barbara, which was published under the title of *Ultimate Concern: Tillich in Dialogue*.[3]

Although Lutheranism is strongly represented in some areas of the United States, the general undertone of American Protestantism is remarkably puritan-Calvinist. This fact made it necessary for Tillich to reorientate himself in presenting and solving problems. The aesthetic-contemplative mysticism of nature which had always attracted Tillich did not fit into the businesslike, technological climate of America. For Americans, historical reality consists of facts which may be seen as having some mutual connection, but it generally escapes them that historical reality is a living and growing whole. Concerning his students, Tillich observes: "Many of the students here had an excellent knowledge of historical facts, but these facts did not seem to concern them profoundly. They remained objects of their intellect and almost never became the elements of their existence." [1]

This last observation is of importance for an understanding of Tillich. Just as there is a physical reality, so too is there a historical reality. In both it is a matter of living, developing reality of which man is part and in which man is vitally involved. One of the facets of historical reality is Christianity as a religion. This reality is subject to numerous influences, as we have seen in the preceding chapters, and is subject to continuous change in which man himself, too, even as a religious person, is involved. Precisely in a time such as ours, many rusty convictions can suddenly become meaningless and untenable. Man, being involved in nature and history, is a changing person, not least in religious respect. Nothing is so dangerous for the position of a Christian, of the Church, and of Christianity, as a static religion in which being a believer is equated with a stubborn conservatism. The Christian must be constantly prepared for new syntheses between faith and the environment of faith: "The way of synthesis was my own way . . . it has found its final form in my *Systematic Theology*." [5] In this respect Tillich was diametrically opposed to

[3] Mackenzie Brown (ed.), *Ultimate Concern: Tillich in Dialogue* (Harper & Row, N.Y. 1965).

[4] Tillich's autobiographical introduction, in Kegley-Bretall, *The Theology of Paul Tillich* (Macmillan, New York, 1952, paperback ed. 1961), p. 5.

[5] *Op. cit.*, p. 10.

Barth. The reflection and the proclamation of the Christian faith must, according to Tillich, be engaged in an uninterrupted dialogue with the changed world where the Christian finds himself. This costs time and necessitates a repeated change of approach.

This explains why the main work of Tillich, his *Systematic Theology*, comprises only three modest volumes which took him forty years to compose. The first part had its origin in the 1925 Marburg lectures but was constantly revised in connection with lectures given since that time in Germany and the United States. It appeared only in 1951. It may serve as a caution to many who are ready to hand out premature and self-satisfied criticism of Tillich to hear that Tillich studied and reflected for a period of twenty-five years before he undertook the publication of the first volume: "The smallest problem, if taken seriously and radically, drove me to all other problems and to the anticipation of a whole in which they could find their solution." [6] This simple sentence typifies the manner in which Tillich looked upon his life's work and the sense of responsibility and seriousness with which he was able to complete it prior to his death. The second part appeared in 1956, and the third part was published in 1963. Elsewhere, Tillich has this to say about the gradual construction of his book: "In Marburg, in 1925, I began work on my *Systematic Theology*, the first volume of which appeared in 1951. At the same time that Heidegger was in Marburg as professor of philosophy influencing some of the best students, existentialism in its twentieth-century form crossed my path. It took years before I became fully aware of the impact of this encounter on my own thinking. I resisted, I tried to learn, I accepted the new way of thinking more than the answers it gave." [7]

This "new way of thinking" which is usually referred to as the existentialist way of thinking, Tillich made his own to the very end. Among other things it is a way of thinking that never ties itself down, that remains open to new discoveries. Actually this way of thinking is not particularly suited for the construction of a system. Apart from his *Systematic Theology*, therefore, Tillich's writings, like those of Heidegger, came about as a result of problems which arose from life and from contact with people. Most of Tillich's writings are collections of lectures and essays

[6] Paul Tillich, *Systematic Theology* (Nisbet, London), Preface, p. ix.
[7] Kegley-Bretall, *op. cit.*, p. 14.

which for Tillich were new insights into the human situation in general and into the religious situation in particular.

It is interesting to note a recent judgment of Karl Barth about Tillich's *Systematic Theology:* "Humanly speaking, no Swiss theologian will ever create a work of the same high standard as that of Paul Tillich's *Systematic Theology*. At any rate, up till now no one of us has been able to do so." [8]

Tillich owes this high standard to his lifelong openness to all sides, to his constant dialogue with his contemporaries, and in particular to the influence of Heidegger and Jung: "The problem of the relation between the theological and the psycho-therapeutical understanding of man has come more and more into the foreground of my interest." "I do not think it is possible today to elaborate a Christian doctrine of man, and especially a Christian doctrine of Christian man, without using the immense material brought forth by depth psychology." [9]

Here, too, it is a matter of the practice of proclamation and pastoral care. It concerns a psychologically warranted judgment and treatment of one's fellow man in which the Gospel can be correctly understood and applied, and in which the frightful errors conventional Christianity has until very recently been guilty of in this respect are understood and prevented. Barth's well-known reluctance with regard to psychologism was entirely foreign to Tillich.

Another problem Tillich occupied himself with after his arrival in the United States was that of the nature and exercise of authority. What is the place of authority in a mature society, and how should authority be exercised? In the environment he grew up in "all democratic elements were rejected, distortedly represented and characterized as revolutionary, which meant criminal." [10] In the United States, on the contrary, there is no question of authoritarian action, neither in the family nor in the school, nor in the Church, state or society. The mentality, the social and religious situation in the United States, says Tillich, are all characterized "by the American courage to go ahead, to try, to risk failures, to begin after defeat, to lead an experimental life both in knowledge and action, to be open toward the future, to

---

[8] *Ex Auditu Verbi* (Kok, Kampen, 1965), p. 37.
[9] Kegley-Bretall, *op. cit.*, p. 18.
[10] *Op. cit.*, p. 7.

participate in the creative process of nature and history." [11] Whatever its truth, this is at any rate a description of the ideal attitude toward life which Tillich made his own in the United States.

We have now arrived at the main principle which is at the basis of all of Tillich's American publications: "Openness for the fundamental question of human existence: What am I?" [12] This is the first question man asks, the real question to which both philosophy and theology try to give an answer. Neither in the proclamation of the Gospel nor in theology are we concerned with abstract speculations about the nature of God, with an increase of knowledge about God in the intellectual sense. This is entirely foreign to the bible. Evangelical witness about God is concerned with how God relates himself to man, how man can be truly a man, and what this means for the mutual relationship between man and man.

Every word in the Gospel points to the inseparable connection between the relationship of man to God on the one hand, and man's relationship to his fellow man on the other. It is here on earth that the relationship between God and man becomes concrete and actual in the manner in which men judge and treat each other. Any person who, because of a legalistic morality or social convention, treads love underfoot, even if it were in regard to the greatest criminal, has no part in the reconciliation between God and man, in the forgiveness which Jesus proclaimed by his word and ratified by the sacrifice of his life. Love of fellow man surely is no mean matter. It supposes complete self-denial which is made possible only by a love which is the fruit of a genuine and deep faith.

It is especially in his sermons that Tillich calls for a radical change in human relationships, and this by reason of the Gospel as Jesus intended it, and as conventional Christianity has all too often denied it.[13] We might recall here what has been said in the second chapter of this present book. It is here a matter of the first and great commandment, the commandment of love in the evangelical sense of the word. Compared to this, a detailed intellectual

11 *Op. cit.,* p. 20.
12 *Op. cit.,* p. 21.
13 Paul Tillich, *The Shaking of the Foundations* (S.C.M. Press, London, 1949; Pelican Books, 1962); *The New Being* (S.C.M. Press, 1956); *The Eternal Now* (S.C.M. Press, 1963).

orthodoxy in doctrine is of little meaning. It is a matter of "being in" truth, and not of "having truth." It is a matter of participating in "the new being-human," as it has been revealed in Jesus as the Christ.

If God is concerned with the salvation of man, then theology also deals with *man*. God's revelation is the answer to the question which is given with human existence as such. It is not possible to learn God's answer if the question has not yet been asked. It is for this reason that theology speaks of God by speaking of man, and by beginning from the human existence and situation to which God is the answer. Only by being truly man will man learn to "know" himself and God. Conversely, it is in "the new Being," in the new being-human of Jesus as the Christ, that God's revelation throws light on what it is to be truly human. The one cannot be understood without the other. In Christian theology it is a matter of "the divine-human relation," of the "mutual interdependence" of the existential question of man and the answer of God.

## Tillich's "Existentialism"

It is debatable whether Tillich should be called an existentialist theologian. It is certain that he is not an existentialist pure and simple. Nor can it be said that he belongs to the school of the early Heidegger. This might be true for Bultmann, but not for Tillich. As we have seen, however, Tillich did appropriate Heidegger's way of thinking, but he put it into practice in his own way.

In Will Herberg's anthology, entitled *Four Existentialist Theologians*, we find Tillich as a fourth in the company of such divergent writers as Maritain, Berdyaev, and Buber.[14] John Macquarrie, on the other hand, includes Tillich in his *Twentieth Century Religious Thought* in one paragraph with Bultmann, Gogarten, and Buri, under the heading "Existentialism and Theology."[15] Finally, in his *Living Options in Protestant Theology*, John Cobb treats of Tillich in combination with Bultmann, H.

[14] Will Herberg (ed.), *Four Existentialist Theologians* (Doubleday Anchor Book A. 141, New York, 1958).

[15] John Macquarrie, *Twentieth Century Religious Thought* (S.C.M. Press, London, 1963), pp. 362ff.

Richard Niebuhr, and Reinhold Niebuhr, under the title "Theological Existentialism." [16]

Cobb diametrically opposes existentialism to any form of speculative theology. In Cobb's opinion, speculative theology since Hume and Kant has been driven into a defensive position, and has lost more and more ground. In our time it is clear to any unprejudiced spectator that speculative thought belongs to an era which has been overcome once and for all: "It no longer dominates the intellectual scene. It has come to seem pretentious and blind to the limitations of knowledge." [17]

Philosophically speaking, the nineteenth century was an age of transition. Soren Kierkegaard and Friedrich Nietzsche were the first existentialist thinkers of that century. Man, and *a fortiori* God, because of his very being stands outside the objectifiable reality of those things which are within the reach of speculative philosophy and science. For Kierkegaard, God was the totally Other, even with regard to man, totally other than anything or anyone that can be conceived. For Nietzsche, the God of speculative philosophy and theology was dead. According to both of these thinkers it was impossible to objectify God, to have objective knowledge of God. But it was also contrary to the nature of being-human to make man into the object of objectifying thought. Man as man belongs to a reality which has its own character, and which cannot be objectified. Man ex-sists, he stands outside objectifiable reality. Hence that which we call "faith" cannot be accounted for in an objective manner: "So vehement was Kierkegaard's hostility to the interpretation of faith as involving rational belief that he taught than any objective evidence for the truth of Christian doctrine would be harmful, depriving faith of its proper province." [18]

Believing, when compared to thinking, is something so different in man that it has nothing to do with thinking. Believing is an act, a leap, a risk, for which no rational arguments can be given. It creates a relation to God as the One who stands outside all imaginable and objectifiable reality. Truth in the sense of a result of thinking, and God as the One to whom faith is directed have

---

[16] J. B. Cobb, *Living Options in Protestant Theology* (Westminster Press, Philadelphia, 1962), pp. 199ff.

[17] *Op. cit.*, p. 199.

[18] *Op. cit.*, p. 134.

nothing to do with each other. Also, the Truth which is Jesus Christ has nothing to do with truth in an intellectualist and speculative sense.

Kierkegaard was the first philosophical and theological existentialist. For Christian theology he meant a radical change. For man, belief in God is a matter of life and death. Without belief in God, man is not man. However, objectively it is impossible to reach God and to be certain of his "existence." Certainty can only be the result of the subjective leap of faith which is based on the certainty of man that without God he is not man. For Kierkegaard, God is, in Tillich's term, *the ultimate concern*, the ultimate goal, and the ultimate sense and meaning of being-human. Believing is that orientation to God which alone makes being-human. Believing is that orientation to God which alone makes being-human possible. Belief has nothing to do with "opinions about God." Subjectively man is absolutely certain because he would not know what else to do than to believe. Not to believe would be the negation of himself as man. Therefore man can do nothing else but believe if necessary quite contrary to all objective data. A person who would want to try to prove the truth of his faith on the basis of objective data will never succeed and will necessarily be left in the uncertainty of faith. Just as man is able to know what love is only by loving, so too can he know what faith is only by believing.

As Heidegger in his first, existentialist period was influenced by the philosophy of Kierkegaard, so was Tillich influenced by the theology of Kierkegaard together with Heidegger's existentialist way of thinking. Tillich's thought always moved on the boundaries between theology and philosophy. Not only on the boundaries between theology and philosophy, but also on those between essence and existence. Tillich was always aware of the one-sidedness of an exclusively existentialist and of an exclusively essentialist way of thinking. The danger of the first was that the significance and function of general concepts and norms are underestimated. The danger of the second lies in the failure to appreciate the completely peculiar character of human existence. To the extent that Tillich, in his approach to the question of God, proceeds from what is completely peculiar to being-human, and to the extent that he sees the realization of "the new being" as meaning and purpose of revelation, he can be classified among the theologians of the existentialist type.

### Tillich's Correlative Method

As far as positing and answering the question of God is concerned there are two opposite methods, both of which Tillich rejects with great determination.

The first method consists in an effort to deduce the answer to the question of God from the question contained in human existence as such and which man asks from his very human existence without taking into consideration any form of. revelation on God's part. With this method, man himself answers his existential question without taking into consideration the possibility or actuality of an answer by God.

The other method consists in the answer which God gives ·in his self-revelation posited kerygmatically without referring it to the question which man asks from his own being-human. Here man really has no question to ask. Only the answer will determine what he possibly might and could ask. The question which man asks on his own is of no consequence and can therefore be disregarded.

The first method bypasses the answer which God gives from himself; the second bypasses the question which man asks on his own. The first method is Heidegger's, the second is Barth's. The first method is exclusively philosophical, the second is exclusively theological. According to Tillich, neither method fulfills its purpose.

In the manner in which he asks and answers the question of God, Tillich strongly emphasizes that it is a question which man asks on his own and an answer that God gives from himself; it is a question which lies within man himself and an answer which lies within God himself. God himself is the answer to the question which man does not pose, but *is*. To man as question God is answer. To the existence of man corresponds the revelation of God. To the question about the secret of being-human, on which philosophy reflects, corresponds the answer of God's revelation on which theology reflects. Question and answer cannot be separated. The one supposes the other. They are mutually related.

Therefore, too, philosophy and theology stand in mutual relation to each other. Tillich's way of approaching and answering the question has a philosophico-theological character. He himself calls his method that of correlation: "It correlates questions and answers, situation and message, human existence and divine manifestation." [19]

The *kerygma* is God's answer to the question contained in being-human. Divine revelation fills the vacuum which is given with being-human as such. Obviously Tillich does not mean this in a psychological but in an ontological sense.

One would show a complete misunderstanding of Tillich's correlative method if a person were to say that, according to Tillich, man must begin by asking about God first, in order that God might be able to answer, and that God is unable to answer if man stops asking. In that case one could call Bonhoeffer to arms against Tillich with Bonhoeffer's question: "What happens when the ultimate questions are no longer there as such, or when they are answered also without God?" [20]

For an understanding of Tillich's approach to the question about God, it is very important to keep in mind the cardinal difference between the hundreds of questions which man can ask and the one question that man himself is. In the course of time man has asked numerous questions to which he thought he could by himself give the answer by "tuning in on God." Bonhoeffer rightly points out that more and more man has undertaken to answer these questions without God. Perhaps then finally no question will be left which man would need God to answer.

However, in Tillich's method it is not a matter of answers to questions which one man may raise, and another not, depending on the level of development he has reached. Tillich's method is concerned with only one question: the question which is *per se* given with being-human as such, without man being able to give an answer to the question he himself is. This he will never be able to do because the situation of being a question without an answer is an inalienable characteristic, an existential if one will, of being-human. Whether there are few or many who are aware of their being a question does not matter to the way in which Tillich approaches and answers the question of God. It is a matter here

[19] Tillich, *Syst. Theol.* Vol. I, p. 8.
[20] Bonhoeffer, *Widerstand und Ergebung*, p. 216.

of an ontological fact, not of a psychological or cultural-historical fact. Therefore Tillich's method has nothing to do with Bonhoeffer's question. Anyone who does not see this appears blind to the dominating difference between the one question about being and the numerous questions about beings.

Man can ask hundreds of questions which are in no way connected with the one and actual question given with being-human as such. Most people fill their entire lives with such questions and with the more or less interesting answers given to them. Unconsciously they are even trying by means of these provisional questions and answers to silence the actual existential question, and to keep the existential anxiety from which the actual question is born at a safe distance for as long as possible. Man is in flight from the question he himself is. Unconsciously he does not want to face that question. He takes care that his life is completely occupied with provisional, inauthentic questions and answers which may be quite interesting in themselves, but which count for nothing when it is finally a matter of *to be or not to be*.

In Tillich's correlative method it is not a matter of answering questions which man may be pleased to posit about God. It is a matter of the one answer to that one question that man himself is. Being-human, when it has reached its ultimate limits, finally ends in the question about the ultimate meaning and firm ground of human existence as such. This existential question is contained in the nature of being-human itself. It will remain thus, even if finally not a single person would be aware of it. Human existence as such continues to cry for an answer, an answer which ultimately is the one, effective and complete answer.

This answer is none other than God himself. God is the answer to man as question. God reveals himself as the answer to the question which rises from human existence. Human existence and divine revelation are mutually attuned to each other. The way in which the question about God must be posited, approached, and answered is at one and the same time a philosophical and a theological one. This does not mean that Tillich wants to return to the relation between philosophy and theology which characterized scholasticism. But it is his express intention to use his correlative method in the abolition of the strict separation between philosophy and theology, so characteristic of Heidegger on the one hand, and of Barth on the other.

*Tillich as Interpreter*

Both the philosopher and the theologian reflect on the question "to be or not to be" and on the answer to this question. As long as Tillich reflects on the question it is not difficult for him to continue speaking as a philosopher. However, it is remarkable how easily and almost matter-of-factly he replaces his philosophical way of speaking by a theological one as soon as he reflects on the answer. A notable example of such a transition from philosophical terminology to a theological one is found in the final chapter of his book *The Courage To Be*.[21] We shall take this book as the point of departure for Tillich's treatment of the question of God. If this book deals ultimately with the courage to accept acceptance, Tillich means acceptance by being-itself (also called the power of being, and the ground of being) and acceptance by God. These apparently mean the same for Tillich.

Both the philosopher and the theologian reflect on the relation of man to his ultimate concern; the philosopher and the theologian basically speak about the same thing. But they approach it from opposite sides, from human existence and from divine revelation. The method is different. So is the language, the terminology. But both are concerned with the ultimate concern of man, with a final effect answer to the secret of human existence as such.

The question approached from human existence would remain unanswered if there were no answer from divine revelation. This answer from divine revelation, however, is not suspended in mid-air but it is the answer to the question which is asked from within human existence. The way of the question and the way of the answer cross on the point where thought becomes belief. It is easy to think and speak about the question in philosophical categories and terms. But it is difficult (and Tillich is a perfect example of it) to continue to do so when it comes to dealing with the answer. Inevitably it is here that a shift is necessary to thought and language which use theological categories and terms.

The real object of Tillich's life's work was to meditate, by philosophizing and theologizing, between modern thinking man

[21] Paul Tillich, *The Courage To Be* (Nisbet, London, 1952). Hereafter cited from the Fontana edition, (Collins, London, 1962).

and biblical believing man (who for that matter can both be represented in the one person). He speaks the language of both, the language of modern man and the language of the believing Christian the language of thought and the language of proclamation, the language of philosophy and the language of theology. As a competent interpreter he shifts without difficulty from one language to the other, sometimes to the great perplexity of some spectators.

Tillich wants to be an interpreter. He is even consciously an apologist. He has made it his task to convince modern man in his own language that he can be a believing Christian even in his own time. Tillich is able to do this because he has and shows that he has an appreciation of the causes as a result of which a proclamation and theology bound up with past culture make it difficult, if not impossible, for modern man to recognize in the appearance of Jesus as the Christ, the answer to the existential question about man's ultimate concern.

If a non-believer asks what a believer understands by "God," Tillich answers that he understands by this the ground of being. On the other hand,, if a believer asks what a philosopher means by "ground of being," Tillich answers that he means God. This is not a matter of a logical identification: God equals the ground of being, as if a believer henceforth does not have to pray to God but to the ground of being. When Tillich preaches, he does not preach about the ground of being, but about God. This is not a question of replacing, but of translating.

For a correct judgment concerning Tillich's objective it is desirable, if not necessary, to compare his philosophico-theological writings with his sermons. Only then will it become clear how well Tillich mastered the art of saying the same thing in two different languages, in the language of philosophico-theological reflection and in that of the proclamation, and in the terminology of the theology of the proclamation.

The fact that God himself is the answer to the question which necessarily arises within human existence in its actual situation is the core of what the bible, the Church(es) and the Christian faith have to say about man and his relation to God. The relation between God and man is the actual concern of being-human: the only and the real ultimate concern.

Since Tillich as a believing Christian is interested in making clear to the secularized person estranged from the Church and from the Christian faith what Christian proclamation is concerned with, his effort should really be applauded in the Christian world. But apparently it is difficult for conventional Christians to discover the original content in the modern translation, just as it was difficult for them to appreciate Bultmann's effort to demythologize the *kerygma* in behalf of modern man.

Tillich himself is convinced that in his philosophico-theological writings it is indeed the same, old, original message of salvation that is dealt with, the same old realities which always were and always will be the concern of the Christian faith. Tillich emphatically denies any connection between himself and the "great critics" since the Enlightenment: "They could be called dangerous. But what I do is something quite different . . . I try to recreate *the old realities* on another basis." [22] The difference does not lie in a new content, but in a new sound, and a new audience. For this reason Tillich speaks in his sermons in the old familiar language of the bible and the Church, since in his sermons he is speaking to the believing Christians who have not (yet) experienced any difficulty in understanding this language: "When I am preaching a sermon—and then I am quite aware of what I am doing—I speak to people who are unshaken in their beliefs and in their acceptance of symbols with a language which will not undermine their belief. And to those who are actually in a situation of doubt and are even being torn to pieces by it, I hope to speak in such a way that the reasons for their doubts and other stumbling blocks are taken away." [23]

In his book *The Courage To Be*, which we shall use in the following paragraph as a point of departure for Tillich's approach to the question of God, the acceptance of acceptance occupies an important place. We shall there meet a typical example of Tillich's art of speaking in two languages.

### The Courage To Be

Courage is the acceptance of a situation in spite of the fact that this situation contains a threat and as a result causes anxiety.

[22] *Ultimate Concern*, p. 192.
[23] *Op. cit.*, p. 191.

Courage means to conquer anxiety in daring to lay hold of and dominate a situation in spite of the threat it contains.

In *The Courage To Be* Tillich does not deal with courage in general, but with existential courage. It is the courage which man necessarily requires precisely as man in the situation of his being-human. No one is an exception to this, whether he is aware of it or not.

Among all existents, man alone knows that he is, he knows that he knows this, and he knows that he knows that he knows that he is. Only man is conscious of being. And at the same time he is conscious of being one with the world (total reality, the cosmos), and of being placed in a given situation: the situation of being-human. That man is (*Dasein*), and that man is man and not something else, that being-human is as it is, that the situation of being-human (*Sosein*) is a given and unchangeable situation, is a fact of which only man as man is conscious. This consciousness is at the basis of his thinking and speaking. That man thinks and speaks, and what he thinks and speaks results from, and is connected with, the immediately given consciousness of being determined, as man, by the human predicament.

However, man is not only a being who is conscious of himself, who thinks and speaks. It is an inalienable and existential characteristic of being-human that being is emotionally or affectively experienced consciously or unconsciously. The manner in which man experiences himself, the other, and the world, causes from the very first moment of the rise of consciousness not only conscious emotions but also affective complexes in his subconscious, which influence and dominate his future life in many favorable and unfavorable ways without his realizing what animates him and without understanding the actual motives for his position and conduct.

Man is conscious of being involved not only in the situation of being-human but also in the particular facts and events of the situation in which he merely happens to find himself (the particular circumstances of his own personal being-human). This involvement always takes on an emotional or affective character. If a man were completely apathetic in everything, without having an emotional relationship to anything or anyone, he would be sick, he would be a psychopath. To be consciously and unconsciously emotionally charged belongs to being-human.

One of the forms of being emotionally charged is that of anxiety. Anxiety is not the same as fear. Man has fear of something that does not belong to being-human itself, of something that does not belong to the human situation as such but that belongs to the world of "accidental" facts and circumstances. This does not mean that such accidental facts and circumstances do not have a cause and cannot be explained, but that they do not *per se* belong to being-human as such.

If someone is in a hotel where a huge fire has broken out, and notices that he cannot be reached by those who would want to save his life, these are circumstances which surely can be explained, and therefore are not "accidental." But they are accidental for man as man. It is not because he is man that a man finds himself in a room in a burning hotel where he cannot be reached. But it is because he is man that a man finds himself in the situation of finitude. He lives, but he knows that he is mortal, that life ends in death precisely because he is man. This knowledge causes anxiety with regard to non-being, existential anxiety.

The particular circumstances in the burning hotel cause fear as well as anxiety. I fear that the situation is hopeless, that the fire will reach my room, that I cannot be reached, that I will not be saved. But this fear also stimulates the thought of the possibility of approaching death. I am confronted with the threat of non-being. This thought does not cause fear, but anxiety. Anxiety has to do with being or non-being. Fear has to do only with all sorts of threats which may arise within the limits of the *So-sein*. Anxiety, on the other hand, has to do with *Da-sein* itself.

Anxiety is of an emotional nature; it has to do with the awareness that being is on all sides surrounded by non-being, that being is threatened by non-being, that being-human is threatened by death. Man knows that he is. But he also knows that he is unto death. Just as the knowledge of being is not always on the conscious level, so, too, is the knowledge that he is unto death not always present in the actual conscious sphere of daily life. It would even seem as if most men are rarely "consciously" aware that they are and that this being is a being-unto-death. As a result it even seems as if man rarely has anxiety of non-being. This anxiety breaks through into the conscious sphere of daily life only when sickness or accident awakens the thought of death. But in the subconscious the anxiety of non-being is always present. This belongs to being-human, and to the human predicament as such.

From the fact that man continues to be, in spite of being unto death, i.e., that he accepts being, it becomes clear that he consciously or unconsciously has the courage to be. Every man possesses this existential courage. Without this courage man would not be able to actualize his being, he could not live it. There may be psychopathic instances where a man loses the existential courage. This results then in an anxiety psychosis which makes life unbearable, if not impossible.

At tl.e same time, this does not mean that the existential courage is an obvious fact for the normal man. On the contrary, every man consciously or unconsciously tries to make this courage possible, and to bring himself to have it. Existential anxiety has three main forms in the life of man. Likewise there are three main forms of existential courage.

Existential anxiety, which is caused by the threat of non-being, is not limited to anxiety about death. Death as well as the inevitable threatens the ontic character of being-human. But man is not man only by being. It also belongs to being-human that man is in a spiritual and a moral way. The threat to the moral being and the spiritual being of man also causes a form of existential anxiety. Fate and death threaten the ontic being of man; emptiness and complete meaninglessness threaten his spiritual being; guilt and condemnation threaten the moral being of man. But fate, emptiness, and guilt do not definitively decide human existence. Death, meaninglessness, and final rejection decide definitively about being or non-being. They are a definitive, irreparable, irrevocable threat to being-human as such. In all these cases existential anxiety is caused by the threat of non-being. In all these cases existential anxiety can be conquered only by the existential courage which affirms and accepts being in spite of the threat of non-being.

Although most men seem to be rarely or scarcely aware of the existential situation in which they find themselves, still most men do have the existential courage which makes it possible for them to "keep going" in human existence. Just as there are three forms of existential threat of non-being, so there are also three forms of the courage to be. This is not a matter of a moral quality in which a person can exercise himself, but of an ontological necessity and fact. In the given situation every man has the courage to be. Otherwise he could not be.

Two forms of the courage to be, however, have only a relative and provisional character. They are connected with man's placing himself in the service of an ultimate concern, which in the final issue may not be a really *ultimate* concern, but only a penultimate objective or interest, such as family, profession, science, riches, art, sport, battles, and so on.

The first provisional courage to be consists in the courage to be as part of a whole; the second consists in the courage to be as oneself; to be an "I," to be a person. The first courage is based on participation, on the security of a community that lasts and that gives meaning to life and that is good. By living in and for the well-being of the community which has been elevated to ultimate concern, man feels protected against the threat of non-being. The second courage rests on the awareness of one's own dignity, on individualization, i.e., on self-confidence, on the striving for a personal ideal, interest, or life-goal which is elevated to ultimate concern, and by which the threat of non-being in all its forms is kept at a distance, banished from the horizon of the useful, successful, active life.

But as soon as man is confronted with one of the three forms in which human existence is threatened by non-being, by death, meaninglessness, and final condemnation, the two forms of courage that are based on participation and individualization, and on a submission to an ultimate concern which is not really ultimate, are insufficient. Man is then seized by the ultimate anxiety of the definitive non-being. This anxiety can be conquered only by the third form of the courage to be, the one complete courage to be in which man is unshaken even in spite of the definitive threat of non-being in the shape of death, meaninglessness, and rejection.

This third courage to be, which is the only completely sufficient one, Tillich calls the courage to accept acceptance. The final chapter of Tillich's book on the courage to be deals with this third courage to be. The chapter is entitled "Courage and Transcendence." [24] Over and above the finite, non-satisfying, and imperfect world of finite things and of unstable human existence there is a transcendent Reality. This transcendent Reality reveals

[24] *The Courage To Be*, pp. 152ff.

itself in, and enters the horizon of our finite and provisional reality. The courage to accept acceptance by the transcendent Reality is the only courage to be which absolutely resists any threat of non-being, and which therefore also conquers any form of existential anxiety.

This also means that for man there is only one ultimate concern which really is ultimate, a concern which to the very last withstands any form of threat of non-being: man's relation to the infinite transcendent Reality which is the only firm ground of his life, of his being. Ultimately there is for man only one *ultimate* concern, not in his being such or so, but in his being as being. All other concerns which man has regarded as ultimate are no longer tenable, they lose their sense and meaning when it is a matter of sink or swim in the confrontation with and the threat of non-being in its ultimate and definitive form. All the various things about which man was concerned are only accidental, arbitrary, provisional. Ultimately only one thing is of absolute interest, only one thing is necessary for every man as man, and that is such a strong grounding in transcendent Reality that no power on earth is able to threaten human existence or harm it in any way.

The two chapters in Tillich's book *The Courage To Be* that deal with the two relative forms of the courage to be may be rich and clarifying. But the heart of the matter appears only in the final chapter which deals with the connection between the courage to be and transcendent Reality, the courage to accept acceptance.

We shall now restrict ourselves to that final chapter, because the courage discussed there is a suitable point of departure for a treatment of the manner in which Tillich posits, approaches, and answers the question of God.

## To Accept Acceptance

The only form of the courage to be which under all circumstances withstands the threat of non-being, and which conquers completely and finally all existential anxiety is the courage to accept acceptance.

Acceptance by whom or by what? Acceptance by transcendent Reality which is the ground, or the cause, the sense, and the goal of the being of beings and in particular of human existence; acceptance by the transcendent Reality which is the beginning and end of all and in which our being-human is rooted and grounded. Our being-human has no sufficient ground in itself. It is not based on itself, but on the ground which gives being to all beings. Not to be left to oneself, but to be completely and unconditionally accepted once and for all, and under all circumstances, by that transcendent Reality to which our being-human owes its being: that is a magnificent thought which indeed gives courage. Not only a thought, but reality as well. It is by no means a scanty consolation, as some of Tillich's critics would have it.

Even though man is unable to form for himself even the least concept of the transcendent Reality because this Reality is immaterial, and even though man is unable to think of a name by which to indicate this Reality, the courage to accept complete and unconditional acceptance by the transcendent Reality is itself a courage of faith. This courage has a religious sense and meaning, even though it is discussed in philosophical terms. But what is most striking of the final chapter in *The Courage To Be* is that Tillich, hard though he may try, does not succeed in continuing to speak philosophically. The reason for this can be discovered when one reads his sermons that deal with the same theme. Miskotte's criticism of Tillich, contained in his book *When the Gods Are Silent*, does not appreciate the true sense and intention of Tillich's reflections about the courage to be.[25]

As long as Tillich, starting with the existential question that is man, successfully continues to express himself philosophically, he uses for the transcendental Reality which gives being to all beings terms such as the power of being, the ground of being, the ground of our being, being itself. He uses these expressions as synonyms, as is clear from some of the chapter headings. Tillich uses the term power of being where on the basis of two previous paragraphs one would expect to see the term ground of being. But what is more striking is that in the final chapter Tillich scarcely uses the philosophical manner of speech, constantly switching as he does to a theological terminology. Because it is very important to understand what Tillich himself thought and

[25] *Op. cit.*, p. 76; cf. p. 223.

intended when he placed such all-decisive emphasis on the acceptance of acceptance, it is necessary to examine how he preached this acceptance in his sermons.

Here I have in mind especially a sermon [26] on the text of Paul's letter to the Christians at Rome: 'For I am sure that neither death, nor life, nor angels, nor principalities, nor things present, nor things to come, nor powers, nor height, nor depth, nor any other creature will be able to separate us from the love of God, which is in Christ Jesus our Lord" (Rom. 8, 38-39).

Christians who are familiar with the language of the bible understand what Paul intends to say. For others, however, it is necessary first to demythologize the text with Bultmann, so that they will not stumble over the angels, the principalities, and the powers. We are forcing the text when we replace the mythological powers with Tillich's threats to being: "For I am sure that neither fate nor death, neither emptiness nor meaninglessness, neither guilt nor condemnation, nor any other threat will be able to separate us from the love of God, which has been revealed in Christ Jesus our Lord." Paul, too, sums up all sorts of powers which might be designed to destroy man, to reduce him to nothing, to non-being. These powers would be able to achieve their goal if they could separate man from the love of God (the love which has been revealed in Christ Jesus our Lord). However, this is impossible. For, as is clear from the biblical context, the love of God is an invincible and ultimate love by which man is completely and unconditionally accepted. This love never leaves man to himself. It always continues to conquer all those powers which are aimed at man's destruction. But these powers are the same, only with different names, as those which Paul Tillich had in mind when in *The Courage To Be* he spoke of the forms in which man is threatened by non-being.

In Tillich's sermon, the power of being is not mentioned, but the love of God is. Yet, in both expressions it is a matter of that by which man is completely accepted forever. When, in his book about the courage to be, Tillich found this courage ultimately on the fact of being accepted, he undoubtedly thinks of the same acceptance of which he speaks in his sermon when he says "Paul's final message is: 'Not even your guilty conscience can separate you from the love of God. For the love of God means that God

[26] *The New Being*, pp. 50ff.

accepts him who knows that he is unacceptable.' " Both in the existential courage to be and in the courage of faith it is a matter of the courage to accept acceptance by the power which ultimately withstands any threat to our human existence. In both instances it is a matter to accept acceptance, only in different languages. When Tillich speaks of the invincible power of being, he means as a believing Christian the love of God. The decision, the act by which acceptance is accepted has in both instances the character of a decision of faith, an act of faith.

God simply is love. The man who, in spite of everything, has the courage to entrust himself entirely and unconditionally to the love of God in the firm conviction that there is nothing (everything that might be aimed at a separation from the love of God is "nothing") that can separate him from the love of God, that man is a believer, a man who, in spite of everything, accepts acceptance.

It is a matter here of the core of the Gospel of Jesus as the Christ; it is a matter of the core of the Christian proclamation of faith. Tillich does not see God as an abstract philosophical concept, an idea, or a postulate. God is the Father of Christ Jesus our Lord. Who will deny that these names are intended symbolically, and that they have a symbolic meaning? Of course, as in all our speaking about God, it is a matter of symbols. But these symbols have a real meaning; they signify, they are directed to, they refer to a reality about which it is not possible to speak in direct terms, but only in symbols. Yet, this does not make reality less real. On the contrary, it is a matter here of the only, the completely unassailable ultimate Reality, the Reality of God, in which everything, including man's being, is rooted and grounded.

That Tillich also had this in mind in *The Courage To Be* is clear from the fact that in his final chapter he is very much aware that, in spite of philosophical terminology, he is the realm of religion. At the very beginning of the chapter about the acceptance of acceptance he relates the power of being to religion: "Religion is the state of being grasped by the power of being itself." [27] Elsewhere we meet this definition in a somewhat changed form: "Religion is the state of being grasped by an ultimate concern." [28]

---

[27] *Op. cit.*, p. 152.
[28] Paul Tillich, *Christianity and the Encounter of the World Religions* (Columbia Univ. Press, New York, 1963), p. 4.

We shall later consider Tillich's vision of what religion is and of the relation between Christianity and the world religions. It can be ascertained that when Tillich speaks in such apparently abstract philosophical terms as ground of being, power of being, being itself, and ultimate concern, he thinks of religion in general, but especially, as is clear from his sermons, of being-Christian in particular.

It is not only on biblical grounds, but also on depth psychological grounds that the contrast between acceptance and rejection occupies such a central place in the belief and thought of Paul Tillich, In fact, this contrast plays a central part in the life of every person, in spite of, or perhaps because of the fact that most men are not aware of it. It is no exaggeration to say that our human existence from beginning to end is dominated and determined by this contrast. Human existence asks for acceptance. For this reason, acceptance in the form of forgiveness and reconciliation is the pivot on which the Gospel of God's revelation in Jesus as the Christ turns. In the answer that God gives, or, better, *is* to the question of being-human it is basically a matter of acceptance. In this central respect too the answer corresponds to the question. Because this central point is so important we shall have to go into some detail.

Rejection or acceptance by the people who influence our lives, plays a great part in our lives, from the very early beginnings. This part is all the more effective to the extent that we are less conscious of it. It is a matter of impressions, traumas, and complexes which have their effect in our unconscious lives, and which, without our being aware of it, determine to a fair extent our thought and action.

Every rejection, or every nonacceptance, in which we are disregarded by people around us or by institutions or organizations with which we have to deal, arouses in our subconscious feelings of antipathy, aversion, and hatred. Aversion to parents and other members of the family, aversion to the parental home, aversion to school, to teachers, superiors, colleagues, aversion to certain expressions of culture: all these kinds of aversion, if they are present, are based on nonacceptance or not being subject to acceptance. On this point many parents and educators, many superiors and employers still commit the most capital errors, in spite of psychological knowledge having become so widespread.

Acceptance is not the same as weakness or as approval of what is wrong. Acceptance can and often must be accompanied by punctuality and strictness. But acceptance is always an "acceptance-in-spite-of." The greatness and benefit of acceptance lies precisely in this, that somebody is fully accepted as man in spite of failures and shortcomings. Never to disparage a person, to belittle him, to disregard him, never to let him feel that he does not count or that he is not taken seriously, in spite of whatever peculiarities or shortcomings; to fully accept every person in spite of stupidities, poverty, party, class, race, or conduct, so to accept him as if he had never done to us whatever he may have done; all this is what Jesus meant when he spoke of love of neighbor. Always and under all circumstances to accept and continue to accept one's fellowman, *in spite of everything*. Not to refuse, judge, disown, or reject in any way—that is love. Because of the absence of this love in the world of conventional Christianity many atheists, unbelievers and criminals will, according to the word of Jesus, enter the kingdom of heaven before us, believing and dutiful Christians. For the only ultimate norm here is love (1 Cor. 13). Expressed in "Roman" terms, the most serious and the most frequent "mortal sins" are not the sins against the sixth commandment which are often rather insignificant, but the sins against charity and love.

In the life of every person nothing has such a lasting and disastrous effect as when he is not fully accepted, even if it is only in respect to one point. Nonacceptance is so contrary to the nature of love that the threat to the love among men and in particular the intimate love between two human beings is never so serious as when it is caused by incomplete acceptance because something or other is lacking. Complete acceptance comprises also complete forgiveness, whatever may have happened. It is only complete forgiveness that is able to renew and confirm the original relationship. Forgiveness, acceptance, and love are inseparably united.

God simply is love, pure, unconditional love. Among us men, at the center of the history of mankind, this love of God has been revealed in Jesus as the Christ. For Tillich too, Jesus is the unique figure in which God's love has been revealed as nowhere else. This must not be forgotten when one tries to form a judgment of Tillich's philosophico-theological translation of the ancient message of salvation into modern language. Finally, in Tillich to accept acceptance by the ground of being, by the power of being, by being itself is only a different expression of the firm belief of having been accepted and healed by the power of God's love. For this reason, however difficult it may sometimes be to love one's neighbor, man can at any rate love God who has first loved us in Jesus as the Christ (1 Jn. 4, 10; Jn. 15, 12; Rom. 8, 37; Gal. 2, 20; Eph. 2, 4; 2 Thess. 2, 16). It is by reason of the power of God's love who has accepted us just as we are, with and in spite of all our past, that we can and must try to love, forgive, and accept our fellow man, every fellow human being we meet somewhere along the way *in spite of everything*.

God is love; God forgives; God accepts. This was the core of Tillich's preaching, and all the work Paul Tillich did during his entire life must be judged in the light of this preaching: "We cannot love unless we have accepted forgiveness, and the deeper our experience of forgiveness is, the greater is our love. We cannot love when we feel rejected, even if the rejection is done in righteousness. We are hostile towards that to which we belong and by which we feel judged, even if the judgment is not expressed in words. As long as we feel rejected by Him, we cannot love God." [29]

Here lies the deepest cause of existential anxiety: to be rejected by God; not to be accepted by God. "But if we have received, and accepted the message that He *is* reconciled, everything changes. Like a healing stream His healing power enters into us; we can affirm Him and with Him our own being and the others from whom we were estranged, and life as a whole." [30] What a radical change. This change touches on our entire human existence in its relation to God, to our fellowmen, to ourselves, to the world, and to the whole human situation. It would therefore be entirely incorrect to say that Tillich did not proclaim the Gospel, and that he did not bring a message of salvation to man in his existential need.

God is the power of love "which tries to destroy within us everything which is against love. To love this love is to love God. Theologians have questioned whether man is able to have love toward God; they have replaced love by obedience . . . They

[29] *The New Being*, p. 10.
[30] *Loc. cit.*

teach a theology for the righteous ones but not a theology for the sinners. *He who is forgiven knows what it means to love God* . . . He who is reunited with God, the creative Ground of life, the power of life in everything that lives, is reunited with life. He feels accepted by it and he can love it." [31] The courage to be, which consists in an acceptance of acceptance by the power of being, by the ground of being, is the same as the act of faith by which the person confronted with Jesus as the Christ acknowledges and accepts to have been accepted by God, and to be secure, in life and in death, in that power of love which Jesus has revealed in himself.

It is in Jesus as the Christ that "the new being" has been revealed. To believe, to accept acceptance, is to have part in this new being. This new being is a "being in love." It enables man to accept his human situation, and to make it fruitful for himself as well as for others. The authenticity or genuinity of faith proves itself in a living in love, in a life of sincere charity toward our fellowmen, in an acceptance of life on the basis of love. The person who really believes in God and who is thereby rooted and grounded in love is the person who accepts life even in its most extreme consequences. His courage to be conquers any form of threat by non-being, and thus any form of existential anxiety.

### Belief in God

Belief in God arises on the point where the way of human existence and the way of God's revelation cross. Faith is born from the encounter between God and man. God himself is the answer to man as question. God himself is the only firm ground of man's courage to be, even if man is not aware of this.

The final chapter of Tillich's *Courage To Be* consists of two parts. In the first part he deals with the power or ground of being as the source of the courage to be. Man's relation to the ground of being may take on two different forms of experience: that of mystical experience and that of a personal encounter between God and man. The first form is characteristic of the Indian religions, the second, of Luther and Lutheran Protestantism. It cannot be denied that in his treatment of this theme Tillich shows

[31] *Op. cit.*, p. 11.

a certain limitation of horizon. The world of Catholicism does not fall within that horizon. The manner in which he deals with the theme is typically Lutheran. At any rate, we shall leave this first part here because for our purpose it is the second part that really matters.

In this second part the courage to be is called the key to the power or ground of being. The fact that the courage to be opens the eye to the transcendent Reality is based on the ontological nature of the courage to be. This courage is an inalienable characteristic of human existence. Precisely because man is not a thing but "man," precisely because he exists and because he is aware of his being which is threatened by non-being, he cannot exist without the existential courage to be. This courage is inherent in being-human as such. Should this courage slip away from man entirely, which seems to happen in some psychopaths, then man will cease to exist as man, his being-human as such will be endangered.

This existential and ontological fact, which is given with the nature of being-human, Tillich considers the key which opens an insight into the transcendent Reality in which everything that is has its ground, and in which is found the power of being that supports all being against the threat of non-being.

This non-being is not nothing. It is an aspect of being. It falls within its horizon. If being were to maintain itself against nothing, this would require no power, and it would be impossible to speak of a power of being by which being maintains itself against non-being. If non-being were nothing, then the threat of this "nothing" could not cause existential anxiety. Human existence as such includes the awareness that non-being really threatens being. For this reason, human existence as we experience and live it, makes it necessary for us to see that non-being is an aspect of being. Otherwise we could not experience it as a living being. For "to live" is precisely the manifestation of the constant powerful tension that exists between being and non-being.

In this train of thought Tillich joins the "philosophers of life" who have always strongly emphasized the dynamic character of reality. For Tillich, this is the point of departure for positing, approaching, and answering the question of God. If we were dealing with pure mechanism, a dead reality, then—supposing that man would ask under those conditions—it would be impossible to make this a point of departure for the question about God and belief in God. In that case atheism could be the inevitable result of a mechanistic concept of total reality. Such a concept is blind to the secret of the tension between being and non-being, to the secret of life.

The first step toward belief in God is for Tillich the acknowledgment that the ground of being is also the ground of life: "Being could not be the ground of life without non-being. The self-affirmation of being without non-being would not even be self-affirmation but an immovable self-identity." [32] Then the ground of being would not be the ground of life. However, total Reality is not dead but alive. We are dealing with a living and dynamic Reality.

Here we have reached the point where Tillich makes a transition from thinking to believing, from philosophy to theology, from a dead ground of being to the living God. Just as philosophy has occupied itself with the dynamic self-affirmation of being itself wherever philosophy did not think statically but dynamically, so, too, theology has done exactly the same wherever it took the idea of the living God seriously. Not all philosophy and theology have done this. It is because of this that philosophy and theology can sometimes be diametrically opposed to each other. But wherever total Reality is acknowledged as a living and dynamic Reality, philosophy and theology have, as in Tillich, met each other as speaking of the same Reality, though approaching it from two opposite sides: from the side of man asking, and from the side of God revealing himself. Philosophy and theology come together when one says: "Non-being (*that* in God which makes his self-affirmation dynamic) opens up the divine self-seclusion and reveals him as power and love. Non-being makes God a living God. Without the No he has to overcome in himself and in his creatures, the divine Yes to himself would be lifeless. There would be no revelation of the ground of being, there would be no life." [33] I do not hesitate to consider this as one of the most important statements written in this century. Without the living God no living person could exist or be thought of. Without the eternal self-affirmation in which God's life consists, there would be no finite self-affirmation; it would be

[32] *The Courage To Be*, p. 174.
[33] *Loc. cit.*

impossible to speak of the courage to be in human beings. This self-affirmation, this courage to be is, however, inherent to being-human as such. For this reason man's existential courage has a revealing power. For this reason, too, it is not intellectual arguments that make the approach to God possible, but the courage to be is the key to being itself, the key to faith in God: "By affirming our being we participate in the self-affirmation of being-itself. There are no valid arguments for the 'existence' of God, but there are acts of courage in which we affirm the power of being, whether we know it or not . . . *Courage has revealing power.*" [34]

However, with all this Tillich has by no means said everything. Thus far he has only tried to clarify that the self-affirmation by which man maintains himself is a participation in the self-affirmation of being itself, and subsequently that this self-affirmation is a manifestation of life. In other words, the ground of being is at the same time the ground of life, and the self-affirmation of being itself supposes not a dead but a living transcendent Reality which for the believer is the Reality of the living God. This living God is a God who reveals himself in the existence of living man.

## Revelation

Man as question calls for an answer. The answer comes from the part of transcendent Reality and is based on revelation. Tillich was convinced that he was in agreement with biblical revelation when he defined revelation as "the manifestation of the ground of being for human knowledge." [35] Later theological misunderstandings which hold that the content of revelation is a complexus of information distilled from bible texts and safely stored as the treasure of the Church, are for Tillich unbiblical concepts of revelation. Revelation takes place in and through human existence. Total Reality as it actualizes itself consciously in human existence has revealing power. We have already seen that Tillich calls the courage to be the key which admits a person to being itself, because this existential courage has revealing

[34] *Op. cit.*, p. 175.
[35] *Syst. Theol.* Vol. I, p. 105.

power. This revelation proceeds from transcendent Reality, from God himself.

In a certain sense God is operatively revealing in the existence of every person. But Tillich certainly would not consider himself a Christian if he were not convinced that this active self-revelation of God in and through human existence, by which this human existence is, as it were, a transparency of God, has found its ultimate and complete expression in the appearance, in the person, and in the action of Jesus as the Christ, such as the New Testament pictures this for us.

In this connection Tillich speaks of "the picture of Jesus as the Christ." It is in and through this picture presented by the New Testament, and in particular by the Gospels, of the existence of Jesus as the Christ that God reveals himself. Tillich prefers the expression "Jesus as the Christ" in order to make it clear that it is not a matter of the life of Jesus of Nazareth in his historical existence, but of Jesus as the Christ, of the picture of his salvific significance as it was alive in the faith-consciousness of the apostles and of the early Christian communities, and as the New Testament has presented this picture.

This picture of Jesus as the Christ has revealing power *par excellence*, more than human existence in general with its courage to be, and more than the existence of any other figure in the history of mankind. To discover, to experience, and to accept this revealing power which proceeds from the picture of Jesus as the Christ is what is rightly called faith in the biblical Christian sense. Any other belief in God found among men finds its ultimate completion and fulfillment in this faith in God which rests on the acknowledgment of Jesus as the Christ.

As every other Christian, Tillich is convinced of the unique character of the appearance of Jesus as the Christ. But this unique character does not lie in the "supernatural" union with God, as the old Church has conceived it and expressed it in its dogmas, but in this, that in the real human existence of Jesus as the Christ in all its aspects, the love of God has been revealed in an entirely unique manner. For this reason the picture of Jesus as the Christ is the final revelation and, as such, the only criterion of everything that has ever been presented or will ever be presented as revelation: "The final revelation, the revelation in Jesus as the

Christ, is universally valid, because it includes the criterion of every revelation and is the *finis* or *telos* (intrinsic aim) of all of them. The final revelation is the criterion of every religion and of every culture, not only of the culture and religion in and through which it has appeared. It is valid for the social existence of every human group and for the personal existence of every human individual. It is valid for mankind as such, and, in an indescribable way, it has meaning for the universe also. Nothing less than this should be asserted by Christian theology." [36]

What all this means concretely has been described by Tillich in the second part of his *Systematic Theology*, while the third part is devoted to the theological reflection on what the bible and the Christian faith understand by "the Spirit" and by "the Kingdom of God." [37] It is entirely impossible within the scope of this chapter to make even the least attempt to summarize the original, rich, and at the same time closely knit content of Tillich's main work. In any case, Tillich saw himself—to refer once again to a sermon —as one "who is grasped, within the Church, by the Divine Spirit and who has received the word of wisdom and knowledge," [38] as one whose task it was to interpret in modern language the paradoxical expression "Jesus is the Christ" and to reflect on all its presuppositions and implications.

### Where Is God?

Where is God? Is it possible for man to meet God and to believe in him on the basis of a real divine encounter? What does it mean when we speak of faith in God? To these questions, which are typical of modern man, Tillich tried to give an answer which takes into account and proceeds from the contemporary difficulties which many people find today in the faith in God.

Tillich was well aware that it was precisely the situation in which man as man finds himself that presents us with an enormous difficulty when there is question of faith in God. Man is completely bound to his being-human. He is man, and not some-

[36] *Op. cit.,* p. 152.

[37] Each of the three volumes has appeared in an American and in an English edition, respectively at the University of Chicago Press, Chicago, and at Nisbet, London.

[38] *The Shaking of the Foundations,* p. 124.

thing else. He cannot but ask in a human manner when he asks questions. Man's questioning is entirely determined by the fact that he is human.

For this reason it is not at all obvious that man can ask about God. From the history of religion it is shown to be a fact that man has always asked about God in one form or another, and that he has always tried to somehow communicate with gods or with God. But who can be sure that this questioning about God and this communicating with God has anything to do with God? To know whether this questioning about God is really a questioning about God, the answer that God himself exists must be known already. The difficulty we have when we posit the question of God is that the question cannot really be a question about God if God is not already known, in other words if the answer has not already been revealed. The question can be legitimately and meaningfully asked only in the light of the answer. This means that the answer must precede the question, and that the question presupposes knowledge of the answer, acknowledgment of God's revealing action.

It seems therefore that we again find ourselves in a vicious circle. Whoever wants to posit the question of God in such a way that it is really the question about God and not about something else, must know the answer beforehand; but a person who knows the answer does not have to ask the question. With a view to this difficulty of the vicious circle Tillich says: "Theology is necessarily existential, and no theology can escape the theological circle." [39] "Every theology presupposes that the theologian is in the theological circle." [40]

But this does not apply to the theologian only; it applies to everyone who believes in God. The arguments for faith in God do not lie outside but inside the circle of faith in God.

With great determination Tillich rejects the pretension of any form of natural theology that it is possible to argue about believing or not believing in God without first believing in God. To account for faith in God is possible only from faith in God itself. Faith in God always rests on a leap into the circle of faith. It is impossible to give rational arguments for faith in God. Therefore

[39] *Syst. Theol.* Vol. I, p. 27.
[40] *Op. cit.*, p. 26.

Tillich's correlative method is by no means intended as a method to present evidence.

Belief in God is not an intellectual but an existential decision; it is not the rational arguments which lead to belief in God, but belief in God rests on God's coming within the horizon of human existence; it rests on an existential encounter between God and man.

On the basis of reflection man can know that man himself is question. That this question is essentially a question about God can come to light only when God is revealed as the answer to the question man himself is, when God enters within the horizon of human existence. Only then does it become clear what the meaning of the question is. Therefore when Tillich takes human existence as the point of departure he does not mean that man could reach God from within this existence. Only later, when from his revealing action God is known as answer, can the question which man is be understood, posited, and answered from the answer which God himself is. This answer which God himself is would, nevertheless, be no answer for man if man as man were not the question to which this answer is the real Answer. This, according to Tillich is the pivot on which the question about God turns: "The answers implied in the event of revelation are meaningful only insofar as they are in correlation with questions concerning the whole of existence, with existential questions. Only those who have experienced the shock of transitoriness, the anxiety in which they are aware of their finitude, the threat of non-being, can understand what the notion of God means." [41]

This notion of God does not derive its content from a reflection on being-human, however necessary this may be as a starting-point, but from revelation on God's part. But the fact that his being-human is an open question stimulates man to a search for ultimate knowledge and certainty. In this regard Tillich distinguishes in his theory of knowledge between a controlling and a receiving knowledge. The first, while it does give certainty, does not have an ultimate sense and meaning; the second can have an ultimate sense and meaning, but does not give certainty. Certain knowledge, which at the same time is ultimate knowledge (knowledge which is connected with man's ultimate concern) rests on revelation. As long as man depends on himself his striving

41 *Op. cit.,* p. 69.

for knowledge will result in a dilemma of knowing: "The threatening character of this dilemma is rarely recognized and understood. But if it is realized and not covered up by preliminary and incomplete verifications, it must lead either to a desperate resignation of truth or to the quest for revelation, for revelation claims to give a truth which is both certain and of ultimate concern." [42]

Left to itself, man's striving for ultimate knowledge and certainty will lead to only two possibilities: either to a resignation to the discovery that the question which man himself is will always remain a question without an ultimate and effective answer (Heidegger), or to a quest for revelation from the transcendent "reverse side" of human existence as answer to the question man cannot answer by himself, the question which man himself is (Newman).

The central question in Tillich's theology is therefore the question about the whether, how, and where of a revelation in which God manifests himself to questioning man, as the answer to the question about being-human. In Tillich's current of thought this revelation cannot possibly consist of the communication of information about God and man, in the communication of revealed truths which are to supplement the truths which man had already discovered by himself. In Tillich revelation has an existential character *par excellence*. God reveals himself within the limits of human existence, in and through the existence of Jesus as the Christ.

It cannot be logically proved that the existence of Jesus as Christ has revealing power. It can become evident for any person who discovers that the answer to the question which he himself is lies within the existence of Jesus as the Christ.

In this respect Tillich's manner of approach shows great similarity to that of Emil Brunner in his book *Man In Revolt* which has quite unjustly been forgotten.[43]

To the question Where is God? Tillich answers: God can be revealed to and known by man in the existence of Jesus as the Christ. Not as if God had revealed, in Jesus, the inscrutable mys-

---

[42] *Op. cit.*, p. 117.

[43] Emil Brunner, *Der Mensch im Widerspruch* (Zwingli Verlag, Zurich, 1937, 1941). English trans. by Olive Wyon: *Man in Revolt. A Christian Anthropology* (Westminster Press, Philadelphia, 1947).

tery of his divine being. Rather, to speak with Kierkegaard, God veiled, in Jesus as the Christ, his being in a complete *incognito*. In the existence of Jesus as the Christ God revealed himself as the answer to the secret of human existence. In Jesus as the Christ light has fallen on human existence. In this light it is clear that the mysteriousness, dissatisfaction, and dissension of human existence are the result of man's estrangement from God and from himself.

Man's existence does not correspond to his essence; it does not correspond to the actual and original essence of man. Human existence not only asks for an answer. It asks to be healed; it asks for salvation. This healing, this salvation man will find in the participation in the new being which has been revealed in Jesus as the Christ. This participation comes about by faith in Jesus as the Christ. This participation means the abolition of the estrangement from God, and the restoration of the relationship between God as Answer and man as question.

The problem of God finds its solution in faith in Jesus as the Christ. But what does it mean when, by faith, man participates in the new being? What does this mean for the knowledge about God? Who is this God whom man meets by believing in Jesus as the Christ?

Tillich declares emphatically that this cannot mean that man now has learned to know a God, and has begun to believe in a God. God is not *a* God. For then God would be a being, and not Being-itself, or ground of all being. The word "God" really cannot be used as a noun. Nor can any idea or any concept, no matter how pure and spiritual, be identified with God. Man can form a concept only of beings which belong to the material, temporal, and spatial aspect of total Reality. But with "God" it is a matter of transcendental Reality which lies hidden behind and transcends material, temporal, and spatial reality. God is not material, he is supratemporal, and extraspatial.

Man cannot form for himself any idea, concept, or image of God. For that reason God is not an imagined divinity, but really "God." Man can really speak about God only in symbols. The symbols point to God. They do not coincide with God. All knowledge about God, also and precisely that which is based on revelation, is symbolic knowledge about God. Any expression or confession of faith is a faith symbol. The early Church knew this. For this reason Tillich resists all concepts of God which are so identified with God that as a result of this identification man does not believe really in God, but in a certain concept of God. In this respect it makes no difference whether man believes in the God (or gods) of monotheism and polytheism or in that of pantheism or theism. The expression "to believe in the God of theism" is—if God himself is meant here—a contradiction in terms.

Belief in God is not belief in "a God" or in "the God of . . ." but belief simply in God. For God is absolute, and cannot be referred to anyone or anything. To refer God to something or somebody necessarily means to relativize God. Belief in a relative God is a relative belief in God. But in a belief in the God who has been revealed in Jesus as the Christ it is a matter of an absolute belief in God. Anything which in any form points to God must be understood symbolically because God is hidden, invisible, nonmaterial, supratemporal, and extraspatial: "Ordinary theism has made God a heavenly, completely perfect person who resides above the world and mankind. The protest of atheism against such a highest person is correct. There is no evidence for his existence, nor is he a matter of ultimate concern. God is not God without universal participation." [44]

In this respect, too, Tillich was firmly convinced that he was in the company of prophets, apostles, and martyrs who took up the battle against a humanization of the figure of God, and against the identification and permutation of finite symbols with the Reality of God to which these symbols could at best only allude. The bible constantly struggles against religion as idolatry: "The Bible is not only a religious but also an anti-religious book . . . the Bible fights for God against religion." [45]

The same is true of the early Church. Were not the first Christians often regarded as atheists? With his expression "God above God" Tillich intended nothing else than to place himself among the Church Fathers in their battle against the paganization of Christianity: "The early Church tried to demythologize the idea of God and the meaning of the Christ by concepts taken from the Platonic-Stoic tradition. In all periods theologians have tried hard to show the transcendence of the divine over the finite symbols expressing him. The idea of 'God above God' can be

---

[44] *Syst. Theol.* Vol. I, p. 271.
[45] *Christianity and the Encounter of the World Religions*, pp. 89ff.

found implicitly in all patristic theology. Their encounter with pagan polytheism, with gods on a finite basis, made the Church Fathers extremely sensitive to any concept which would present God as being analyogous to the gods of those against whom they were fighting." [46]

God is supratemporal and extraspatial. God is far above any concept of God we might want to form of him. God is not here or there: "God is present in what we do as citizens, as creative artists, as friends, as lovers of nature, as workers in a profession, so that it may have eternal (i.e. ultimate) meaning." [47]

This of course does not mean to say that God is not real. Nor that an end has come to the religious era. Tillich calls the idea of "the end of the religious age" an impossible one: "The religious principle cannot come to an end. For the question of the ultimate meaning of life cannot be silenced as long as men are men." [48]

In the chapter that follows we shall consider the implications of Tillich's belief in God with a view to the relation between Christianity and the non-Christian religions.

At the moment it would seem that Tillich's influence in the United States is decreasing. Bonhoeffer's vision of an approaching religionless era and of the necessity of a rapid secularization of the Christian proclamation has attracted many. In reference to recent publications of Altizer, Hamilton, Vahanian, Howlett, and others, the public press speaks even of a God-is-dead-movement. A few weeks before his death Tillich said of this: "This is going too far." Therefore at his death he left us with the question whether it is indeed possible to go too far, whether a development once begun can come to a stop halfway, or whether it perhaps lies in the very nature of things that a development once accepted must, according to internal laws which dominate it, go as far as it can.

At any rate, at the beginning of his book *The Gospel of Christian Atheism*, Thomas Altizer assures us emphatically that he owes his Christian conviction mainly to Tillich, and that he considers his own vision of the gospel of Christian atheism as the ultimate and inevitable conclusion from the principles of Tillich's philosophical and theological thought.

[46] *Op. cit.*, p. 91.
[47] *Op. cit.*, p. 94.
[48] *Op. cit.*, p. 96.

# 9. Confrontation with the Non-Christian Religions

Before proceeding to draw up the balance sheet we shall first have to devote a chapter to an aspect of the undermining of conventional Christianity not thus far mentioned: the confrontation with the non-Christian religions.

Christianity could be called the world religion *par excellence*. Today there is not a country where Christianity has not penetrated and where it has not been able to win at least a few for itself. But apart from this actual spread all over the world, Christianity had from its very beginning an ecumenical character. Even if the words of the risen Lord with which he commissioned his disciples to proclaim the Gospel to the whole world, to all peoples, and to the end of time had not been uttered by him in a literal and historical sense, even then these words would still be an expression of the awareness of being sent to the whole world and for all times which characterized the Christian Church from the very beginning.

This missionary awareness was by no means the fruit of a provincialism unable to look beyond the boundaries of its own small world. Rather, we are dealing here with the breakthrough of an awareness of vocation and responsibility so wide and supranational that it was able to draw all the peoples of the world within its horizon.

Nor was this ecumenical missionary awareness the bitter fruit of an exaggerated self-esteem and self-sufficiency or, worse still, of the lust for power or self-interest. It originally rested exclusively on an awareness of vocation and duty, and on a real concern for the lot of mankind in general and of individual man in particular.

The Christian missionary awareness did not rest on human weakness, as if the Christians considered themselves better than others, knowing everything better than others. It was not based

253

on an exaggerated self-esteem but on the content of the Gospel itself.

If a person is convinced of the truth of the Gospel message this neccessarily includes, because of the very content of that message, the conviction that the message is destined for all men of all times and in the whole world. It also includes the conviction that there is no other salvation for mankind than the salvation proclaimed by the Gospel.

It is as in a case of a sickness unto death against which suddenly an effective medicine has been discovered. When a doctor in his practice deals with a patient who suffers from that sickness he simply has to be absolute and exclusive in his decision. Because of his vocation and duty he will not be able to do anything but prescribe this medicine absolutely as the only means to save this person. He will necessarily have to tell his patient that this medicine, and none other, will effectively save him from an otherwise certain death.

From the very beginning it was also like this with the proclamation of the Gospel. The claim of absoluteness and exclusivity which has always characterized the Christian proclamation is based on the completely unique and definitive character of the content of the Gospel, and is necessarily given with this content.

Three facts are of decisive significance for a proper insight into the relation between Christianity and the non-Christian religions. The first fact is that in the Christian proclamation it is not a matter of a certain vision of the relationship with God, but it is a matter of a real event that is decisive for this relationship. It is not a matter of a teaching of Jesus of Nazareth which states that God is love and that therefore every person, no matter how low he has fallen, may be convinced that in spite of everything he is fully and unconditionally accepted by God. It is a matter of the reality of an act by which man has actually been redeemed and saved because God has effectively accepted man.

The Gospel is a message of salvation, a message of healing and saving brought about by God himself. The Gospel is a message of misery and salvation, a message of distress and deliverance. The Gospel proclaims that mankind, and with it every individual without exception, is in a state of such radical estrangement from God and of such ultimate and complete deprivation that God alone has it in his power to save man. According to the Gospel, the human predicament has the character of an existential situation of distress in which the *to be or not to be* of man is at stake. From this situation of distress God himself has saved man by an act, by a salvation event.

The Gospel proclaims that God sent his Son into the world, not only to bring a message to man, but also effectively to reconcile man to God and thereby to save him from disaster. According to the Christian proclamation Jesus Christ is the only savior and redeemer because he effectively took up man's cause, and by his sacrifice on the cross reconciled mankind once and for all to God and saved it from its state of sin and deprivation. This act of reconciliation, redemption, and salvation was ratified by God when he raised Jesus from the dead. The reality of salvation falls or stands, in the biblical proclamation, with the reality of the resurrection.

This leads us to the second fact. What the Christian proclamation says on the basis of the biblical witness about the person, the origin and birth, the life and death, the passion and the resurrection of Jesus Christ was, from the very beginning, understood, not in a symbolic but in a literal sense, not in a mythological but in a historical sense. All of the Christian proclamation stands or falls with the historicity of the salvation event, of the history of salvation. It is clear from the fifteenth chapter of Paul's First Letter to the Corinthians that from the very beginning this was true also of such a seemingly incredible story as that of the resurrection, a story diametrically opposed to the general experience of all mankind that a person who dies and is buried does not rise again. Paul tells the Corinthians that if it is true, as some people say, that the dead cannot rise, then Christ has not risen either. But if Chirst did not really rise from the dead, then "our preaching would be without meaning and your faith groundless."

It is precisely on the basis of the fact that Christ's work of salvation was a unique and effective event in the history of mankind, by which mankind was once and for all restored to the proper relationship with God, that the Christian proclamation has a completely exclusive character. "Neither is there salvation in any other. For there is no other name under heaven given to men by which we must be saved" (Acts, 4, 12). This exclusivism is not based on some form of narrow-mindedness or self-exaltation of the Christians, but it is inevitably given with the character of the content of the proclamation.

But the third fact is, if possible, of still greater significance. It is the fact that from the very beginning the Christians carried this treasure of salvation in vessels of clay (2 Cor. 4, 7). Among other things this means that Christianity as an empirical religion may under no circumstances be identified with the biblical and Christian proclamation. In any case, this proclamation is itself expressed in human words. As far as the form of expression is concerned it is human and temporal. It is not a matter of the form but of the content of the message. But all the more does this apply to Christianity as an organized, stabilized, and even uniform religion. As a religion, Christianity is a time-bound product of culture with a human pattern, sometimes all too human. Without distinction this applies to all the Christian Churches. It is therefore not without reason that the great missiologist and philosopher of religion Hendrik Kraemer expressed the necessary distinction between religion and faith in the title of one of his books: *Religion and the Christian Faith.*[1]

The relativity and the limitation of Christianity as world religion does not contradict the absoluteness and exclusivity of the message of salvation. But insofar as the message of salvation finds real expression in the teaching, theology, and liturgy, and other forms of Christianity, Christianity shares in the absoluteness and exclusivity proper to the message of salvation because of its own content and character. This does not have to exclude the possibility and the actuality of the fact that God wanted to prepare all mankind for the message of salvation through the action of the Holy Spirit, and that the non-Christian religions in general, such as the religion of Israel in particular, are the fruit of the action of the Holy Spirit. About this matter, Christians of different Churches have, in the course of time, thought quite differently.

### Condemnation of Non-Christian Religions

Numerous passages can be found in the bible which clearly show that according to the biblical and evangelical norm the fact of not belonging to the chosen people of God does not automatically mean the exclusion from any relationship with God. In the Old

---

[1] Hendrik Kraemer, *Religion and the Christian Faith* (Lutterworth, London, 1956). Cf. E. D. Soper, *The Inevitable Choice* (Abingdon, New York), pp. 138ff.

Testament, Melchisedech, by whom Abraham was blessed, is called "priest of the most high God," and the Persian king Cyrus is called "the friend" and "the anointed" of Yahweh. In the New Testament several Roman officers are called blessed because of their great faith such as Jesus had not found even in Israel. This of course does not imply a judgment about the religion to which these believing men belonged, but it shows that God's final judgment about man does not depend on the doctrine or religion to which he "officially" adheres.

In the course of time several attempts have been made to ascribe a positive meaning to the religiousness of non-Christians in the general picture of the history of salvation. Such attempts were made, among others, by Clement of Alexandria and Origen in the second and third centuries, by Nicolas of Cusa in his work *De Pace Fidei* [2] in the fifteenth century, by representatives of the modern science of religion in the nineteenth century, and finally by several missiologists and dogmatists, both Roman Catholic and Protestant, in our own day.

But in general, conventional Christianity has adopted a negative attitude with regard to the values of non-Christian religions. Not only adherents of these religions, but "heretics" as well were simply excluded from eternal salvation. The revival of missionary zeal in the Roman Catholic Church since Francis Xavier, and in the Protestant Churches since the rise of pietism and methodism of the seventeenth and eighteenth centuries had its origin in a deep concern about the salvation of the souls of pagans and of all those who did not believe in Christ and did not belong to his Church. At the same time, some missionaries have made great contributions to a better knowledge of the religion and of the way of thinking of the primitive peoples.

In the course of this century the theology of Karl Barth has had a noticeable influence, particularly in the circles of the International Missionary Council, on the attitude toward the non-Christian religions, in particular through the book *The Christian Message in a Non-Christian World*, which Hendrik Kraemer wrote in preparation for the International Missionary Conference of Tambaran in 1939.

Barth's position with regard to the non-Christian religions

[2] Nikolaus von Kues, *Philosophisch-theologische Schriften; Lateinisch-Deutsch* (Verlag Herder, Vienna, 1964), Vol. III.

does not differ essentially from that with regard to any form of faith-conviction and piety within Christianity such forms are based on something human instead of God's revelation in Jesus Christ alone. Religion is preeminently the area in which man's pride and lying, his rebellion against God, in short his godlessness and self-exaltation, find expression. Man-made religion is not faith, but unbelief; man-made piety is not communion with God but flight from him. God's revelation in Jesus Christ is not the completion or ratification, but the abolition of man-made religion. This applies to many expressions of Christianity as well as to doctrines and practices of the non-Christian religions: "In our reflections about 'Religion as Unbelief' we have purposely left aside the distinction between Christian and non-Christian religions, because we think that everything that could be said there, applies similarly to the Christian religion." [3]

God's revelation in Jesus Christ is the judgment and definitive end of every religion and piety: "Religion is never and nowhere true as such and in itself. Rather, God's revelation denies that any religion is true, that it is in truth the knowledge and worship of God and the reconciliation of man to God." [4] This applies in the same degree to Christianity as organized, stabilized religion, bound to history and culture, as to any other religion: "All the activity of our faith, all our Christian concepts of God and of divine things, our Christian theology, our Christian worship, our Christian forms of community and order, our Christian morality, poetry and art, our attempts to give individual and social forms to Christian life, our Christian strategy and tactics in the interest of our Christian cause, in short our Christianity, to the extent that it is precisely *our* Christianity as our own human undertaking . . . all this in its totality and in its individual elements . . . is not a work of faith and obedience to God's revelation, but the purpose and action is here no less seriously human unbelief, opposition to God's revelation. It is therefore active idolatry and self-righteousness." [5]

Therefore faith in Jesus Christ means deliverance from religion, from the unbearable slavery of religion. For religion imposes all sorts of burdens on man which are too heavy to carry. The person who is not reconciled to God in Jesus Christ tries, by

[3] Karl Barth, *Kirchliche Dogmatik*, I 2, p. 357.
[4] *Op. cit.*, p. 356.
[5] *Op. cit.*, p. 358.

means of penitential exercises, sacrifices, and pious practices, to reconcile himself to God, or to place himself in safety against God. Religion is preeminently the expression of the state in which man finds himself when he is not in Jesus Christ. Religion is a sin.

Barth's position can only be understood and judged in the light of his anthropology (*Church Dogmatics*, Vol. 3). In the relationship between man and God, that which alone counts is God's attitude toward man. Man is so unfaithful to his being as creature and as covenant-partner of God that he is entirely incapable by himself of establishing any relationship with God. Any attempt he makes in that direction, in whatever religious form, is not only in vain but also blasphemous pretension. Man's salvation can be found only in God's eternal and unwavering fidelity. This fidelity of God applies to all men. The relationship between God and man is not determined by the religion to which he adheres, but by God's fidelity. This fidelity has been revealed and has, as it were, actualized itself in Jesus Christ. In him God has shown man, of whatever religion he may be, his own eternal fidelity and has, as it were, ratified his covenant partnership with God. In Jesus Christ it appears that God is not against man, but for him. Jesus Christ means God's complete acceptance of man as he is, and in spite of everything. This is the salvific fact which on Christ's authority must be proclaimed. Christian faith is man's acknowledgment and acceptance of this message of salvation.

In Barth's position with regard to religion there is question of a twofold distinction. The first distinction is the one between man and any religion which stands outside Jesus Christ. Just as decisively as God detests and condemns any man-made religion as a rebellion against God, as idolatry, and as pseudo-religion, just as decisively does God in Jesus Christ accept man as such. God condemns religion precisely because he loves the man who has fallen victim to religion, with an infinite love and fidelity, and has accepted him in Jesus Christ, in spite of the fact that man has no knowledge of this acceptance. Therefore, when Barth speaks of the utter rejection of any religion which stands outside Jesus Christ as a pseudo-religion, this does not mean a definitive rejection of man but, on the contrary, his preservation.

The second distinction Barth makes is between the Christian proclamation and the Christian faith as based on it on the one hand, and Christianity as religion on the other. Not only the non-Christian religions, but Christianity as world religion in its various Catholic and Protestant forms as well are under the judgment of God's Word and under the discipline of Jesus Christ as the only Lord. Only where the domination of Jesus Christ is accepted and honored, and where any other sort of domination of whatever human form is rejected, only there the kingdom of God is truly present, as Berkhof states.[6] Christianity as a product of culture, as world religion, has often and in many ways obstructed the arrival of God's kingdom more than it has promoted it.

Ultimately therefore it is not a matter of comparing or confronting Christianity with non-Christian religions, but rather of confronting all religions (including Christianity) with the Gospel of Jesus Christ and with the Word of God to which the bible and the Church give witness. The priority of Christianity and Judaism with regard to other religions is based on the historical fact that Christianity and Judaism are the two religions which have tried to give expression to the Word of God: Judaism to the Word of God in its provisional and prophetic form; Christianity to the Word of God as it has received a definitive form, has become incarnate, in Jesus Christ.

Therefore faith in the biblical sense if not faith in one or another Church form of Christianity; faith is always and exclusively faith in Jesus Christ. Whatever presents itself as divine faith apart from Jesus Christ is a pseudo-faith. It is here important to realize that faith in the Old Testament prophetic Word of God is in principle also faith in Jesus Christ, and therefore genuine faith.

Wherever the influence of Barth's theology has penetrated, it is not so much a matter of determining the relation between Christianity and the non-Christian religions as of a confrontation of all religions and all forms of religiousness with the Gospel of Jesus Christ. The Gospel has the only and final norm of judgment. By positing the problem this way Barth has undoubtedly brought light and order in the obscurity and chaos into which we had fallen with regard to the approach and mutual comparison of religions from the viewpoint of Christian faith.

In general it can be said that the Protestant mission is less

[6] H. Berkhof, *De Katholiciteit der Kerk* (Callenbach, Nykerk, 1962), p. 89.

inclined than the Catholic mission to ascribe a positive value, even merely preparative to the non-Christian religions. Nor is it necessary for a person to be a professed disciple of Barth if he wishes to deny any content of truth to all non-Christian religions. A clear example is the recent book of the well-known Methodist historian of religion and missiologist, Edmund Perry who gained a great name for himself in the United States and Canada. The book is entitled *The Gospel in Dispute*, and deals with the relation of the Christian faith with other religions in missionary areas. Perry considers the non-Christian religions under the aspect of their aggressivity in regard to which Christianity has been forced into a position of defense.

Perry thinks that it should be a conviction in principle of every Christian that the non-Christian religions are not only quite incapable of making any positive contribution to a genuine faith in God, but that all non-Christian religions also lead man further and further away from God. All non-Christian religions lead man to serve idols instead of the one true God who has revealed himself in Christ. Anyone who doubts this in the least has already in principle denied his faith and thus jeopardized his Christian existence: "Since from the viewpoint of Gospel-faith the one true and only living God is the God of Abraham, Isaac and Jacob, the Father of our Lord Jesus Christ, and since the Gospel alone brings man to this God, all other faith- claims and -systems lead men away from him." [7]

The word "religion" according to Perry as a phenomenologist of religion, is simply the general and collective term for the universal phenomenon which aims at leading man, individually and collectively, away from God. In other words, religion as such has a demonic character, for every religion is "a concrete manifestation or actualization of a particular people being led away from God in a particular way by a particular schema." Religion as a collective term is the general expression of "the unity of human life being oriented and organized *away from* the God of Gospel-faith through the diversity of creeds, codes, myths, rituals, cults, and many ways of worship." [8] In other words it is only on the basis of Gospel-faith that mankind can

[7] Edmund Perry, *The Gospel in Dialogue* (Doubleday, New York, 1958), p. 88.
[8] *Loc. cit.*

become one; religion, on the other hand, in all its contradictory forms cannot but divide and separate mankind. In this viewpoint, ecumenism can be realized not by bringing the religions closer to one another, but by radically rejecting them and replacing them by Gospel-faith: "The primary essence of all non-Gospel religions is the scattered germ of sin, willful substitution for God, the death or repentance of which is the death of religions, the mission and goal of Gospel-faith." [9]

It is obvious that Perry does not mean that this radical rejection of any form of religion other than Gospel-faith implies that the Christian may not or should not respect and take seriously as men the fellow human beings who have fallen victim to this or that religion. On the contrary, the Christian cannot and may not exclude anyone from the love of Christ. But the Christian must know what he is doing when he begins to occupy himself with non-Christian religions. For a person who does not know what he is doing, this is playing with fire. Under no condition may the study of a non-Christian religion lead the Christian to look for positive values for the enrichment of his personal religious thought and life. This would be nothing more nor less than apostasy from the Christian faith. It is quite impossible to have a reconciliation and communion between the Gospel-faith of the Christian and the pseudofaith or unbelief of the non-Christian.

This attitude, which for that matter is similar to that which Roman Catholics adopted for centuries toward Protestants, and Orthodox toward liberals, is still rather widespread among Christians. It is the attitude which generally was adopted by conventional Christianity as self-evident.


## Dialogue of Religions

It would not seem that the conventional attitude of rejection has been the final word in the relation between Christianity and non-Christian religions. An encounter between religions has become inevitable, also as a result of the fact that we find ourselves in a nascent world on the way toward a new world culture comprising all peoples and bringing all peoples into more and more contact. Everywhere it is possible to notice a gigantic exer-

[9] *Op. cit.*, p. 94.

tion to conquer, in spite of everything, the extremely dangerous contrasts between the different races, ideologies, and ethnic groups. This has evoked a new phenomenon, that of the dialogue. Nations and social groups are more and more trying to use peaceful discussion in the mastering of situations which only recently usually led to discord, conflict, and force of arms. The only way out toward a possible solution is that of the dialogue.

The religions and the Churches cannot escape this general tendency. The ecumenical movement which nowadays comprises practically all the Christian Churches is already beginning to develop into a general human movement which brings representatives of all religions, as well as humanists and atheists, together in dialogue about belief or non-belief in God.

A change can also be noticed in the relation between the Christian Churches and the non-Christian religions. The dialogue has begun between Israel and the Church. The Second Vatican Council has established secretariats for the promotion of dialogue with other Christian Churches, with Israel, with non-Christian religions, and with groups of fellow men who do not believe in God. This means a sincere mutual acceptance of one another on the basis of fellow human-being, and in spite of existing religious contrasts. In this respect it is undoubtedly possible to speak of a radical, possibly a Copernican, revolution in the sphere of human relations. This revolution is one of the many symptoms of the end of conventional Christianity.

In his last book *World Cultures and World Religions* Hendrik Kraemer used as sub-title *The Coming Dialogue*.[10] From the positive tone of appreciation with regard to everything sincerely intended as religion, including theosophy and other syncretist movements, it is clear that Kraemer has begun in this respect to take a wider standpoint, without, however, weakening in his personal Christian convictions. The book presents a general analysis, based on extensive factual material, of the present world situation with regard to religion.

Here we touch on an important point: the foundation of analyses on objective reproduction of a generally oriented, factual material. The judgment about non-Christian religions should be based on a real, more than superficial, encounter, and at least

[10] Hendrik Kraemer, *World Cultures and World Religions* (Lutterworth, London, 1960, 1963).

on a serious reading of the holy books concerned. I myself am one of those who never visited an Asiatic country, and who gained his knowledge of other religions from books about those religions. This makes it necessary to consult writers with long personal experience and firsthand knowledge.

Barth's position with regard to non-Christian religions is based on arguments derived exclusively from the content of the Christian faith itself. It begins with the supposition that the biblical vision of man and the content of the Christian proclamation are of such a nature that they justify and even demand an attitude of pure rejection and a crushing judgment, even though the person making the judgment might not have any thorough knowledge at his disposal of facts concerning those religions. Until recently, the judgments of the Christian Churches about each other were made on the basis of the doctrine of each particular Church, and no trouble was taken to try to get to know the other as he really was. In like manner the judgment about non-Christian religions was based on the Christian faith itself, regardless of the actual content and intention of those doctrines and practices, which were *a priori* condemned. There was no awareness of the fact that man should never, on whatever basis, condemn that which he does not know. Not too long ago it was not at all unusual to hear sermons in the most different churches, and not least in the Roman churches, categorically condemning other Churches, religions, and parties, purely on the authority of hearsay, and without any basic knowledge of the facts.

To form a judgment about the faith or about the religious practice of another person, no matter to what religious community he belongs, is morally justifiable and in agreement with the love which we Christians owe to all our fellow men because of Christ's "new commandment," only if this judgment is based on exact and profound knowledge of the facts, on personal encounter, and on sincere respect. Here we touch upon one of the most current sins of conventional Christianity, a sin from which we have to convert ourselves at any cost and with open heart.

But the more seriously we exert ourselves to do justice to the person of another faith, the more we discover how extremely difficult, if not impossible, it is, and how much patience and perseverance is required to learn to know another religion or a different form of piety, and to understand them as they are really intended. One of the main obstacles on the road to an ecumenics which comprises all men in true unity and in sincere community, is that we judge lightly and know only superficially. We all tend to think that we understand and judge the other correctly when we have only begun to take the first step in that direction.

There is a daily multiplication of circumstances because of which Christians and non-Christians are forced to come to an encounter and dialogue. But at the same time it is also true that a really meaningful and fruitful dialogue must be based on an existential encounter, and through this on an exploitation of the circumstances which make such an encounter possible. To those who can foresee that they will become involved in the dialogue of the religions perhaps no better advice can be given than to consult the extensive warnings in Gerald Cooke's book *As Christians Face Rival Religions*, with the subtitle *An Interreligious Strategy for Community without Compromise*. The great advantage is that this book places the dialogue of religions in the midst of the religious situation of all mankind at present. His criticism of extreme positions to the left and to the right (respectively Hocking, Toynbee, and Barth, Kraemer) is reduced to two directives: (1) "Neither close-minded exclusivism nor extreme and perhaps empty tolerance is acceptable." [11] (2) "The tension between divine revelation and human reason will never be satisfactorily solved by exalting either at the expense of the other." [12]

A first acquaintance with the non-Christian religions may give the believing Christian a jolt that might lead to indifferentism, relativism, and uncertainty of faith. This type of jolt will in the future await every Christian as world citizen, for encounter and dialogue are inevitable in the long run. Cooke speaks of two shocks from opposite directions: the shock of similarity and the shock of difference.[13] In this connection he devotes, in admirable impartiality, about fifty pages to an accurate analysis of the similarities as well as of the differences between Christianity and the other religions.

As an antidote against possible confusion which might result from a first acquaintance, he prescribes an exercise. The reader is advised to exercise himself in discovering that on further reflec-

[11] Gerald Cooke, *As Christians Face Rival Religions* (Association Press, N.Y., 1962), p. 150.
[12] *Op. cit.*, pp. 151ff.
[13] *Op. cit.*, pp. 50ff.

tion differences may still be found in what appear to be similarities, and that, on the contrary, similarities may still be found in what appear to be differences. He illustrates this exercise by examples taken from a great number of different religions.

Dialogue and encounter suppose each other. But at the moment we have not yet reached the point where we can speak of an encounter and dialogue between the religions themselves through official representatives. The encounter takes place on the personal level of human relations. The dialogue—in so far as it manifests itself to the outside—is still restricted to some individual adherents of different religions, individuals born and educated each in his own religion, but who on the basis of the fact that the present world situation has brought them together in encounter sense the need for dialogue. This, of course, is nothing new in history. In past centuries, too, discussions on religion have taken place between Christians and non-Christians in those countries where the circumstances gave rise to encounter and discussion.

Kraemer's book, which we have mentioned earlier, is devoted entirely to the problematics of dialogue. There are mainly two facts which give rise to dialogue. One is the growing need for collaboration in various fields which brings together increasing numbers of representatives of the different religions, thus almost forcing them to encounter and dialogue. The second is the character of the nascent world culture, as a result of which all religions without distinction are beginning to find themselves in an ever increasing situation of crisis which is similar for all. "All religions," writes Kraemer, "have—whether their adherents have noticed it or not—entered a period of lasting and fundamental crisis. The more clearly and more honestly their authoritative representatives acknowledge this, the better it will be for the world, for religion, and for culture. Such an acknowledgment includes that they are all faced by the necessity to reinterpret their unchangeable, fundamental positions without which they would lose their identity." [14]

In this connection Tillich distinguishes between religions and quasi-religions. By quasi-religions he understands ideologies such as communism or fascism, in which the ideal of a new welfare state has so much acquired the character of ultimate concern that it takes the place of God. These quasi-religions, together

[14] H. Kraemer, *World Cultures and World Religions*, p. 310.

with secularism, have conquered the world to such an extent that they threaten the continued existence of all religions. The quasi-religions give a new answer to the question about the meaning of life, about the real and ultimate goal to which man's existence can and must be directed. Neither God and God's design and commandment, nor heaven and a future heavenly bliss occupy even the least place in the world of thought of the quasi-religions.

What is common to the old, classical world religions is that for all of them and all over the world their existence is increasingly threatened by the quasi-religions and by secularism which is the inevitable result of the direction in which the nascent world culture is developing.

For the time being, this conflict also has its good sides. It stimulates the world religions to reflection and action. Kraemer especially is in this respect filled with courage and confidence. This is not only based on his belief that God has the last word in the history of mankind, but also on what he sees and experiences. He flatly denies that "we live in a religion-less world" and that "the Christian Church, for example, is dying all over the world." For Kraemer, the contrary is true, and he finds that both the great non-Christian religions and the Christian Church are experiencing a revival.[15] It is precisely this revival which again confronts the religions, presenting them with the choice between conflict and dialogue.

It is undoubtedly true that the present world situation and the nascent world culture promote an encounter of the religions and make dialogue inevitable. But the question is whether a dialogue of the religions is actually possible, and whether it can be fruitful. If such a dialogue would be condemned to be fruitless from the very start, it would be a waste of time to engage in it. The first question which presents itself is what the conditions are for a dialogue between the religions, what motives and aims must form the basis for the dialogue, and what the least expectations must be.

Here again it is not a matter of my personal vision, but of the direction in which the situation is actually developing. What is the opinion about these questions on the part of experts who have already been personally engaged in the dialogue? I am thinking of the numerous discussions which Kraemer had during his entire life with representatives of all the world religions in practically

15 *Op. cit.*, p. 312.

all the countries of Asia and North Africa; I think of Benz' visits to Japan and India, and of Tillich's visit to Japan. What do they have to say about the prospects of the coming and inevitable dialogue?

In the first place, they begin with the present world situation. Never has there been a period such as ours in which so much has happened all over the world, quite unexpectedly, and in a short time, so much which anyone would have considered utterly impossible only a few years ago. We are living in a time of surprises that follow each other in rapid succession. In a very short time we have learned not to consider anything impossible. Things simply happen, and the end of it cannot be seen. It is like this, too, with the dialogue of the religions.

This, however, does not mean that there are not certain conditions which must be fulfilled if it is to be a fruitful dialogue. Tillich names four pre-suppositions for all representatives in the dialogue.[16]

1. The partners must take each other's convictions seriously, and acknowledge that the other's contribution has a positive value. For there is not a single religion which is not ultimately based on a revelatory experience. It is unreasonable to begin with an *a priori* supposition that this would be true of one's own religion, but not of that of the other. This revelatory experience may be of a different nature, and therefore does not of itself mean that all religions are *one* already, as if one could not say anything new to the other.

2. The religion which each of the partners represents must be a personal and existential matter for them (their real ultimate concern), so that they will be able to clarify to the other in a convincing manner what is the actual character of the religion they represent. In view of the fact that in our time all religions experience a revival, adaptation, and renewal, the partners must take seriously also those who have something new to say which may not coincide with the traditional, orthodox, and conventional concepts in the religions concerned. For example, a person who distrusts the Ahmadiyya movement in Islam because of its open

[16] Tillich, *Christianity and the Encounter of the World Religions* (Col. Un. Press, New York, 1963), p. 64. Cf. Tillich's posthumous book: *The Future of Religions* (Harper and Row, New York, 1966), in which Tillich discusses this subject.

and general humanistic attitude would also have to consider many a Christian sect as nonrepresentative of Christianity.

3. There must be a common ground for the dialogue. There must be sufficient agreement as to what the various partners understand by "religion." It is not sufficient that all use the word "religion." This word must have the same sense and meaning for all. As we have seen in the previous chapter, Tillich defines religion very generally as the state of being seized by the power of being, or by ultimate concern. The definition could be made more concrete by saying that religion is the expression of the way in which man conceives and maintains his relation to God (to the divine, the holy, the mystery of Reality). In this respect, religion everywhere seems to fulfill a similar function in life, even though this may be in many different forms. These differences do not facilitate the dialogue. But the dialogue is possible when the partners realize that with all the differences and possible contrasts their religion is a matter of a similar necessity and function of life. We shall return to this after indicating the fourth presupposition.

4. It is inevitable that real or supposed (lack of knowledge and prejudice) characteristics of the religion of one partner will evoke criticism by other partners. All partners must be ready to listen to these criticisms. The partners must be prepared and willing to receive mutually from each other, even if it were initially only to obtain a new and deeper insight into the meaning of their own religion. No matter how convinced the various partners may be of the truth and value of their own religion, the dialogue must in no instance aim at the conversion of the other without taking seriously the value which the other ascribes to his religion.

## Common Ground

The question can be asked whether in fact there is a common ground for a meaningful and fruitful dialogue. Many will deny this, even though they may do this on *a priori* bases and without any real knowledge of the religions which are *a priori* rejected.

The most difficult obstacle to dialogue is the phenomenon of orthodoxy. Precisely because religion concerns the most important factor in man's life it is an unbearable thought that one's own religious convictions and practices are assailable and insufficient, and that those of another may be true and trustworthy. In religion, it is a matter of to be or not to be. It is clear that this is the background of religious fanaticism, religious wars, persecution of those of other faiths, and restriction of religious freedom. But all this is basically inspired by a self-defense against the existential anxiety of not being safe and secure in one's own religion.

Even within the world of Christianity itself there are as many orthodoxies as there are types of Church. The more orthodox a believer is, the less he is prepared even to consider the idea that his orthodoxy is not absolutely infallible, and that other Churches might be closer to the truth or more in agreement with the practice of the Gospel. But the phenomenon of orthodoxy is not only found in Christianity. The other religions of Semitic origin, the Jewish and the Islam religions, know this phenomenon also. Both in the Jewish religion and in Islam the phenomenon of orthodoxy has given life to two other phenomena: the organization of sects and liberalism. The man of the sect dissociates himself from orthodoxy because he overemphasizes a certain aspect of his religion, especially if he thinks that the orthodoxy expresses this aspect not at all or insufficiently. At the same time, a sectarian can be extremely orthodox within his own sect.

Liberalism, on the other hand, resists any restriction of the freedom, openness, and spontaneity of religion. Liberalism makes a sharp distinction between the heart of the matter and the more or less arbitrary, time-bound, human, relative form. Liberalism distrusts any authoritative discipline meant to protect orthodoxy, and defends the right and duty to examine freely and judge all things, and to be free to accept them or not. Obviously, liberalism is a danger to orthodoxy. But on the other hand, it promotes dialogue between representatives of different orientations, Churches and religions. Liberalism is especially open to the achievements of science and philosophy and to the development of culture in general. It considers orthodoxy, stemming from earlier centuries, as antiquated in many respects and as no longer acceptable. Not only Christianity, but the Jewish religion and Islam also know the orthodox and the liberal type of faith.

Orthodoxy obviously involves a position of antithesis. This position is typical of the religions of semitic origin. The religions of Indian origin, on the other hand, are characterized by a synthetic position. They easily incline toward syncretism, they can more easily adapt to new circumstances, in the Western world they often present themselves in Christian dress, and they are remarkably less fanatical in their attitude toward other religions, unless the latter provoke them.

On the basis of all this it is impossible to say in general whether or not there is actually a common ground for a dialogue of the religions. This depends on the question about what religions one is speaking, and what religious groups within a certain religion are considered as representative.

At any rate, the first serious acquaintance with non-Christian religions in our time has been a considerable shock and threat to conventional Christianity, particularly as a result of the many surprising similarities which are found and must be admitted.

In the first place, it is impossible to lightly pass over the fact that all world religions possess holy books, the content of which is ascribed to divine revelation and inspiration, and which are considered unassailable and having authority. The obedience to and respect for the Koran in Islam does not yield to that which a Jew pays the Torah (the books of the Old Testament acknowledged by the Jewish canon as the books of Moses), nor to that which the Christian pays to the Bible and in particular to the Gospel. Hinduism considers as holy and authoritative the book of the Vedas, and often also that of the upanishads; and Buddhism does the same with regard to the Tripitaka.

Those who were born into the various religions and educated in them have no doubt about the truth and authority of these holy books, just as the Christians has no doubt about the truth and authority of the bible. In all religions one finds an exegesis of the sacred texts, and a doctrine or theology based on this exegesis. Orthodoxy is found everywhere, and councils have been held to determine and safeguard the doctrine in its purity; likewise is liberalism found everywhere as a reaction to orthodoxy; sectarianism is found everywhere as a phenomenon; everywhere a Protestant type can be found which places all the emphasis on the reading and contemplation of the sacred text, and everywhere a Catholic type can be found which reserves a large place for cult, devotions, and various religious practices. Each one of the world religions is represented at the universities of the respective country by a theological faculty. In all religions those who bear authority watch over the integrity of the religion, often in collaboration with the state.

In none of these respects does Christianity differ from other religions. But the forms, too, in which religious life, individually and in common, is expressed are the same everywhere: prayer and sacrifice, preaching and meditation, adoration and worship. Added to this is also the fact that as a result of the present world situation, of the increasing secularization, and of the threat of what Tillich calls the quasi-religions, all religions find themselves in a hitherto unknown crisis, thus having to struggle with similar problems. The common ground for the dialogue of religions lies in the common situation we have just described, as a result of which all religions are "in the same boat," and in the various other points of similarity we have mentioned. This dialogue presupposes an attitude of love and sympathy for one's neighbor. Only in situations where self-interest or at least an egocentric attitude of life predominates, are dangers perceived in the other religion; only there is the other seen as the opponent.

*Positive Evaluation*

An exclusively negative and condemnatory attitude, based on purely *a priori* arguments, toward the non-Christian religions may be the result of a lack of sense for reality. It cannot be denied that these other religions do exist. If there is an omniscient, all-wise God who has designs for mankind which are inscrutable for us, is it not obvious that all religions are in some way or other contained in God's plan? Besides, is not conventional Christianity itself the result of a process of assimilation by which certain elements were borrowed from other religions and made to serve one's own structure? Is the theology of the Church Fathers actually anything else than an expression of the Gospel in terms and categories of Greco-Roman antiquity?

The well-known Spalding professor of Eastern religions at the University of Oxford, R. C. Zaehner, in his book *At Sundry Times* applies the first words of the letter to the Hebrews (After God, in times past, spoke *at sundry times and in divers manners* to the Fathers by the prophets) also to the positive meaning of the Greco-Roman world in God's plan of salvation, and finally to all existing world religions. Early Christianity made grateful use of the rich inheritance of Greek thought and of Roman life when an expression had to be given meaning for those times of the Christian life and faith. In like manner Christianity of our time should, in its mission to the world, continue to build on the valuable elements which are present in all religions, and assimilate these. "Today it would be utterly unrealistic, uncatholic in the widest sense of that word, and absurd to persist in confining ourselves to the legacy of the Greco-Roman world alone. Since Christianity claims to be a universal faith, it can only survive by showing that it can assimilate . . . also whatever in Oriental religion seems to point the way to Christ." [17]

"To point the way to Christ." If it is true that the non-Christian religions somehow point the way to Christ, then it would simply be foolish and irresponsible if the Christian mission were to pass by these signposts because of a kind of self-sufficiency or a feeling of superiority.

The obvious question which is to the point is whether, in how far, and in what way the non-Christian religions show any signs of pointing to unity in Christ.[18] In the third part of his book *The Faith of our Baptism*, Schooenberg even arrives at the somewhat unusual notion of the reality of a supernatural revelation which is general among pagan peoples, and which finds expression in the non-Christian religions. According to his notion there would be question of a "general supernatural revelation" in the non-Christian religions; "general" in contrast to the special divine revelation in Christ, yet supernatural inasmuch as that revelation shows an orientation to salvation in Christ.[19]

This does not mean that the Christian revelation is seen as the completion of that general supernatural revelation in the same way as it is a fulfillment of the Old Testament prophecy. What it means is that in the non-Christian religions somehow a positive meaning must be acknowledged in God's plan of salvation. This is something that has been declared also in the decree of the Second Vatican Council concerning non-Christian religions. Obviously this is a judgment from the point of view of the Christian

---

[17] R. C. Zaehner, *At Sundry Times* (Faber and Faber, London, 1958), p. 166.
[18] P. H. J. M. Camps, *In Christus verbonden met de Godsdiensten der Wereld* (Dekker & v.d. Vegt, Utrecht, 1964), p. 12.
[19] P. Schoonenberg, *Het Geloof van ons Doopsel*, III (Bois-le-Duc, 1958).

faith. This positive evaluation has left out of consideration the question of God's existence, as also the fact that certainly the non-Christian religions are not satisfied with such a subordination to Christianity.

## The Study of Religions

In today's nascent world there is a growing tendency toward a confrontation of Christianity with the non-Christian religions. The people who adhere to these religions have, from a material point of view, undergone the influence of the West. But from the spiritual and religious point of view they all resist the danger of westernization. The ideal of the great Methodist missionary: "the world for Christ in this generation" has not been realized. The non-Christian peoples show no sign at all of surrendering to Christianity. It rather looks as if the tables are being turned. In almost all the large cities of Europe and the United States there is a moderately successful, increasing missionary activity of Islam and particularly of Buddhism, whereas in turn the Christian mission in Asia and Africa is meeting ever more serious obstacles.

In his book about the coming dialogue between East and West and between Christianity and the non-Christian religions, Kraemer speaks of a firm determination of the Asiatic people to remain true to their own type. This applies to culture in general, but also in particular to the point of religion. If it is a matter of capitulation, Kraemer thinks not only that there is no sign in the East of any inclination to capitulate to Western civilization and Christianity, but that in fact a subjective mood can be noticed in the West of capitulation to the East.[20]

Kraemer thinks that in Western Europe, even from the eighteenth century on, there has been a growing feeling of uneasiness about the value of Western culture and religion, and as a result, an increasing tendency to self-examination and self-negation. Many were hoping to find in the East a richness to combat their own spiritual poverty. There is still a growing interest in Islam, in the philosophy of the Hindu religions, and in particular in Buddhism in its various forms. The result is that the East is more and more ready to answer the call from the West, and unfolds an ever growing and more successful missionary activity.

[20] Kraemer, *World Cultures and World Religions,* p. 203.

This phenomenon is more a consequence than a cause of the undermining of conventional Christianity. For many, the bible has many unintelligible, many points of doctrine are considered incompatible with the achievements of philosophy and science; for many, Christianity has become far too complicated, too divided within itself, and is too often misused in the service of politics. In this situation many expect from one or another Eastern religion, and in particular from Buddhism, a more satisfactory answer, if not to the question of God, at any rate to the riddle of human existence. Many who today occupy themselves with the study of non-Christian religions are not driven by curiosity but by the need for a security which they are unable to find in Christianity, and by the hope that the particular religion under study will be able to supply a less unstable and less assailable foundation to the interpretation and experience of human existence than Christianity is able to do in its present crisis, insecurity, and division.

The study of non-Christian religions has long since stopped being the exclusive activity of experts and scholars. The theosophist movements of this century, and various other religious movements of Eastern origin have contributed to an increase of interest in the West in non-Christian religions. At any rate, at a time when encounter and dialogue are becoming more and more inevitable it seems that no one who is in step with the times can any longer afford to be completely uniformed about the great non-Christian world religions.

There are, however, great difficulties with regard to a possible study of non-Christian religions. The Eastern and Islamitic missions usually present themselves in a typically Western-Christian attire. Actually a person should try to come to know and understand the non-Christian religions in their own environment and by means of personal contact. But this possibility is reserved to only a few. Yet, even then one meets with an almost insuperable difficulty. In 1959 a book appeared in Chicago, containing a collection of eight essays by the most prominent scientists of religion in the world.[21] Quite correctly, this collection opens with an essay by Enst Benz, the strongly ecumenically oriented Marburg historian of Church and dogma. He deals with the ques-

[21] Eliade-Kitagawa (ed), *The History of Religions, Essays in Methodology* (University of Chicago Press, Chicago, 1959).

tion whether, and in how far, it is possible really to understand alien religions. The study is based on experiences during his stay in Japan and India. Using many examples, Benz treats of the premature suppositions of the Western Christian, and of the great difficulties which stand in the way of a real understanding of the alien religion.

One of the Western presuppositions, according to Benz, is the great significance we give to the theological dogmatic aspect of religion. Our whole concept "religion" is in fact of a typically Western-intellectualist make. In this connection we might also mention a recent book which could be said to be indispensable as an introduction to the study of religion. This is the book by Wilfred Cantwell Brown, the director of the center for the study of world religions at Harvard University, entitled *The Meaning and End of Religion*.[22] Brown also contributed an essay to the collection we have just mentioned, about the science of comparative religion. We might point out that the collection also contains essays by Friedrich Heiler, Mircea Eliade, Jean Danielou.

### The Problems of Religion

The "official" practice of the modern science of religion in its various branches, and the more private manner in which many study "alien" religions are in themselves a very special way of approaching the question of God. The philosophical approach has an abstract and speculative character because it is an approach from speculative thought about God. The theological approach is concrete and of a practical nature, but it takes place from a definite conviction of faith which corresponds to the revelation accepted in that conviction. The approach of the science of religion does not touch on all this. Its starting-point is that there have been many religions which now belong to the past, and that at present there are also some world religions which are spread all over the world.

The first aim of the modern science of religion and of the interest in religion is to find out what kind of phenomenon religion actually is, and what function religion apparently fulfills in

---

[22] Wilfred Cantwell Brown, *The Meaning and End of Religion, A New Approach to the Religions of Mankind* (Macmillan, New York, 1962).

the life of individuals and of peoples. What is the concern of religion? Is this concern the same in all religions, or are there profound differences and contrasts in this respect? What is understood by revelation, by inspiration, by illumination; what is understood by faith, prayer, meditation; what by mysticism, asceticism, and penance; what by sacrifice, cult, and devotion? In all this, what is in the mind of man; on what grounds, arguments, and intentions are religious convictions and practices based; what influence does religion have on the life of the individual and of society? An examination based on a comprehensive collection of facts about these questions is bound to lead to a deeper insight into what religion is and into the place religion occupies in man's life.

There are two main groups of questions which increasingly intrigue today's man, unless he is entirely indifferent with regard to religious questions. To conclude this chapter we shall have to say something about each of these groups.

The first group includes the question about the relation of the religions to one another; the question about the relative and the absolute; the question whether one definite religion is the only true one or at least the one that is most true, or whether one religion is better for one individual or one people, and another religion better for another individual or another people; and finally the question whether it is possible or desirable to "design" a generally accepted world religion to which all the existing religions make a valuable contribution.

The second group comprises the question of what religion actually is; the question whether religion is based on an objectively given reality or on the imagination; the question whether religion is perhaps nothing but a certain form of expressing the manner in which man experiences, actualizes, and interprets his human existence, making this existence possible, bearable, and acceptable; the question whether religion belongs properly to being-human as such or whether religion perhaps belongs to a past stage of culture which man is now leaving behind. In other words, the question whether the old, classical world religions have not now had their time, and whether they will not have to capitulate in their stubborn but nevertheless hopeless battle against the modern quasi-religions and against secularism.

It is of course quite impossible to deal with these two groups of questions in a few pages. It is scarcely possible to keep track of all the existing pertinent literature, and its list is constantly growing. But we should make some observations connected with the main theme of this book, as a conclusion to the present chapter and as a preparation for our final considerations about the present and the future.

As far as the first group of questions is concerned it is important to return for a moment to the distinction of which we have spoken, between the religions of Semitic origin and of Indian origin. In the first (the Jewish religion, Christianity, and Islam) what is mainly concerned is the answer to the question of God, God's will, God's commandment and purpose; in the second (Buddhism and certain forms of Hindu philosophy in particular) what is concerned primarily is an insight into the nature, the meaning, and the manner of experiencing human existence. In other words, the first are theocentric, whereas the second are anthropocentric, or humanistic. This latter applies above all to the religions of China.

Some other remarkable differences are closely related to this cardinal difference. The first religions are based on revelation, the second on illumination; in the first it is a matter of faith and obedience, in the second of insight and wise conduct; in the first religions it is a matter of a personal relationship to God, in the second, of a mystical union with the infinite, eternal ground and reality in comparison with which things visible are only deceptive semblances; in the first religions the life of religion is maintained principally by prayer, in the second group meditation is the main means to arrive at harmony or union, as the purpose of religion.

Within the first group, the most important question which the Jewish religion asks of Christianity is whether history has not clearly shown that Jesus of Nazareth is not the expected Messiah. Apart from the fact that the early return of Jesus the messiah which the disciples were expecting did not take place, it is clear that Jesus of Nazareth was not the prince of peace who established the kingdom of God on this earth forever. The Christian nations have not distinguished themselves as peaceful nations. Moreover, the world-mission has failed. What are the facts that have shown Jesus to be the messiah who announced and introduced the effective breakthrough of the kingdom of God in the history of mankind?

But the most complete contrast in the relation between the religions is that which exists between Buddhism and Christianity. The questions which Buddhism asks of Christianity are basically the same as those which nowadays a growing number of Christians ask themselves and one another. The new way of reflecting on faith in God, and the predominant attention to human existence with its questions create, as it were, an access for Buddhism, or at least a special receptivity to the teachings and practices of Buddhism.

Not only conscientious pacifists but many others with them appreciate the fact that Buddhism has had to endure many severe persecutions, but that it never tried to propagate itself by forceful means. Buddhists have never burnt their adversaries at the stake. At most they have burnt themselves in protest.

From discussions with Christians who became Buddhists it appears that the principal reasons for their transition lie in the fact that Buddhism has no discipline based on sanctions which threaten man's spiritual freedom and independence, and which constantly involve man in conflicts of conscience as a result of the exercise of force on the conscience; that Buddhism does not oblige anyone to hold as true, on the basis of authority, certain incredible teachings and stories which cannot be reconciled with modern thought; that Buddhism gives an explanation of human existence, as it presents itself and as it is experienced, which fits into the framework of the idea of evolution, and which does not, as does the teaching on original sin, clash with the achievements of those sciences that occupy themselves with research into the rise and development of man and his civilization; that Buddhism leads man to continue working at his perfection and redemption, because it allows man to be independent in ethical respect and does not make him trust in the vicarious life, passion, and death of Christ.

It is clear that these and similar motives are of a negative nature. They are based on the personal experience that conventional Christianity as it has been taught at home, at school, and in church is in so many respects in conflict with the thought and knowledge, with the psychological insight, with the moral awareness, with the general experience and environment of the life of our time, that a person who does not base his religious life on convention but on a personally acquired insight into total reality, finds it impossible to accept it any longer. It belongs to man's very nature to ask questions about the whence, whereto, and foundation of being-human. For this reason many find it impossible to remain bogged down in a skeptical view of life and world; and hence they look for an answer to their life's question among the non-Christian religions.

At the same time, the non-Christian religions have, just as Christianity, different and divergent variations. This applies also to Buddhism in particular. Kraemer considers Japan as the real bulwark of Buddhism,[23] and undoubtedly as the center of the Buddhist sciences.[24] Yet, in no other country has religion been so seriously threatened by secularism, and in no other country have new religious movements been able to spread so rapidly as in Japan.[25] In spite of all this, Buddhism is, more than any other religion, a real and formidable competitor of Christianity in its effort to gain the West for itself, thus to become the preeminent world religion. At the same time we must not forget that our concept "religion" is in itself a Western concept. Actually it is not a matter of replacing one religion by another, but of a gradual impregnation of the "Christian West" with the Buddhist vision of human existence.

The second group of questions comprises all the problems concerning the origin, the character, the facets, the sense, and the value of religion in general. This entire problematic also affects conventional Christianity in all its expressions. Phenomenology of religion traces all the various points of similarity and difference between the religions. It also attempts to establish an order of values by investigating how the religious awareness and the religious formulation have developed.

Subjects which recently have come to be at the center of interest are: the history of the development of images of God; the question whether and in how far every image of God is a projection of the way in which man sees himself, in other words, whether man does not create God or gods to his own likeness; the question about the necessarily symbolical and mythical character

---

[23] Kraemer, *World Cultures and World Religions*, p. 147.
[24] *Op. cit.*, p. 150.
[25] Offner-van Straelen, *Modern Japanese Religions* (Brill, Leiden, 1963).

of all human thought, speech, and action with regard to God; the question about religion in the light of modern psychology, particularly that of Jung; the question about the connection between language and religion; the question about the revelatory character of religion; and finally the question about the future of religion.[26]

Conventional Christianity is more than fifteen centuries old. It is therefore quite obvious that the forms of this Christianity which have been able to maintain themselves for centuries by force of habit cannot, in our time of specialization in all the areas of methodical and utterly modern science, escape the touchstone of profound criticism.

The causes which have been treated in this book as having led to the undermining and the definitive end of conventional Christianity are, *mutatis mutandis*, also operative in all other religions. It is a matter of questions which are asked of religion in general and of each religion in particular from the viewpoint of philosophy, the modern sciences, the present pattern of culture and environment, and the general human experience. Which religion will appear best capable of standing up to the test?

One thing is certain, all contrasts and frictions between the religions themselves are of little significance when compared to the life-struggle which all religions have to wage against the increasing secularism and against what Tillich called the quasi-religions: "All religions, whether they know it or not, have entered a period of lasting and fundamental crisis." [27] "All religions have the common problem: how to encounter secularism and the quasi-religions based on it." [28]

And yet, there are indications that this crisis is more a purification than ruin and destruction. In this connection, Bleeker speaks of the rhythmic movement of the history of religions. From each crisis a revival is born.[29] Whether he likes it or not, man cannot help being religious.

[26] F. Sierksma, *De religieuze Projectie* (Delft, 1957). Mircea Eliade, *Images and Symbols*, transl. by Philip Mairet (Sheed & Ward, New York, 1961). John Hutchison, *Language and Faith, Studies in Sign, Symbol, and Meaning*, (Philadelphia, 1963).

[27] Kraemer, *World Cultures and World Religions*, p. 310.

[28] *Christ and the Encounter with World Religions*, p. 77.

[29] C. J. Bleeker, *Christ in Modern Athens* (Brill, Leiden, 1965), p. 138. Cf. also *Relations among Religions Today: A Handbook of Policies and Principles*, edited by Moses Jung, Swami Nikhilananda and Herbert W. Schneider, (Brill, Leiden, 1963).

# 10. Toward a Responsible Belief in God

The religious, theological, and ecclesiastical changes of the past twenty years, and more particularly of the conciliar and postconciliar years, have rarely been equaled in number and significance.

As a result of recent ecclesiastical events the contrast between Rome and Reformation is visibly weakening. Moreover, the achievements of biblical science and exegesis, as well as the new problems and tendencies of contemporary theology have caused the controversial differences of belief to lose much of their relevancy. And besides, a new contrast is beginning to overshadow the former. The present contrast, much more radical and serious, is one between belief and unbelief.

The critical religious situation in which we find ourselves today is characterized by a continuous tension between reorientation and conservatism, between adaptation and indifference, between renewal of faith and loss of faith. We are afraid of losing the stabilities of bygone days, but we are equally afraid of suffering a loss in our existential commitment to the world of today, which is our own world. All of us have become hesitant and doubting believers, and yet we feel we must be believing hesitators and doubters.

As a result of the cultural stage which mankind has reached we have arrived at a religious impasse. An ever-growing discrepancy has come about between the forms of our belief in God and the forms in which we experience and live our human existence today. It seems as if we are facing a precarious dilemma: either to renounce our being in this world for the sake of our belief in God, or to renounce our belief in God for the sake of our commitment to the world of today. The unity which for centuries was considered and experienced as self-evident by conventional Christianity has in our own time come to be, for millions of people, an almost unbearable disruption.

Is this the fault of Christianity as it has developed in the course of the centuries? Or is it the fault of the direction which our modern world culture has taken? Or does the blame lie in both of them as they intertwine and as they depend on one another?

Today these and similar questions are actual and urgent, as is clear from a good number of recent publications.[1]

In this connection we are also inclined to think of the Second Vatican Council and its consequences. What is involved here is of a much deeper significance, reaching far wider than merely the originally intended *aggiornamento*. This is evident not only from the Council itself, but also from the ever-growing aftereffects which cannot be stopped or disregarded.

The Council gave the impetus to a reorientation and renewal in the whole wide area of biblical exegesis, dogmatic, moral, and pastoral theology, the liturgy, religious life, the life of the priest, the Church's place in the world, and human relations. And behind all this lies the necessity of preparing a way toward a belief in God which in its various forms of reflection and practice will be tenable and responsible not only at present but in the future. What is at stake is the very belief in God. This fact lies at the basis of the present religious unrest, uncertainty, and restless activity.

Some time ago a Dutch publishing firm issued a new-book catalogue which gave a kaleidoscopic view of publications concerning the subjects that interest and occupy man's mind today. It showed how remarkably the Pope of Rome, as well as a host of writers are moved to ask the question: "What has happened to God?"

This is indeed the actual religious question modern man asks himself, if he still thinks of God at all. It does not require a genius to dispose of this question with the facile answer that nothing has happened to God, but that something has happened to man. Of course something has happened to man too, even before he was able to ask himself this question. It is a typically modern question asked by modern man. Not without a certain feeling of perplexity does he ask himself what has happened to God. And he does not like being told that he should not ask such a question. On the

---

[1] Lehman (publ.) *Ist der Glaube krank?* (Quell V., Stuttgart, 1966); Buhr, *Der Glaube—was ist das?* (Neske Pfullingen, 1963); Haendler, *Zwischen Glaube und Unglaube* (Vandenhoeck-Ruprecht, Göttingen, 1966); Schaefer (publ.) *Der Gottesgedanke im Abendland* (Kohlhammer, Stuttgart, 1964).

contrary, he expects a satisfactory answer. Therefore the question deserves to be taken seriously. Any person who does not consider it a terribly serious question is obviously still entangled in the self-evidence of thought patterns from which modern man has long since become estranged, and he still proceeds from suppositions and premises in which modern man is no longer interested.

The most radical authors—and this by no means implies that they are also the most eminent and excellent ones—produce an answer to the question about what has happened to God which in short amounts to this: "In the twentieth century the same thing has happened to the God of conventional Christianity as what happened in the fourth century to the gods and goddesses of what was then the conventional Greco-Roman religion." They hold that just as at that time the non-Christian peoples experienced the entirely unforeseen death of their gods and goddesses, so too are the Christian peoples of our time experiencing the unforeseen "death of God"; this was unforeseen except by a handful of visionary poets and philosophers of the last century.[2] They say that the particular experience of such poets and philosophers has in our modern time become a general human experience.

It is not my intention here to elaborate on the important differences in the way in which the expression "God is dead" is interpreted and dealt with by the various representatives of the theology which bears this name. Rather, I intend to clarify somewhat, first, what are the principal backgrounds to the contemporary discussion concerning the question of God; secondly what aspects of belief in God are mainly involved as a result; and thirdly what prospects are opening up for the possibility of a new form and practice of belief in God which modern man, standing in the nascent world of our time, can consider responsible.

*Backgrounds*

I understand modern man to be a man who in his manner of life and thought has not become stagnated in a past stage of the development of culture, but who consciously and completely

[2] Rehm, *Jean Paul—Dostojewski, Zur dichterischen Gestaltung des Unglaubens* (Vandenhoeck-Ruprecht, Göttingen, 1962); Glicksberg, *Modern Literature and the Death of God* (Nyhoff, The Hague, 1966).

lives in the world of today. Some people are of the opinion that religion in any form is a matter that has had its day, and that now merely belongs to the past. If this were true, then modern man would not be able to be religious, and a religious person would not be able to be modern. In any case, one thing is certain, and that is that a religious person, insofar as he is modern, cannot escape the question of God as it imposes itself on us from within modern life and thought. In this connection I would like to point out three different backgrounds, a general human background, a philosophical, and a theological background.

In any religion man originally considered it as self-evident, in the different anxieties and needs of human existence, to have recourse to gods and goddesses or to God by means of sacrifices, penitential exercises, and prayers. Modern man, on the other hand, experiences this less and less as something obvious and self-evident. There are many reasons why God has gradually been crowded out of reality as it is experienced in everyday life. Some of these are the achievements of science and technology, the way in which these achievements are communicated to the people at large by means of the press, pocketbooks, radio, television, and travel. Other reasons are the frightening events of war, the equally frightened means that are supposed to prevent a new world war, the new forms and possibilities of modern existence, as also the enormous sufferings in the world, with which everyone is confronted as a result of the modern means of communication. Modern man is no longer able to see how all this could have anything to do with God. He no longer encounters God in this reality. He cannot imagine how the question whether God exists or not could make any difference to everyday reality.

Modern man has experienced and discovered that his cry for help to God is left unanswered. Nor does he receive answers to the many urgent questions about life itself. He has discovered that God (if he does exist) will not take the blame for the various human affairs. In short, modern man has reconciled himself to the fact that he must learn to live as if God did not exist. If a person wants to call this "atheism," it is at any rate an atheism born from existential need, and not an atheism as the fruit of an old-fashioned and superficial rationalism of the Enlightenment.

The second background is formed by the character of the

newest, postwar philosophy. This philosophy is no doubt closely connected with modern man's situation as we have sketched it out roughly above. It is not of a speculative, idealist, romanticist, vitalistic, or even existentialist nature, but it has a sober, business-like, and realistic character. After a first start in the form of an all too narrow-minded logical positivism, this philosophy continues to unfold itself under the title of a linguistic or analytical philosophy. One of its principal founders is Ludwig Wittgenstein.[3]

Analytical philosophy is noticeably Socratic. It examines the possibilities as well as the limitations of language. It inquires into the exact meaning of each word and into the real sense of any statement. The terms used are purified from all conventional and illegitimate associations that are irrelevant. It is obvious that precisely in the religious area many words are open to the suspicion that they have their origin in a past stage of culture, that they have been devaluated, that they are still being used even though they have lost their original meaning, that they are passed on as old coins even though nobody remembers their value. Such are, for example, the words "God," "spirit," and "soul." Do these words have their origin in a far distant past, when primitive man thought himself surrounded by gods, spirits, and souls? But what does modern man mean when he cries out to "God," or when he speaks of a "spirit," or of the "soul"? The same goes for such words as revelation, sin, grace, faith, or belief. What meaning do these words still have, and how can they be so manipulated that they really have a meaning?

Finally, the present-day concentration on the question of God also has a specifically theological background. Because we cannot determine exactly how he would have worked out his sporadic but visionary statements made in his letters from prison, if he would have had the chance to do so, we are abstracting here from Bonhoeffer. But we must certainly mention the three Protestant giants, as Macquarrie calls them.[4] These three giants who dominated, or at least stimulated and influenced the discussion for nearly half a century, are Karl Barth, Rudolf Bultmann, and Paul Tillich.

[3] van Peursen, *Ludwig Wittgenstein* (Wereldvenster, Baarne, 1965).

[4] Macquarrie, *Principles of Christian Theology* (Charles Scribners' Sons, New York, 1966); cf. p. ix, where Macquarrie mentions Brunner, instead of Bultmann, as one of the three giants.

Each of these three giants has in his own and original way contributed to the fact that a definitive end has come to the conventional manner in which belief in God was for centuries built up and interpreted.

During the entire existence of mankind belief in God or in gods has always been the fruit of the way in which man thought he experienced the world or himself. All sorts of phenomena in the world or in his own emotional life led man to believe that all this pointed to the existence and intervention of God or gods. In this connection we usually speak of a natural belief in God which upon further intellectual reflection can form the basis of a natural theology. In short, belief in God has its roots in the general human experience of the whole of reality and in a reflection of this reality.

Karl Barth uprooted this kind of belief in God through his denial that such a belief in God could have anything to do with God. As far as Barth is concerned this kind of belief has to do only with pseudo gods and idols. Today mankind has reached a stage of culture in which it loses belief in these gods. A natural belief in God will sooner or later end up in atheism. The one and only way toward a real, legitimate, and authentic belief in God begins with God and develops through God's salvific action in and by Jesus Christ, according to Barth.

Bultmann, too, holds that man cannot reach God by himself. Belief in God is always based on God's salvific actions, on the Christ event. Bultmann does not deny that this event has a foundation in an objective reality outside man. But man has no access to this reality and is in no way capable of determining the historicity of the event of salvation. All man can do is to ascertain that the message of salvation, the *kerygma*, has reached him. Belief in this message is a gift, an act on the part of God. It effects a radical transition in human existence, because it convinces man of God's love, thus liberating him from the restraints and inhibitions that prevent him from understanding and realizing human existence in an authentic way as originally intended by God. Thus the event of salvation is an event within the world of human existence. No windows or gates lead from this world to an objective reality other than the reality of man.

Finally, Paul Tillich has, by his correlative method, made an effort to construct a bridge between man as question and God as answer. He tried to show that there is a revelatory power in the manner in which man experiences his being-human. In this light all religions have a positive significance. But it is only a confrontation with the Christ event that makes a true belief in God possible. Yet, Tillich's contribution to the undermining of conventional belief in God is to be found especially in his effort to separate belief in God from any form of theism and supranaturalism and to lift this belief in God from any such form. For Tillich, God is not a "someone" who resides "somewhere" above, beyond, or in reality such as we know it. In a recent article, Nels Ferré, the well-known author of the book about language, logic, and God, points to Tillich as the actual founder of the God-is-dead-theology.[5]

The three giants, Barth, Bultmann, and Tillich did not only prepare the way for the present crisis in belief in God. They closed a theological era which now definitely belongs to the past.[6] Their influence will continue to make itself felt. But they still were making use of thought categories and conventional terminology which evidently have become unintelligible and unacceptable to modern man.

*Aspects*

We have now arrived at the question of how the discussion concerning the question of God has such an extremely urgent character. We also have arrived at the aspects of belief in God which are mainly involved in this.

In 1961, the same year when Pope John XXIII was beginning with the preparations for the Second Vatican Council, the United States saw the publication of Gabriel Vahanian's book *The Death of God*,[7] which was later followed by other books of the same author *Wait without Idols*,[8] and *No Other God*.[9] Shortly after the publication of the first book, people in the United States began to speak of a new, radical God-is-dead-theology, although

[5] Ferré, *Tillich and the Nature of Transcendence*, Religion in Life, (Winter) 1966, Vol. 35, p. 662, ff. Note: The title of Ferré's book is: *Language, Logic, and God* (Eyre and Spottiswoode, London, 1962).

[6] Ogden, *The Reality of God and Other Essays* (Harper & Row, New York, 1963, 1966 [3rd ed.]), pp. 53ff.

[7] Vahanian, *The Death of God* (Braziller, New York, 1961).

[8] Vahanian, *Wait without Idols* (Braziller, New York, 1964).

[9] Vahanian, *No Other God* (Braziller, New York, 1966).

it soon became apparent that this course of affairs had by no means been intended by Vahanian.[10]

More or less simultaneously a new discussion on the question of God was started in Germany by Herbert Braun [11] and Helmut Gollwitzer.[12] They were later joined in this discussion, either directly or indirectly, by other theologians. In the meantime, Dorothee Sölle has spoken of her book *Stellvertretung* [13] as "a chapter of theology after the death of God," and as "a design of a post-theistic theology."

What is taking place under our very eyes is something far more serious than merely an attempt at reformation or an effort to arrive at a new belief in God or at a new religion. According to Heinz Zahrnt's diagnosis, it is too late for this. In his latest book Zahrnt tries to show that modern man's belief in God has been attacked at its very roots and that it has been fundamentally undermined to the very core.[14] According to Zahrnt the facts show that a definitive end has come to the conventional forms of belief in God: "It will never be the same as it once was . . . Something new is being announced which we can at most only surmise but of which we cannot form any idea yet." [15] It seems impossible to express more clearly and more frankly what situation Christianity finds itself in, whether consciously or not.

As is clear from the discussion, there are mainly four different aspects of belief in God involved. These four aspects I would like

[10] *Ibid*, p. xi, "So-called 'Christian Atheism' glories precisely in what I deplored when I first used the term 'death of God.' "

[11] Braun, *Gesammelte Studien zum Neuen Testament und seiner Umwelt*, (Mohr, Tübingen, 1962, 1967).

[12] Gollwitzer, *Die Existenz Gottes im Bekenntnis des Glaubens* (Kaiser Verlag, Munich, 1964). English translation: *The Existence of God as Confessed by Faith*, tr. by James W. Leitch (S.C.M. Press Ltd., London, 1965). Cf. p. 81, where Gollwitzer states the problem as follows: "How far it is still legitimate to speak of the being, existence, and reality of God or whether to speak in that way is already to fall into the objectivism of which traditional metaphysics is accused." Braun's answer to Gollwitzer is contained in *Zeit und Geschichte, Festschrift for Rudolf Bultmann* (Mohr, Tübingen, 1964), pp. 399ff.

[13] Dorothee Sölle, *Stellvertretung* (Kreuz Verlag., Stuttgart, Berlin, 1965).

[14] Zahrnt, *Die Sache mit Gott, Die protestantische Theologie im 20. Jahrhundert* (Piper und Co., Munich, 1966). With Macquarrie's *Twentieth Century Religious Thought* (S.C.M. Press, London, 1963), and Cobb's *Living Options in Protestant Theology* (Westminster Press, Philadelphia, 1962), this book belongs to the best publications in the field of religious thought and Protestant theology of this century.

[15] Zahrnt, *Die Sache mit Gott*, p. 177.

to indicate with the words authenticity, possibility, expression, and expectation.

The present approach to the question about God has, in the words of Vahanian, an iconoclastic character. A new iconoclasm is taking place, in which one must decide for God and against the idols. In other words, it is once again a matter of the authenticity of belief in God.

Vahanian's books deal with this aspect of belief in God.[16] He asks whether religion, including religion in its conventional Christian forms, is deep-down not really concerned with idols instead of God. He asks whether the rapidly spreading unbelief is not fundamentally an unbelief in idols rather than an unbelief in God, and whether the death of God is in fact nothing but the death of idols.

In the bible the word always has an iconoclastic character; it is always directed at the destruction of idols, not only of idols of stone, silver, and gold, but also of idols of the mind, all images of God and the teachings and practices based on them, which present a false picture of God. Not only Moses and the prophets, but Jesus and the apostles, too, were engaged in an uninterrupted conflict situation with the religious milieu of their times. Would it be any different in our own time? Does the current belief in God still have anything to do with the God of the bible?

Vahanian holds that one must speak of idolatry whenever the personal ego stands at the center of religion, whenever God is used as a means—for example, to solve problems, to satisfy religious needs, to subdue existential anxieties. One must speak of idolatry whenever man replaces God's unfaltering fidelity by human certainties such as a tradition, ecclesiastical authority, infallible or pure doctrine, confession, convention (in short all orthodoxy), or by any certainties at all which can be ascertained and easily manipulated. When these human certainties collapse— as is happening in our own day—then all those who had built their hope on these idols experience this as the death of God. In reality, however, God is in our own day busy liberating us from the hands of the idols.[17]

Secondly, what is also involved in the present discussion is the *possibility* of belief in God, as also the *problematic character* of

[16] Cf. especially: *No Other God*, chapter four, pp. 37ff.

[17] Zahrnt, *Die Sache mit Gott*, p. 185: "God frees us from the hands of the idols."

the question of God. Johannes Körner has tried to bring the discussion on the question of God, particularly as it is going on in Germany, under one common denominator.[18] He sees this as a tension between reality and the possibility of expressing this reality. When people begin to reflect on whether God is a Reality or not, then they are inevitably also faced with the question whether it is at all possible for them to be in any kind of relationship to a reality that is in all respects completely other than the reality we know in our human condition. They have to face the question whether it is at all possible to say anything meaningful about a reality which is beyond the human grasp.

It is told that Buddha, when asked by his disciples to tell them something about God, used to put his finger on his mouth, maintaining a noble silence. For that matter, in the history of Christian theology, too, we can find a negative theology, in which an effort is made to say something about God by saying what he is not. Mystics even make mention of a dark night of the soul in which God is experienced as completely absent and inaccessible.

Thus the realist of our own day is inclined to ask himself whether that which is presented as a revelation from God is anything more than the result of our human phantasy or projection, born from the need of explaining the inscrutable mystery of our reality against the background of another reality which is supposed to be at the basis of our own.

While it is true that what has just been said creates a difficulty, it nevertheless remains a fact that religion and belief in God have always existed in the most varied forms. God has many names. Belief in God finds *expression* in the most different ways. Here we are faced with the third aspect of belief in God which is involved in the present discussion on the question of God.

An accumulation of discoveries and experiences of various kinds has brought us to the beginning of a new stage in the history of mankind. Whether this will become a "religionless era" is open to debate. At any rate, what Bonhoeffer meant when he used this expression is not far from the truth.[19]

[18] Körner, "Wirklichkeit und Aussagbarkeit Gottes," in *Theologische Rundschau*, 32 (Feb. 1967), Vol. 1, pp. 43ff. Cf. "Die transzendente Wirklichkeit Gottes," in *Zeitschrift für Theologie und Kirche*, 63 (Dec. 1966), Vol. 4, pp. 473ff.

[19] Bonhoeffer, *Widerstand und Ergebung* (Kaiser Verlag, Munich, 1951), pp. 178ff.

In the thought, life, and belief of mankind profound changes are taking place which necessarily will leave a lasting impression also on the Christian belief in God. Particularly in Western Christianity a process has started which, by way of demythologizing, desacralization, and dehellenization, will end up in a complete secularization of belief in God.[20]

Demythologizing is mainly a matter of ridding belief in God from primitive, magical, and mythological images of a cultural stage which we have definitively left behind. Desacralization is closely connected with this. Sacred persons, objects, and places have lost their intrinsic sacredness. The total reality of man and world is a profane reality. Or better, all of reality is sacred. What was previously called belief in God is being replaced by awe and reverence on the part of modern man with regard to the inscrutable mystery of the being of man and of the world.

However, at present the discussion concerns mainly a dehellenization of belief in God. What is involved here is a liberation of belief in God from the grasp of an essentialist, substantialist, and objectivizing consideration of God.[21] The contrasts between supernatural and natural, this-worldly and other-worldly, transcendent and immanent, have lost their meaning for modern man. So have all static images of God lost their meaning for him. Modern man no longer knows anything of a God who dwells somewhere, and who exists in himself, quite apart from and beyond the total reality of man and world.[22] Insofar as there is sense in speaking of "God," this must be related to a God who is closely involved in our reality, which is and remains a dynamic and evolving reality: "God's Being is in becoming." [23]

It is getting to be more and more evident that a purification process has been started in which the most different forms and expressions of belief in God, for centuries the heritage of conven-

[20] Stallmann, *Was ist Säkularisierung?* (Mohr Tübingen, 1960). Cf. Smith, *Secular Christianity* (Collins, London, 1966); Callahan, *The Secular City Debate* (Macmillan, N.Y. 1966); van Buren, *The Secular Meaning of the Gospel* (S.C.M. Press, London, 1963). Translator's note: Cf. also Richard, *Secularization Theology* (Herder & Herder, New York, 1967).

[21] Ferré, *The Living God of Nowhere and Nothing* (Epworth Press, London, 1966), p. 41: "Substance-thinking distorts and disturbs all theological problems which are posed in its terms."

[22] *Ibid.*, p. 32, p. 72.

[23] Jüngel, *Gottes Sein ist im Werden, Verantwortliche Rede vom Sein Gottes bei Karl Barth*, p. 117.

tional Christianity, are one by one being eliminated as no longer relevant. It seems an arithmetically progressive subtraction, and there are many who ask themselves whether a core of belief in God will remain, and what it will look like.


*Prospects*

In the course of events I have sketched out roughly it will also be necessary to search out the point of departure for a correct interpretation of what is called the God-is-dead theology. The radical theologians could also be called consistent theologians. In the existing process of reduction they are filled with a sense of factuality and veracity. Leaving nothing unturned they draw ultimate conclusions. It never even occurs to them, as modern men, to proceed abstractly in a speculative reasoning process. Hence it is not by such a process of reasoning that they arrive at the conclusion: "God does not exist." They ascertain facts, proceeding concretely and existentially. When they say that God is dead, this is a frightening and painful experience of life for them. They experience the final point of the process of reduction as the death of God. They are, furthermore, convinced that in all Churches there are thousands of Christians who, even though they do not speak of the death of God, are in fact undergoing the same experience, with varying degrees of reflection or nonreflection. The sensational saying "God is dead" may go out of fashion, but the experience to which the saying refers will continue.[24]

It is therefore not in the least astonishing that the question arises: "What can be expected in respect to religion, and what possibility of hope and prospect remains for the future?"[25] Here we are faced with the fourth aspect of belief in God, an aspect which in the present discussion concerning the question about God has received a new and grave accent. Eschatology is not just a final chapter of the Christian belief in God and of Christian theology. In fact, as such, and in all respects this belief and this

[24] Altizer-Hamilton, *Radical Theology and the Death of God* (Bobbs-Merrill, Indianapolis—New York, 1966). Cr. Altizer, *The Gospel of Christian Atheism* (Westminster Press, Philadelphia, 1966).
[25] Dewart, *The Future of Belief; Theism in a World Come of Age* (Herder & Herder, New York, 1966). Cf. Schilling: *Glaube und Illusion* (Ev. Presseverband, Munich, 1960).

theology are of a thoroughly eschatological nature. In other words, the principal aspect of belief in God is that of hope, of *expectation*, of eschatological prospect. This applies also the God-is-dead theology.

It is therefore not without reason that Jürgen Moltmann, in his book *Theology of Hope*,[26] devotes an extensive and positive reflection to the God-is-dead theology. There are many points of resemblance between these two theologies when it comes to looking forward in expectation to the resurrection and to the future of God. In both theologies this expectation and looking forward is based on the death *and* the resurrection of Jesus. His death and resurrection are seen as a unity. The death on the cross derives its sense and meaning from the resurrection, and the resurrection derives its sense and meaning from the death on the cross.

The radical theologians see the cross of Jesus as the symbol *par excellence* of the cross of each and every man, as the cross of all mankind. It is the cross of being completely abandoned by God. The existential need of each and every man, and of all mankind, is exemplified and representatively expressed by Jesus' cry on the cross: "My God, my God, why have you abandoned me?". To this cry of distress no answer has echoed on this side of death, on this side of the utmost limit of human existence.

Since the death of Jesus, who built all his confidence on God, mankind in general and each man individually knows that God is silent, that God is dead. According to the radical theologians, in Jesus' death on the cross it had once and for all become clear that within the human condition on this side of death there is no other possibility than to live as if God did not exist.

Yet this is not the final word. Even among those who speak of a "Christian atheism" there is hope, expectation, and the prospect of a new possibility on the other side of death. And here the spatial-temporal representation must be considered as an unavoidable symbol.[27]

Since the death of God, within the limits of the human condition, Jesus takes the place of God. But what must be kept in

---

[26] Moltmann, *Theologie der Hoffnung, Untersuchungen zur Begründung und zu den Konsequenzen einer christlichen Eschatologie* (Kaiser, Verlag, Munich, 1964, 1966 [fifth edition]), pp. 150ff. Cf. also the contributions by Dorothee Sölle and Moltmann in Kutschki (publishers) *Gott Heute* (Kaiser Verlag, Munich, 1967).

[27] Altizer-Hamilton, *op. cit.*

mind—and this is the central thought of Dorothee Sölle's book to which we have referred—is that Jesus as God's representative also keeps the place of God open. For belief in Jesus involves both death *and* resurrection. On this side of the borderline everyone experiences, just as Jesus did on the cross, the silence, the death of God.

But belief in Jesus of Nazareth stands or falls with death *and* resurrection. However, this resurrection in which Christians of all times have believed is not—as opposed to the historical event on the cross—a historical event in the same sense as that in which other events are historical. The resurrection is an eschatological event, an event that does not take place on this side of our human existence. The resurrection must be believed. It cannot be ascertained or proved. Belief in the resurrection is a hopeful expectation of, and looking forward to the event that takes place at the utmost limit of our existence, death. It is not a void that awaits us there, but the love of the living God. In this expectation, to believe means to live and work in the present moment of our human existence.

We can now draw the following conclusions:

1. If scholastic theology was mainly concerned with a knowledge of God in an intellectual sense, and if the authentic reformation theology was concerned mainly with a belief in God in an existential sense, we have now arrived at the beginning of a new era in which it will be mainly a matter of waiting for God in an eschatological sense.

2. In all of mankind a sociological, cultural, and religious process is at work, as a result of which belief in God as well as theology will look different from their appearances so far in conventional Christianity.

3. Even in the radical theology of the death of God, and in fact wherever there is a tendency to build belief in God exclusively on the death *and* resurrection of Jesus, we can find traces of the lasting aftereffects of the radical exclusivity of Karl Barth.[28]

4. In every respect mankind is busy settling accounts with the past, and orienting itself toward a new future. Religion, Church, and theology will not escape this transition. The past is

[28] Engelland, *Die Wirklichkeit Gottes und die Gewissheit des Glaubens,* (Vandenhoeck-Ruprecht, Göttingen, 1966), pp. 188ff.

gone forever, and only the future lies open. This is the future of God. This is the future that awaits us and we can go forward to meet only if we have the courage to eliminate those ties with the past which prevent us from running the course that lies ahead.

5. At the beginning of this chapter I mentioned the former contrasts and problems which have for centuries separated Christians. As a result of the process which I have described in this chapter these differences hardly continue to be operative. Accordingly there is no sense in placing them on the agenda of a laborious dialogue. Ecumenically speaking, there is still too much tilting at windmills going on. We have now arrived at the post-ecumenical era in which the solution will present itself against the background of a new and responsible belief in God.[29]

6. In our time we are experiencing the collapse of a pantheon of all sorts of Christian and ecclesiastical idols. As Bonhoeffer stated, it is thus that the way becomes open again for the God of the bible. The more unbelieving we become, the more believing we become. In this transition now taking place it is important that the Church and theology, instead of blocking the road, keep it open to that God for whose coming we are waiting. Wait without idols! [30]

Wittgenstein thinks that the whole of reality is of such a nature that, no matter what may befall us, nothing can ultimately happen to us. This philosophical perception finds its fulfillment and completion in the Old Testament certainty of faith: "When the sun sets, the light breaks through" (Zach. 14, 7), and also in the New Testament confidence: "The sufferings of this present time are not worth comparing with the glory that is to be revealed to us" (Rom. 8, 18).

[29] Oxtoby, "The Post-Ecumenical Era," in *Theology Today*, No. 3 (Oct.) 1966, Vol. xxiii, p. 374ff.

[30] Zahrnt, cf. note 14 of this chapter; Vahanian, cf. note 8 of this chapter.